# THE CHURCH IN *THIS* PLACE

A History of the English Church
illustrated by its life in *this* Parish
of Saint Gregory the Great
in Dawlish in Devon

from its beginning,
until the Year of our Lord 2000

This story is compiled with the help of many friends
and advisors,
by
Muriel Bradshaw

*for Peggy
with love from Quack
(Muriel)*

First published in 2007 by the author

Dr Muriel K Bradshaw

'Vailima'
78 West Cliff Park Drive
Dawlish, Devonshire
EX7 9ER
Telephone: 01626 865286

Typeset in News Gothic and New Roman

Printed in Great Britain by

Swiftprint Ltd
High Street
Dawlish, Devon, EX7 9DB

Copyright Muriel Bradshaw 2007

ISBN 978 095256430 1 7

# CONTENTS

List of Illustrations .................................................................. iv
(The Illustrations are set between pages 108 and 109)
Foreword................................................................................. v
Author's preface and acknowledgements........................... vi-ix

Text Chapters: *Part One: The Growth of Church and Town*

1. The Dawn of Dawlish ................................................... 1
2. Gregory and Augustine ................................................ 8
3. The Coming of the Normans ...................................... 14
4. Village and Church in Mediaeval Times .................... 27
5. A Strong Tower ........................................................... 33
6. Letting in Light ............................................................ 39
7. Building and Furnishing a new House of Worship ... 46
8. Changeful Times in the Church Catholic .................. 54
9. Life in Georgian Dawlish ............................................ 65
10. Raising the Roof ......................................................... 77
11. Restless Years in the early 19th Century ................. 86
12. Is there an Ideal House of Worship? ...................... 101

*Part Two: Understanding the Christian faith through the Furnishing and Adornment of the building*

13. The Ministry of the Word......................................... 114
14. The Sacrament of Baptism ...................................... 123
15. Furnishing the Sanctuary ........................................ 137
16. The Inspiration of Light and Colour ....................... 145
17. Making Music for the Lord ..................................... 159
18. On the Keeping of Records..................................... 169
19. Towards the Present Day ....................................... 180
20. At the end of the Second Millennium ................... 196

Glossary and Appendices 1-6. These follow page 209.

INDEX   (Final pages)

iii

## THE ILLUSTRATIONS (Picture section page numbers)

1. St. Gregory's Church south-west view (St. Mark's day 2007)
2. Ground plan, colour-coded to show development of building
3. The Norman corbel stone lying by a north buttress, and an example of a corbel table at Kilpeck, Herefordshire
4. The 1400 Tower, cleaned and re-pointed in 1897 to mark Queen Victoria's Diamond Jubilee. (The author abseiling!) The Flag keeper, Miss Diane Coombes, on the tower roof
5. From the tower: Views of the Town, and of the Graveyard, which includes the Hoare Family burial garden
6. The 1438 Capital on north pillar 2, (Upper Narthex view) The Nave Arcade and barrel roof seen from the narthex
7. The Dissenters' Pit in Bradley Wood, Newton Abbot (1962)
8. The old Church and Tower from 1438 (north aspect), and a south view after the rebuilding in 1825 (increased height)
9. The Nave in 1850: 'auditory church furnishing', contrasted with St. Mark's Chancel (emphasis laid on the Sacraments)
10/11. Dawlish Sea Front: Steam Special visits us in 2006
12. The new Chancel (1875) in St. Gregory's Church, as it was on Easter Sunday 2000 after Festival Parish Communion
13. In the Chancel: the High Altar (Festival colours), and the north wall revering the Great Prophets
14. The Font, and the Pulpit
15. Patron Saints: St. Gregory and St Michael
16. The Lady Chapel: the Raphael window and the Altar
17. The Lady Chapel exterior and the ancient Cross stump
18. Palm Sunday Procession 2000, led by The Reverend William Lark (with donkey) and the robed Choir; then we enter the west door (near the ancient yew tree)
19. Making Music for the Lord: Organist and Choirmaster George Elliott at the organ console
20. Easter Eve 2000: "The Lord is risen: He is risen indeed".

The photographers are identified by their initials near the pictures: FC...Fred Comber, JB...John Bradshaw, MKB...Muriel Bradshaw, PH...Pam Howells, RMQ...Ruth M Quick (the author's mother), OU...Origin uncertain, CDM... Courtesy of Dawlish Museum.

## FOREWORD

This book is much more than a guidebook to a building: it is the social and spiritual story of a community. It belongs to the modern way of presenting history: by entering into the feelings, beliefs and hopes of individuals in each generation, rather than simply imparting two-dimensional lists of dates and details. In short, by making history live.

Some of my happiest years were spent as vicar of Dawlish, and I thought I knew the place inside out. But Muriel Bradshaw's research has opened my eyes to much that I never knew or understood, not only about town and church, but even about the wider evolution of Christianity in England! I marvel at her humility as she sat listening to me week after week without a word of criticism!

Every stone in St. Gregory's church speaks to Muriel's mind and heart. She knows why it is there, when it was put there, what is its symbolism, and the living faith that lies behind it. You will discover the story of the church tower from someone who loves it so much that she has abseiled down it! Through all the centuries she watches the life and growth, ups and downs of church and people nourishing the hopes and aspirations of the whole town.

This is an easy read, and a must for anyone who knows and loves Dawlish, Devon, and the Christian Church.

WILLIAM LARK.

AUTHOR'S PREFACE: *This book tells a story.*

    The author of 'Treasure Island', Robert Louis Stevenson, spent the last few years of his life seeking better health by making his home in Samoa, a tropical island group in the south Pacific area. There, he was affectionately known as 'Tusitala', which means, in Samoan, the 'Teller of Tales'. Years later when my husband John was Principal of Malua Theological College where Samoan and other Island ministers were being trained, we spent 10 action-packed years among the people of Samoa. We were invited to visit many of the villages all over the islands, to share in worship and in village life. On each such occasion, our welcome included the privilege of sharing in the traditional Kava ceremony.

    This took place in the large, thatched and open-sided house of the village Chief. Most of the adults and children of the community would gather around outside to watch and to listen to everything that was going on. What they saw and heard was an age-old ceremony which *told the story* of the Universe and related it to the very people of Samoa, and to that specific village where we were meeting. In beautifully elegant word pictures, the formal sequence of speeches told the story of the great 'Mornings' in the life of this people: beginning with the Morning of Creation itself. Then we recalled the epic voyages which had brought Samoan ancestors to their present home, and then the great chiefs under whose leadership their land was protected from would be rivals. Then the speech would 'home in' on the Great Morning when the Christian Gospel was brought there in 1830 by John Williams and his co-workers; and so on to the establishment of peace between warring tribes, and the new understanding of the God of love whose Spirit brought joy and peace and not fear. Ultimately they celebrated *this* Morning when "you, our esteemed visitors have come to share Kava, to eat, and to worship and be with us". It was a humbling (and exhausting!) experience, which magnified the importance of *story telling* in the preservation and transmission of the life saga of the people to the next and future generations.

In the village on that day, those listeners were being taught to value their past and to know that they were a real part of the story—the story of something extending far beyond themselves.

It remains true that vocal story-telling by careful and committed orators, (and these include mothers and fathers at home), can have an immediate, colourful and lasting effect on the listener. Long may the speeches of the Kava Ceremony continue to survive! And long may the *telling* of Bible stories flourish and influence the hearers both young and old!

But we also give thanks for all the ways in which stories are available to us today through printed and electronically recorded works. 'Permanent' records have great value: and their availability is widespread. Through the printed word we have easy access to stories corresponding dramatically with those told in the Kava Ceremony: they are collected together in The Holy Bible.

So I have tried to write my book in the form of the *story* that gathers up the great 'Mornings' in the life history of Dawlish and the Church in *this* place.

'RLS', the teller of tales, would gather his household of Samoan and European members together for family prayers every evening. They were summoned, not by a bell, but by the blowing of a Conch shell. Formerly used to gather men for battle, this cleverly prepared instrument had come to be a call to peaceful gatherings. RLS named his house 'Vailima', the Samoan term for 'five waters' which drained the hillside behind his home. When we came to live in Dawlish we noticed, from the map and our walks, that Dawlish Water too has five main sources in the hills around us. So we call our house 'Vailima', a little tribute to RLS and his lively stories, and to the warmth and hospitality of the people of Samoa. I am glad to bring them so happily into my story. Though I write of 'The Church in *This* Place', we are all members of the *Church Universal*.   May God bless us all.

Muriel K Bradshaw

# ACKNOWLEDGEMENTS

I owe a great deal to the friends who have assisted me in many different ways during the writing of this book.

The Reverend William Lark first encouraged me to write articles for the Parish Magazine. These were welcomed by the then Editor, Mr. Jack Batten, a former Churchwarden, (who later undertook a comprehensive proof-reading of this book typescript). William Lark suggested that I might draw these articles together in book form, and so offer a more detailed record than was possible in the current brochure 'History and Guide to the Church of St.Gregory the Great, Dawlish'. From that point onwards I was committed to undertaking a much bigger historical, architectural and social study than I had at first anticipated. And I quickly recognised that I was immersing myself in the total story of the Christian Church from its beginnings on the first Easter Day and at Pentecost: the real birth of the Church in Dawlish.

I have had no formal training in Theology, but have lived 'with' it all my life: and am deeply grateful to my Congregationalist Minister father whose rugged theology and strong sense of Liturgy never failed him. The Rev'd Howard Partington prepared me as I confirmed the vows made for me at my baptism, and inspired me with his warm sense of being in a Church that is worldwide and has unbroken continuity; it led to my offering, as a qualified medical doctor, to work with the 'younger churches' abroad.

This I did, not only as a doctor, but as a wife and mother, for I was by then married to the Reverend Dr. John Bradshaw. Throughout our life together John has shared with me his own thinking and reading, both in Theology and Psychology. He has exercised enormous patience and support during the generation of my two books. He has helped me through my mistakes and exasperation as I wrestle with computer intricacies which I do not understand or like! More positively, he has contributed some fine photographs to this book, including the cover picture, taken from our sitting room window. Thank you John!

In my retirement years I was fortunate in being able to attend several high quality extra-mural courses in the University of Exeter. My thanks are due to Dr. Steven Taylor for his lectures on Church History and Architecture, well illustrated and full of his infectious enthusiasm and encouragement to visit and enjoy intelligently the many places which he has appreciated. His helpful 'Reading lists' introduced me to the works of Eamon Duffy (and others, of course). There are few detailed accounts of the church life in the past which help us to appreciate so vividly the devotions, fears and struggles of our forbears, as Duffy's books 'The Stripping of the Altars' and 'The Voices of Morebath'.

In compiling the pictures for this book, I have been most ably assisted by Mr. Fred Comber of St. George's Church in Holcombe. As an experienced printer and photographer, he has devoted much time and energy in works for the Churches, and will help to oversee the production of this book.

Most authors need inspiration, support and correction during the evolution of their work, and these gifts come from members of the communities of which the writer is an integral part. I wish now to acknowledge the interest, the warmth, and the care I have received from my fellow members of St. Gregory's Church and of other churches in Dawlish; also from Dawlish Local History Society, Dawlish Museum, and the many people who have shared their personal memories and records freely. Thank you all!

Lastly, a chance to pay humble tribute to a special helper, The Reverend Canon Colin Evans, who in his 'retirement' has ministered quietly to many people, using a lifetime of pastoral experience and carefully nurtured wisdom and discerning love. Colin has scrutinised every word I have written as the years of the book's gestation have run their course, and has offered generous portions of his immense knowledge of the Faith and the complex ways of Church Institutions, to help me on my way. I have needed his teaching and correcting and calming, but always had this good friend's support and encouragement to write in my own way.

This book, and all the worship and work offered in St. Gregory's Church, is dedicated to the GLORY OF GOD.

# PART ONE

*The Story of the coming of Christianity to Dawlish, and the inter-twined growth of Church and Town*

# CHAPTER ONE

## THE DAWN OF DAWLISH

What does the name Dawlish conjure up for you? Bucket and spade holidays on sunny beaches backed by red, red cliffs? Or a little river tumbling down a series of wide waterfalls in the middle of a green open space within a small town of family owned shops? Perhaps black swans and exotic ducks, or noisily aggressive seagulls; railway trains gliding along the seafront and in and out of tunnels? In casual conversation with strangers anywhere in the world you can mention that you live in Dawlish and then watch the face of your listener broaden into a happy smile and offer the response "Oh, that's where the trains rush along the water's edge isn't it?" (Just imagine what would happen today if Isambard Kingdom Brunel proposed such a route for the Great Western line: 'God's Wonderful Railway'!)

Older people might say "The smell of sweet violets", for Dawlish fields once produced thousands of bunches of violets for sale in Covent Garden market in London. The growers depended on the early morning trains to take their harvest to major supply outlets. As did the many market gardeners of the area whose livelihood was the working of the sheltered inland fields and warm hill slopes.

Long before the railway brought increased prosperity and population to the Dawlish area early in the 19th century, this was a place of settled habitation at least as far back as the Iron Age, and probably well before that. If like the Psalmist the dwellers here expressed thanks to a fatherly Creator God, they too would have sung:

"The lines have fallen unto me in pleasant places
yea, I have a goodly heritage."

Psalm 16 v 7

For in this part of Devonshire there is good, kind land. All along the Devon coastlands the Iron Age peoples had, for 500 years before the time of Christ, built their protected villages where they could guard livestock and use the fertile land below their hillside enclosures. There were walled pounds for cattle outside the residential family area, and the entrance to the complex was, naturally enough, close to a source of water. So we have our own Castle Dyke high up on the south-east facing Little Haldon Hill, close to one of the source streams feeding the Dawlish Water.

The Haldon Hills form a barrier protecting our Dawlish valley from the prevailing westerly gales and fierce Atlantic weather. They are capped with the remnants of porous chalk-with-flints and Greensand rock which are slow to yield to weather erosion. Where these rest on the older, less permeable red sandstone, springs of water emerge. Five main streamlets find their way down into the valley to form the Dawlish Water. They supply and drain a fertile basin of very desirable land which must have attracted settlers from time immemorial. The tribal families who were fortunate enough to find this spot must have enjoyed a relatively good life for they had lush grazing for cattle, productive farmland, and woodland for timber and firewood and wild game. Only a short way farther down the valley was the sea for fishing, salt and travel by water. Yes, they had a goodly heritage to hand down from generation to generation.

Those of us who live in Dawlish today are indeed their successors, so with a very proper sense of curiosity we can ask: What were these people like? What did they believe? How far were they like us in their hopes and fears?

In writing this story I am trying to feel my way back into what it was like to live in this beautiful valley in former times. I am looking for *continuity* in the links that join us to our forefathers, and I am trying to trace the story of how the Parish Church of St Gregory the Great was established and has tried to serve the needs of Dawlish people for at least ten centuries. I hope you will enjoy the search and know that you too are part of the story.

*Man has always had a sense of wonder*

To be human is to wonder, to ask questions and to seek meaning in the very experience of being consciously alive and aware of the apparent boundaries of life and death. While in prehistoric times men constructed vast stone circles and avenues whose detailed significance we still struggle to understand, it seems to us now, that people have always wanted to find a *meaningful pattern* in their natural surroundings. Survival was only possible if they acted in harmony with the seasonal cycles of the mysterious planet where they lived. Trusting those patterns was a vital part of their way of life and their religious thinking.

Iron Age man subscribed to a form of religion which was his attempt to find answers about his existence, and to protect himself. He did not embrace the idea of one true God, but we would be seriously mistaken if we did not respect his search for understanding. The Pagan religions included an awe-inspired respect for the natural world which seemed to these people to be under the control of spirits which had power to bless or confound their hold on life and health. They sought to obtain the blessing of the spirits of earth, air, fire and water, and to placate them when disaster struck. Sun, moon and stars set out the seasons of their life. But above all, for them, *water* was the essence of life and also a revered and necessary source of healing.

So, in addition to choosing to site their dwellings near a spring of good clear water, they also enclosed streams to form *sacred pools*. Trees forming a *sacred grove* sheltered many such holy places. High up on Little Haldon Hill there is such a spring which even now has the aura attributable to a place of special use. In Mediaeval times it attracted a religious recluse and pilgrims. Legends of strange healings (and also less desirable happenings) were handed down by word of mouth, and a chapel was built there. This is now a fragmentary ruin, and is difficult to find, but maps still show the name Lidwell and mark it as a *Holy Well*. Some now say they think the name 'Lidwell' is a corruption of 'Our Lady's Well'. If so this is a good example of the long continued use of an old, and probably pre-Christian, sacred site.

From the hillsides encircling the fertile basin many streams ran down and joined to form the main Dawlish Water. This cut down quite deeply into gravelly soil, and lower down, the banks became clothed with overhanging trees which made this a dark place. But the water was good and the riverside level terraces afforded room for a sizeable settlement. This took the name of its sombre river: *DAWLISH*, which is thought to mean *DARK WATER*.

*Our own sacred pool?*

Now within the village that grew up here were several more springs draining the steepish hills on either side of the lower valley of the Dawlish Water and its largest tributary the Aller Water. One of these (it is marked on the 1: 25,000 Ordnance Survey map) rises at the spot where the west end of the Parish Church now stands. Until 1981 this was where, inside the building, the baptismal font stood. (In 1981, when the narthex screen was installed, the font was moved to the north transept.) When it was in its original position, consecrated water from the font drained into a stone-sided and covered well below the floor of the church and so back into the natural earth and stream, and on into Dawlish Water. Is it too great a leap of sensitive imagination to surmise that the first Christian church was built on this spot because *it was already a holy place* by virtue of a sacred pool made by damming the natural stream in pagan times? I don't think we can ever know with certainty, but the idea that holy water in this actual place forms a link between early (pagan) worshippers, many seeking healing, — and the devotions and needs of the present day congregation, is an attractive one to me.

*The coming of the Romans*

Early in the century in which Jesus was born in Bethlehem, and while he lived his wonderful life in Galilee and Jerusalem, the Romans who already ruled the lands of the Near East were busily extending their empire to include Britain in the far North West. Their skills in establishing themselves as the dominant power in this newly invaded land are well recorded. Not only did they conquer by using superior fighting methods, but they also very quickly organised the making of fine and durable roads for rapid communication and movement of troops and stores.  They introduced the arts of building in stone, locally baked bricks and prefabricated timber fortifications.  The resident Britons may have watched with amazement the installation of sophisticated plumbing, sanitation and heating and even mosaic pictorial floors in grand houses, public buildings and temples to the Roman gods.  Even humble soldiers had the use of a heated bath-house in each settled town.  A new and highly organised way of life was being introduced all over the land.  It is likely that the Romans had reached Exeter by the start of the $2^{nd}$ century A.D. and had set up there a fortified military trading and administrative post.

*Two centuries of Roman domination in Dawlish*

Roman policy seems to have been to shift the burden of administration on to the shoulders of loyal local leaders as soon as was possible.  Such co-operation was to the mutual benefit of both parties to the agreement: the Roman garrison in Exeter needed steady provision of food, timber and fuel, and local people gained the protection of Roman law.  Dawlish families would have been required to provide labour and goods and to submit to the dictates of those who made the domestic arrangements for the support of the fighting militia based in Exeter.  I wonder if there were trading agreements, and if so, maybe Dawlish residents may have enjoyed the chance to sample imported Mediterranean delicacies.  Perhaps they were introduced to dates and figs, wine and olive oil and luxuries such as jewellery and fine pottery.

This period in our local history was marked by several changes of great significance :

Firstly, the start of *widespread use of currency.*
Secondly, an increase in *knowledge of the world beyond Britain.*
Thirdly, the acquisition of *the skills of reading and writing.*  This last was perhaps one of the most important changes that divide the time since the Romans came, from all that had gone before.

Finally, along the routes of trade and legal transactions with the Roman Emperor and his minions, and the travels to and fro of soldiers retiring or newly appointed, there was brought to Britain again, word of *the Good News of Jesus Christ.*

It must have been hard indeed to be a Christian Roman soldier in a foreign land, surrounded by men who worshipped and made sacrifices to the many Roman gods, and who venerated the Emperor himself. They faced ridicule and ostracism and, more than likely, punishment and the death penalty. We know there was persecution, for there are records that tell of a Christian priest who fled and found shelter in the home of a Roman citizen who had become a devout Christian in Verulamium (St. Albans). When the hide-out was discovered, Alban the Roman dressed himself in the priest's clothing and went out instead of him, to face torture and death by beheading. So Alban became the earliest known Christian martyr in Britain, in about 250 A.D.

We have no records of any priests, nor of Christian groups in the Exeter or Dawlish areas during the Roman occupation, and it is generally agreed that Christianity had little hold in many parts of Britain before the 4$^{th}$ century. Then, after Constantine the Great became Emperor in 306 A.D., Christianity became an approved religion, and then the official one throughout the Roman Empire. Constantine concerned himself with internal struggles of the Church as it strove to describe and record its belief and practice, so that its teaching should remain consistent and universal, and true to that of our Lord Christ. One of the great Councils to which Constantine summoned the leaders of the Church was held in Nicea, (in what is now modern Turkey), in 325 A.D. This was the first of a series of meetings from which came, eventually, the Nicene Creed that we use during the Celebration of the Eucharist. We learn that bishops from Britain took part in the later councils; from this we may surmise that organised Christian churches existed in many parts of our country, and that there was priestly care and instruction, perhaps even in the Dawlish area.

*After the Romans*

The Roman occupation of Britain came to an end early in the 5$^{th}$ century. For a while some Britons or Romano-British people tried to maintain the style of living which they had so admired, but most of the fine buildings gradually fell into disrepair as local communities re-determined their own legal and social systems. Practical skills learned from the Romans were forgotten, and the use of imported materials faltered and died. So too with Christianity, which seems to have faded away as the older pagan religion retained its hold in rural and urban society.

Britain was left to fend for itself against the already threatening attacks of the many land-hungry invaders from the continent. Angles, Saxons, Jutes and Danes saw their opportunity and year by year, came over the seas to harry and subdue, but often just to marry and settle here. Their different cultures, art and languages contributed to the eventual formation of an *English* nation after many years of turmoil and enmity. Resistant Britons moved westwards into Wales and Cornwall and Ireland, some taking with them a loyalty to the early Celtic form of Christianity brought from Ireland, together with some features of Roman life.

Devon lands and people, on the other hand, were destined to become part of the Anglo-Saxon kingdom of Wessex. We need to remember that the invaders of Britain were largely from a broad cultural group which included German, northern French and southern Scandinavian peoples. These 'Germanic' peoples were almost certainly illiterate for the first two centuries of their occupation of Britain. Historically accurate accounts of this part of the 'Dark Ages' are largely wanting. There are huge gaps in our knowledge, and question marks over information supplied by hostile Britons and ill-informed foreigners. It was a time of fluctuating fortunes, and survival was through small community loyalties and careful agricultural hard labour. Again the favourable, relatively remote position of the Dawlish lands would have helped our ancestor families to survive as a community.

This must have been roughly the situation here when, in 597 A.D., Augustine and his 40 monks came to Kent with a specific mission, namely to *re-establish* Christianity in *England*. (Celtic Christianity had been established in Ireland and had come to Northumbria, Scotland and Wales some 100 years earlier).

*Who sent the priest Augustine, and why?*

This will be the subject of the next chapter in the history of Dawlish and its Parish Church of St. Gregory the Great.

# CHAPTER TWO

## *GREGORY and AUGUSTINE*

Augustine, priest and monk, was Prior of the Monastery of St. Andrew in Rome. In 596 A.D. he and 40 monks were directed by the then Pope, Gregory the First, to travel to Britain to re-establish Christianity there and to set up an organised Church under the auspices of the Popes of Rome.

Pope Gregory became known as Gregory the Great and eventually as Saint Gregory. He was born in the year 540 in Rome, the son of a senator. He first pursued a government career and became a Prefect of Rome. But he was not satisfied with the kind of life into which he had been led, and when his father died he resigned from his political position and became a monk. As a Christian he longed for the contemplative life which the monastic discipline seemed to offer him, but he was soon called upon to serve as a statesman of the Church. This apparent conflict of personal vocations he resolved in a successful blend of worship, study and effective leadership.

He was a fine theologian, and an excellent musician. He gave his name to several hymns dating back to his time, and also devised what are now treasured as the Gregorian Chants. He paid great attention to ways of worship and forms of liturgy. Much beloved by his fellow priests and people, he was elected to the office of Pope, but refused all grandiose titles, asking only to be a *"servant of the servants of God".* His mission was to save souls by spreading the Christian faith to all parts of the extensive Roman Empire.

Legend has it that when Gregory saw fair-haired boys for sale as slaves in the market place in Rome and asked where they had come from, he was told they were from Britain and were Angles. "Oh not Angles, but ANGELS!" was his comment. We don't know whether this is fact or fiction, but it is said that this incident was the trigger for Gregory's longing to send Christianity to Britain. Indeed, he himself wanted to come here, but he bowed to the wishes of his advisers who felt that his prior work was in Rome. This did not detract from his strongly held intention. His great zeal enabled him to send Augustine, who, with his band of 40 monks set out to journey through Gaul. There they met with much hardship and their doubts and fears made them want to turn back. After receiving letters of encouragement from Gregory they pressed on and came into Kent, and were safely received by King Aethelberht, and his wife who was a Christian from northern Gaul. The king later became a convert; land was set apart for the new community of monks, and then a church was founded in Canterbury. From here a robust Christianity began to spread out into Anglo-Saxon Britain.

Pope Gregory wrote frequently to the younger churches, and over 800 of his letters remain precious and relevant for Christians today. His book "The Pastoral Office" describes the qualities essential for the 'shepherds of the Church': how they should live, how they should instruct the people, and that they must always remember their own frailty. Truly he was a faithful shepherd and we remember him with gratitude. When his dedicated life ended he was buried in Rome and the following epitaph (in Latin of course) was inscribed on his tomb:

> Wisdom was in his words, and all he wrought
> was as a pattern, acting all he taught.
> To Christ he led the Angles, by God's grace
> swelling Faith's armies with a new-won race.
> O holy pastor, all your work and prayer
> to God you offered with a shepherd's care.
> Triumphant now you reap your just reward
> raised to high place, the consul of the Lord.

*******************************************

At this time, the Anglo-Saxons were spreading out to take control over many of the British kingdoms, and over the next three centuries they reached Devon which became part of the Kingdom of Wessex. During this same period, from its earliest footholds Christianity spread from Canterbury into Wessex lands as well as in other directions. To Devon lands, then, came the form of the

Christian faith and liturgical worship that was ordained by the Popes in Rome.

Devon was at this time a stronghold of the pagan religion. How would the missionary monks set about presenting the new faith in a place like Dawlish?  We do know that when Augustine was consulted about how to deal with pagan sacred sites and where to build a church, this was his reply :

*"Do not destroy sacred places of worship, but purify them from the worship of demons and dedicate them instead to the service of the true God.  In this way, we hope that the people, seeing that their temples are not destroyed, may abandon their error and, flocking more readily to their accustomed resorts, may come to know and adore the true God"*

It is this advice which prompts me to think there is some substance in the idea that the first Dawlish church was built on the site of a former pagan sacred healing spring.

*Early Church Foundations*

Athelstan was king of Wessex in 926 when he founded the monastery of St. Mary and St. Peter in Exeter, on the site where the cathedral now stands.  From there, Christian groups were taught in many of the surrounding villages which were part of the Royal Manor lands, and eventually a house for worship would be built.  A new local church in the early days of Christianity was often built over the tomb of a martyr who would be regarded as the fatherly Saint who could offer to God helpful prayers for that particular place or community.  In line with this type of belief, the people in the new Dawlish church chose Gregory as their patron saint because they were well aware of the self-sacrificial and major part he had played in bringing the Faith to them. Dedication of a church to St. Augustine or St. Gregory often signifies that it was established in Anglo-Saxon times, and we have good grounds for thinking that our Dawlish church came into existence as early as this.  Documents exist which testify that in 1044 King Edward the Confessor, one of the later Saxon kings, gave the manor of Dawlish to his chaplain and secretary Leofric, a devout Christian who is thought by some (without firm evidence) to have taken up residence in the good land at Holcombe.

Leofric later became the appointed Bishop of Devon and Cornwall, a huge area which he cared for from his 'seat' at Crediton. In 1050 this was transferred to the safer, walled city of Exeter, and records show that Dawlish, Holcombe and also Teignmouth had to raise revenue for the support of the cathedral canons. Although this was a secular requirement of the whole population of the manor, we can be reasonably sure that churches were in existence by then, and that the people had access to places of worship. The earliest written record of any of these is one which mentions St. Michael's Church Teignmouth in 1044.

*The Saxon Parish*

It was in these Anglo-Saxon times that established villages and homesteads became organised into secular *parishes*. A parish was a group of settlements whose people cultivated their fields in common, and served the lord of the manor. Saxon parish boundaries have persisted to this day in many parts of the country and there are good records of our local one of Dawlish. The parish was an administrative unit whose economy was based on a system of *tithing*. One tenth part of the parish produce, in money or 'in kind' was required as a sort of tax. The need for substantial storage space led to the building of the 'tithe barn'.

*The first church building in Dawlish*

As Christianity spread, it was the lord of the manor who organised the building of the earliest Christian assembly hall and claimed the right to appoint the priest of his choice, often his own chaplain, a married man rather than a celibate monk.

We can confidently suppose that our church meeting house in Dawlish, like the tithe barn, was built in the local style, and so having a timber frame with 'wattle and daub' panelled walls (or possibly Devon cob walls), and with a reed thatched roof. All locally available materials. We have no known remains of Saxon buildings of timber or stone in this area, but we can be sure that the meeting house stood out in strong contrast to the humble dwellings of the families in the parish. It would have been built to worthy standards by the best local craftsmen. The Venerable Bede, a Northumbrian monk, scholar and scribe, in his book 'The Ecclesiastical History of the English People', praises the high quality of Saxon workmanship in the timber-built churches.

These timber structures are reminiscent of the mighty Halls where Anglo-Saxon warriors feasted and rested after battle, as portrayed in the Beowulf narrative. But in Christian times these wonderful skills in the selection and working of woodland trees were put to more peaceable uses. The site of the Dawlish building would have been beside, or even over, the bubbling spring which had marked the place as sacred, set apart and holy, as far back as anyone could remember. I wonder if they used the spring and pool water for Christian Baptism?

We are told that, alas, many of these fine timber buildings were destroyed by fire, and some would in time suffer natural decay especially in damp places like the bottom of the Dawlish valley. Some must have been re-built several times during the Saxon era. In Dawlish it seems unlikely that there was a stone structure, but we just don't know! If funds had permitted the making of such a high status building, it might have looked like the one which still exists in Bradford-on-Avon in Wiltshire. This has a narrow, high-walled simple nave, and a small chancel with squared off east end. The English preferred this shape to the rounded east end recess which was more usual on the continent.

*A little bit of word history*

I'm told that our word 'church' comes from the Celtic form 'chirich' or 'cirice' which referred to the *churchyard* where burials took place. Even earlier, the Greek words 'kyrikon doma' meant *the house of the Lord*. In English the 'ch' form was retained, giving us *church,* while in Scotland we have *kirk* and in German a mixture which gives *Kirche* These related words in the several languages all continue the feeling of reverence for the burial ground and the house of worship within it. The Greek word 'ecclesia' referred to the *assembled Christians*, and this is closer to the spirit of the earliest Christian communities before there were special buildings. (hence 'église' in French and 'eglwys' in Welsh, and 'ekalesia' in Samoan). We often use the word church for the building, but a better practice is to apply it to the *people* who use it. Today this is often emphasised by conferring upon the word the dignity of a capital 'C' when it refers to the people.

*Keeping the records and spreading information*

Other familiar words such as 'clerk' tell interesting stories. Many legal records pertaining to land tenure and boundary agreements survive from these Anglo-Saxon times. Comparatively few people could read, but even fewer were those who could write. Those who had learned the art were much in demand for making permanent records of legal matters, and for the copying of manuscripts. Where did they learn to write?

It was in the monasteries that the art of copying was most highly developed. A monk who had been taught to achieve a high standard of writing and illustrating would make this his life's work, his own offering to God. In the monastery school children and young men were taught to read and write and so to become *'clerks'*. Some would go on to take Holy Orders while others could find work beyond the walls and discipline of the monastery. The simplest meaning of the term 'clerk' is 'one who can write', or a 'penman'. This came to indicate a man of learning who could keep written accounts of legal or business affairs. A clerk who was ordained priest was then described as *'a clerk in Holy Orders'* which is still the official designation of a *clergy*man today.

*Growing towards an English nation*

Anglo-Saxon society had already established its own local and regional structures for the administration of law and order. Its courts dealt with land tenure and taxation for supporting defence measures. In general, land owners and villagers alike had come to feel themselves part of a much larger overall community with extending trading possibilities. The development of its own common spoken language was a huge step towards the realisation of an English nation.

But a comprehensive and momentous change was to come.

# CHAPTER THREE

## *THE COMING OF THE NORMANS*

1066 and all that!  Once again our land was invaded.  The Saxon kings were over-ruled by the newcomers, men whose origins lay in the northern lands but who had taken up residence in French land just across the Channel.  There was bitter but ineffective resistance and resentment, and the Normans had to *impose* their rule, rather than succeed by gaining the co-operation of lords, bishops and leaders of Saxon institutions.  The invaders set out to take over those institutions by replacing their former leaders with Norman incomers and suppressing the use of the 'Old English' language that was becoming standardized and in use as a unifying feature of the country.  Norman French became the language we had to acquire if we hoped for any kind of status or authority.  Also the Catholic Church in England came to be increasingly under stricter supervision from Rome.

With the passage of time some working together was slowly achieved, and here in the south-west our own Bishop was one of the few who were allowed to retain their appointments and lands. So there was less disruption in land tenure and the Church than in many parts of the country, and Dawlish could settle down again.

The Normans were highly organised and determined to know in detail what were the resources of land, productivity and manpower.  So the Domesday Book was compiled in 1084, based on a thorough and widespread inspection, and probably making use of the Anglo-Saxon records already in existence.  Its written catalogue has an entry for Dawlish which describes it as being 'Land of the Bishop of Exeter', and valued at £8. This implies that it was a rather flourishing community within the King's manor.

The royal manor embraced a number of villages, each of which was administered by a landlord loyal to the King, and, if required, was forced to provide military manpower.

*Village life in the 12th Century*

In these times the vast majority of people were living in villages and were engaged in agriculture and its attendant occupations. The primary object of farming was to supply the simple needs of the family, and to pay the required tithes to the local landlord, for a man did not own the land upon which he depended. The lord of the manor reserved for his own use a portion of the total estate, and this *demesne* or home farm was cultivated for him by his dependent tenants in return for their own holdings. The lord, with his manor house, large home farm and the judicial court over which he was required to preside, stood for power and authority in the village.

But the priest, with the Church, filled a similarly essential place in the life of the villager. The church building and the churchyard were the setting for much village activity. There the people gathered not only for religious observances on Sundays and the many Holy Days, but also for their merry-makings which included dancing and singing. This was a focal point for the exchange of news and general discussion and pleasurable talk. Here a market might be held for sale or barter of goods.

Although the priest was often of lowly birth, sparsely educated and seldom wealthy, he enjoyed a high status because of his solemn duties. But on weekdays he was working, like any other peasant, on his *glebe,* parish land given over to the married priest and his family. In Dawlish this was possibly only the land around his house, though some might lie in *field strips* among those of his parishioners. If so, what a splendid way for the priest to know and converse with his people! Beside cultivating his land, he had another important duty in the village farming interests: he was expected to oversee the maintenance of the parish bull and parish boar, and sometimes the ram and stallion as well! For on these valuable beasts the village depended for all its animal stock and hence its prosperity in general trading.

*Norman efficiency expressed in impressive buildings*

As the manorial landlords became firmly established under the rule of King and Bishop, and their financial assets increased, they took up the practice of building places of worship in stone and to patterns devised by Continental architects. Many Saxon timber buildings were destroyed and replaced with stone ones of *Romanesque* design which featured the Roman round arch and massive walls and narrow window apertures. Norman Romanesque building is done in the 'grand manner', conceived and boldly executed by men of tremendous energy, in a massive and menacing style as if to underline the power and authority of the conquerors over their compliant cultivators of the land.

Still, parish life in rural areas like Dawlish was not suddenly drastically altered. Our parish priest continued to cultivate his 'glebe' and to perform his vocational duties in worship, instruction and care of his flock. But there were important developments, for under the increased authority of Norman government and the Pope in Rome, Anglo-Saxon writing became replaced by Latin or Norman French for all formal purposes, and the language for church services was Latin as in the monasteries. This was, of course, the universal (= catholic) language of the Church, but for the villagers attending worship in their own locality it must have raised an almost insuperable barrier to their understanding and real participation. If, formerly, the priest had used the local tongue in parts of the Mass, it was now forbidden. I find myself wondering how it was that the people were persuaded to accept the new ways, and then I realised that they were simply told to do so by the lord of the manor and the Bishop!   Perhaps that authority was no bad thing in a community which depended on strong leadership to keep its productivity and coherence at the highest possible level.

## Our first recorded church re-building

What makes it certain that the Church in Dawlish and its meeting house and burial ground had been established for a long time, is the fact that we have it on record that Dawlish saw the *re-building* of the parish church in the year 1148. Our manorial landlord (under the Bishop of Exeter) had enough wealth to erect what was probably our first stone-built house of worship. Had there been a stone Saxon building, some of it would probably been incorporated in the new Norman structure, but there are no records of this.

So it seems certain that we had a new building in the heavy Norman style with thick walls, round headed arches and tiny windows. The largest arch would be the one which divided the nave from the chancel, and it was probably made of carved sections to make a chevron design.

A strong building indeed, but how dark and oppressive, even forbidding! In winter and maybe all through the year, many candles or burning torches on wall brackets would have been necessary in order for the congregation to see any decorative colours on the roof beams and arches and to make out the pictures of saints and Bible characters applied as frescoes to the walls. A person's first duty was to *kneel and listen* as the priest celebrated Mass at the altar at the far east end. His words, in Latin, and his actions, would remain a mysterious ritual unless he took the trouble to instruct them in their own familiar language. No doubt a goodly number of priests did so with great devotion. For most certainly the Mass and the rites of Baptism, Holy Matrimony and Burial were valued and significant highlights in the lives of all his parishioners.

*Inside the new Norman church*

The essential 'furniture' within the building would be the stone slab altar at the east end, and the font at the west end. There was the great arch separating the chancel (where the priest performed his duties) from the nave (where the people gathered). There were no pews or seats except that perhaps there was a stone ledge around the inside of the walls where the old or infirm could sit and rest their aching legs: this may be the origin of the phrase *'The weakest go to the wall '*.

The Normans developed the art of carving stone far beyond the simple but powerful depictions of angels, saints and representations of the crucifixion, which Saxon workmen had achieved. Saxon buildings had square, straight lines. The Norman masons used the *axe* to shape square blocks of sandstone into curved pieces which they could assemble to make rounded pillars.

Individual arch sections were decorated with bold zig-zag designs before they were hoisted into place. In some Norman churches the patterns didn't quite match up, and the *'chevron'* design was a bit irregular!  (When I visit an old church and see these marks of the differing degrees of skill of individual workers it warms my heart and I think of those toiling masons with great affection. They become real people to me and remind me that not one of us is perfect).  The *capital* at the top of a pillar was wider than the pillar because on it rested a roof support.  Here was another site where axe-carved designs, often geometrical motifs, could be used.

In these times a doorway was often surmounted by a semi-circular *tympanum* using the space enclosed by the top of the arch.  Here was a favourite site for showing Christ in Glory, or the struggle between good and evil, or the tree of life.  Such more detailed work was carried out with mallet and chisels various: the refined tools and delicate craftsmanship that we expect of a master mason.  The doorway was often the most prolifically carved feature of the building because it signified the important journey of worshippers from the 'ordinary' everyday life towards the contemplation of the 'extra-ordinary' world which embraces "….all that is, seen and unseen…." and for the Christian, a welcome to enter and accept his unique place within it.

*The Norman corbel stone*

At the top of the outside wall, where the roof rested on an especially strong course of projecting stone (called the corbel table), the masons often carved decorative and symbolic figures. Today we may find it hard to understand what these figures were meant to convey.  Some of them were of Biblical characters while others showed frankly pagan subjects, or a local mason's joke or his self-portrait.  Sometimes there were overtly sexual motifs which everyone would understand.  Grotesque, amusing, shocking or superstitious as they were, they remind us of things that have always been important in an ordinary person's life.  These include fertility of people and their crops and livestock, fidelity in marriage, appreciation of plants for their beauty and healing properties, an important recognition of wild animals as either friend or foe.

There were many (to us) strange ideas about the powers of birds and animals; these were often portrayed as caricatures in stone. Above all was the over-riding hope of *the victorious power of good over evil*, which might be represented by combat between the 'Great Beasts' of Norse mythology, or an angel and a writhing serpent, or St. Michael standing in triumph over a vanquished dragon.

There *is* some evidence that our Dawlish Norman building was adorned with such carvings arranged just below the roof support. We have in St.Gregory's churchyard one *corbel* stone which has survived to the present day. I wonder how many or how few of us know about it? What a story it could tell! At present it stands on the ground, tucked away in the corner made by a buttress and the north wall of the present building. It depicts a ram's head, and reminds me of Abraham's obedience to God's command to him to sacrifice his son Isaac. He makes all the preparations to do so, and at this point, God calls again and tells him to stay his hand and sacrifice instead the ram he sees caught in a thicket. Abraham had demonstrated wonderfully his obedience to God, who would now make him the father of a great nation. This is but one of the many Bible stories which the 12th century Dawlish village congregation would have been taught until they knew it by heart, but they would be *reminded* of it every time they came to the church and looked up at the series of carvings just below the roof.

Our Norman church was, we think, built of fairly local red sandstone, probably from the large Whipton quarries near Exeter, and limestone from the far side of the Exe estuary. The carved 'ram' corbel is of Beer stone from the extensive workings in East Devon which would supply great quantities of material for the interior structures in many churches like Ottery St. Mary and in the rebuilt Cathedral from 1270 onwards. While Beer stone is relatively easy to carve when freshly extracted, it is not sufficiently durable for exterior work. (Tragically, a similar 'soft' stone was used for the images on the west front of the Cathedral which are now only a shadow of their former glory). These very useful limestones from Beer and Salcombe Regis and Dunscombe were always distributed to building sites by sea, this being far more practicable than hauling it all the way by cart along the rough 'roads' of the time.

Our 'ram' corbel stone no longer has the crisp edge lines it had when freshly carved. It is more than likely that most of its fellow sculptured beasts had crumbled to unrecognisable shapes by the time the Norman church had served us for 300 years. It is my hope that this remaining stone will be treasured and carefully preserved for future generations to appreciate this tangible link with the Norman church on this site.

## Dawlish clergy and congregation

During this span of time (1148 – 1438), we have access to only a few shreds of information about the building and the parishioners, but we know rather more about the clerical incumbents. In the year 1272 the oldest surviving record of the names of the Vicars of the parish begins with the single letter 'W' written at the edge of the damaged record. After this, the record is complete up to the present day, apart from the (recently noted) omission of John Street, 1523. (The list can be read in the appendix to this book, and on the wall of the lower foyer in the present building). Before 1272, clearly the record was either not kept or it has since been lost.

"A record of 1282 suggests that by that date the Dawlish Church, dedicated to St. Gregory the Great, was the mother church whose vicar had authority over the chaplains at Cofton and East Teignmouth". (A.R.Thompson: see below)

Under the Normans, special *ecclesiastical courts* were set up. These operated in parallel with the *secular courts* but dealt with so-called 'crimes against God', namely disputes within the church, or over church property, or reported misconduct of the clergy. They also "had authority over lay people in respect not only of marriage and divorce but also of slander, breach of promise, witchcraft, and sexual misconduct, and in Dawlish where the lordship of the manor was in clerical hands, disputes over wills and tenancies".

We learn also that "The local priest was a significant figure receiving taxes and rents for the church, particularly the tithe on all produce, which he shared with his lord. By the end of the 12th century the right of many churches to take this tithe, had been appropriated by monastic houses which enjoyed the revenue and appointed *vicars* (clerical deputies) to carry out parish duties". Or a *rector* (an incumbent entitled to have the major part of the church tithe) was appointed by someone high up on the ecclesiastical ladder. He would take the 'great tithes', those of corn, hay and wood, whilst the vicar received the 'small tithes', those on other produce (which were more difficult to collect)!

Happily, "from the early 13th century vicars usually received an adequate stipend from tithes and the cultivation of glebe land, and enjoyed security of tenure …

"In 1301 the parishioners told Bishop Bytton that although the vicar visited them he did not reside in Dawlish but left the village in the care of Sir Adam, a chaplain, who appears to have given good service. There was also another curate, Randolph, who … had been leading a blemished life for over ten years and although often admonished was quite unrepentant! "

(These quotations are from "How Dawlish Lost Its Independence" written by Dr. A.R.Thompson. Dawlish Local History Group. 1998).

The title 'Sir' was accorded to an ordained chaplain or priest in Mediaeval times; it did not imply knightly status.

*A Visitation and Inspection*

As we have heard, in the year 1301 Dawlish Church was visited and assessed by Bishop Bytton of Exeter. In his report the Bishop wrote:

"The statue of St. Gregory on the high altar is badly represented and has one hand missing."

Perhaps it wasn't a sign of general neglect, for the rest of the report, detailing the church furniture, vestments, communion plate and the building fabric and roof was satisfactory, and there was praise for *the newly built chancel.* The building was being enlarged or modified, perhaps as the congregation increased.

But what had happened to the people of St. Gregory's Church, that they hadn't found it important to keep a decent statue of their patron saint? Could the people, and especially the vicar, have failed to remember, or lost interest in, the story of how the Gospel came to England and so to them? (Perhaps the statue was a wooden piece that had become badly worm-eaten).

We don't know what happened to that particular statue, but the gratitude for St. Gregory has been renewed and kept strong. Every time *we* go into the present building we can look up and see a rather lovely statuette of St. Gregory and the Anglo-Saxon slave boy, on the chancel arch. It is Italian workmanship and was presented to the church in 1961. We can imagine that in 1301 the Bishop's report was a wake up call to the people, and that they set about making a new and more worthy statue. In doing so no doubt there were special prayers said and votive candles burned nearby as they *retold the story.* This *recollection* of the patron saint eventually became an annual festival. It is still celebrated in the 21st century, because we know *our* memory is fallible and we are enriched by thinking again about such great moments in our common history of the Church.

*Some thoughts about remembering: a little digression!*

Before reading became a skill available to the many, the ordinary person depended far more on his memory than we do today. Knowledge and traditional culture and belief were handed on by word of mouth, by pictures, sculpture in wood and stone, and by ritual dance and seasonal observances, all of which were, and are, *memory triggers*. Think about the importance of the pattern of events in the Christian Year which we continue to observe, and the teaching that is given as each stage is celebrated. In the Middle Ages this regularly repeated *recalling* was even more beneficial than it is today for us who, if we recognise our need, can read and study the story of our salvation privately as well as being dramatically reminded in our worship together.

A good teacher is a valuable asset in any community and particularly in a non-literate one as the congregation of St. Gregory's Church would have been at that time. To be effective a teacher or priest had to be adept at using methods which fixed stories, commands and instruction in the memory of the listener. These methods are still very familiar to us in the way we learn 'by heart': from the *repetition* of nursery rhymes and chanted multiplication tables when we were young, to the songs telling of our history, common experience or loyalty, that we sing together again and again. We never forget what is thus so firmly imprinted in our memory. And this is the method used in synagogue schools and Islamic seminaries to ensure that students *learn and retain* the Scriptures. How else did Jesus himself learn them but at his mother's knee and in the synagogue school and worship? It used to be, and I hope will always be, part of a basic teaching method in nearly all British homes and schools, and those of us who grew up experiencing this discipline remain deeply grateful for the treasure store we gained and which is here to hand at any time now and will still be ours even when we can no longer see or hear.

Some of the strongest memory aids come from pictures. 'Picture' memory and thought are ours before we begin to think in words, and we remember some of those scenes with a wonderful clarity. So the ability to raise a *picture* in our mind is a mark of the best storyteller. *Rhythm and pattern in speech* are also of immense importance in making sayings both beautiful to our ears and in helping us to recall them accurately. How much easier it is to memorise poetry than prose! Why else are hymns, work-songs and folk-songs enjoyed and perpetuated?

How blessed *we* are to have the Scriptures in our own language, and to be able to read and listen to them. Thanks to the care of translators we have this treasury of stories *memorably* told, and songs and ideas set out in *unforgettable poetry*. As we read the Gospel narratives, we can sit at the feet of Jesus, the greatest Teacher who ever lived!

*Teaching the local congregation*

As for our St. Gregory congregation worshipping in the Norman building, spare a few moments to wonder how *they* learned their Bible stories, and the essentials of Christian belief and how to live by it. The main act of worship was the Mass celebrated in Latin; the Bible readings and prayers also in Latin. We must conclude that the priest *taught the people in their own local tongue*, telling them over and over again many stories from the Bible and about the saints, instructing them constantly in the Gospel truths and how these should shape their everyday lives. The picture aids were there on the walls and in the carvings and must have been constantly used.

There is an inscription carved on the 14th century font in the church at Bradley, Lincolnshire which reads:

"Pater noster, Ave Maria, Criede,
Leren the childe yt is nede"

(Our Father..,Hail Mary..,the Creed...you need to teach the child).

Clearly the teaching of a member of the church begins when the Sacrament of Baptism is administered. The message on the font is addressed to the parents and Godparents, with the overall help in instruction given by the parish priest. All of this would lead to Confirmation and adult belief. So a great deal depended on the priest who taught both the parents, (probably unable to read), and the child. The teaching ministry of the priest was very important, second only to his authorisation to administer the Sacraments.

*The duties of the parish priest in the 13th and 14th centuries*

There was an important and authoritative meeting in Rome in 1215 which laid down certain rules that must be followed by every parish priest. Among these was the order that he should hear the Confession of each parishioner at least once every year. This gave him the opportunity to examine a person's moral condition and his knowledge of the Catholic faith and practice.

The priest was to test everyone's competence in the articles of the Creed and his ability to recite The Lord's Prayer.

Another council in 1281 drew up a scheme for instructing lay people, and stipulated that *four times a year* the priest was to teach them, *in their own language,* subjects which included The Creed, the Ten Commandments, our Lord Christ's summation of the Commandments as 'Love God and Love your neighbour', the Seven works of mercy, Seven Virtues, Seven Vices, and the meaning of the Seven Sacraments. This was all very well if the parish priest was sufficiently educated and trained ... by no means could this be taken for granted!

## Training the Priests

In a largely illiterate society, the establishment of a large number of parish churches and the need for a priest in most of them, led to the situation where any man of good standing and having a sense of vocation might be ordained priest to answer this need.  The bishop would be aware of the need to train such a person in matters of liturgy, pastoral care and theological guidance ... an immense task when required in respect of men of simple education or only basic literary ability.  We can wonder what sort of a man was our first recorded priest "W" in 1272 in Dawlish, or his successor "Robert".  But the fact that their names are recorded shows us that literacy was gaining ground steadily. Of course, all records at this time were hand written as were all the copies of the Bible and the Missal (prayers and hymns and detailed requirements for the ordering of public worship). The production of *literature to help the parish priest* had already begun.  There were manuals of instruction on how to conduct Confession and administer the other Sacraments, and how to teach lay people.  Gradually an increasing breadth of knowledge and deeper understanding of the riches of the Faith was available to priests and was then passed on to their congregations.

In these early Mediaeval years, we can have some confidence that the parishioners of St. Gregory's Church were cared for and nourished in their faith, and that the ceremonies of worship and festival were thoroughly integrated with the local agricultural way of life, a life that was intimately understood by the priest who was himself a part of it.

The next chapter dwells further on the place that the Church occupied in the daily life of the families which made up a village like Dawlish, and on the sense of community which carried its members through times of crisis and change.

# CHAPTER FOUR

## *VILLAGE and CHURCH in MEDIAEVAL TIMES*

Life for most families in those days was one of hard and unrelenting toil in the fields and forest of the landlord. Every member of the family joined in the struggle to feed and clothe and provide warmth and shelter for all. In times of great trouble neighbouring families would help as best they could; and they would share their delight when things were happy and prospering.

Throughout the Mediaeval centuries, disease, injury, seasonal malnutrition, death and bereavement could interrupt or destroy family life. Whole communities could be struck down by natural and social disasters which they did not understand and over which they had no control and little in the way of remedy. Small wonder that there was recourse, not only to the rich store of folk medicine and herbal wisdom, but also to echoes of pagan magic. There was a longing for miraculous cures. The belief in the healing power of the bones and other relics of the Saints drew those who had the means and opportunity to go on pilgrimage to wherever there were tales of special healing.

For the ordinary villager reluctant to believe that his suffering was to be accepted as the 'will of God', there was, close at hand, the holy, consecrated water kept all the year round in the font in the church. We know that many succumbed to the temptation to steal some and use it with spells and incantations, in a desperate attempt to procure healing. This practice was so deplored by the Church authorities that in 1236 Edmund Rich as Archbishop of Canterbury issued an order requiring all fonts to be kept locked and sealed. In Dawlish, this was enforced by Exeter's Bishop Quivil whose edict in 1287 stated that every church in his diocese must have a "stone font well sealed". Then our font was fitted with a flat oak cover; iron staples were inserted into the stonework and sealed in with lead, and a strong iron bar passed through the hoops and secured with the padlocks of those times.

I often wonder what sort of support was or was not offered by our landlord to afflicted families in those days when life could be so hard. Did he care? I like to think that on the 'land of the Bishop of Exeter' the local landlord was encouraged to exercise a degree of kindness to his tenants. There was, of course, the rigid system of duty to the land owner (and through him to the King), from which no-one could escape, but it was a reciprocal provision of the means of livelihood and prosperity. Lord and peasant needed each other and loss of manpower would harm the interests of both, but there was a pretty firm class distinction! If in one year there was a good yield of wool or corn it was not to be assumed that the peasantry would benefit as well as the wealthier landowner.

By contrast, it was the Church that was at the centre of local communal life and which tried to have for ordinary people a concern for their bodily needs as well as offering some meaning and pattern in their lives. And to foster a sense of wonder at the marvels of the created world, and to strengthen the conviction that each person was of significance in the eyes of an all-seeing and loving God, even if their ordinary lives were hard and short.

*Broadening the outlook of 'ordinary' parishioners*

In the fine Norman stone church in Dawlish in the 12th, 13th and 14th centuries, the village community came together to worship God in a building that was of a richness quite unknown in domestic dwellings. The skills of masons, carpenters, sculptors and woodcarvers were on display together with those of weavers, needlewomen, gold and silversmiths, mural artists and the copiers and illustrators of sacred manuscripts ... all these arts were offered with the result that the church building was full of colour, and a place of wonder. This formed the background to the elaborate ritual of the Mass and its symbolic images, candles, banners, and priests wearing splendid vestments. Such a feast must have brought another dimension into the lives of humble folk, whose horizons might so be extended to let them have a vision of heaven and feel the aura of the Holy God. The village church building, like the new great cathedrals, could call forth awe and the desire to worship "in spirit and in truth".

Nevertheless, the people had their feet on the ground too, when they shared much more down to earth matters, as the following extract suggests. It tells a lot about how the Mediaeval Church functioned in a place like Dawlish:

"It was supported by all; it relieved the sick and needy; it was used as a parish hall; the church house (nearby or in the churchyard) was the meeting place of the guilds; and even ale was brewed on the premises, sold for the church funds, and drunk during dances and fairs in the churchyard.

"The sexton, parish clerk and the churchwardens were far more important persons in those days (than now in 1945). The sexton acted as a kind of town-crier, proclaiming the 'obits' (prayers for the dead) and Masses for the morrow. The parish clerk assisted the parish priest, when Mass was said daily. He rang the bell, prepared the altar, led the responses and preceded the procession with holy water (as the priest entered to begin the service). When the priest visited the sick the parish clerk led the way, carrying the bell and candle if the priest was taking the sacrament to the dying. On Sundays and great Feast Days he went round the parish, entered the houses and sprinkled the people with holy water.

"The churchwardens were entrusted with more varied duties than today. They had to keep accounts of everything connected with church funds, collect rents of lands and houses left to the church, farm the church stock of cattle, sell wool and cheese and gifts in kind made to the church, organise 'church ales' and administer the funds for the relief of the needy, church repairs, etc., prosecute such offenders against ecclesiastical law as adulterers and Sabbath-breakers; they also acted as bankers and pawnbrokers, the valuables entrusted to them being stored in the church; they were responsible for the safe custody of the Maypole, and of the bells and coats used in the Morris-dancing...

"It must be remembered too, that the church was often a place of refuge against marauders.........sometimes it served as a shelter from the blasts of storms".

These quotations are taken from the Introduction to:

How to Study an Old Church. A.W. Needham. 1945

(Batsford Books)

Everyone living in the village was involved in the day to day care of the church and in attendance for worship. Many would hear early Mass before heading off to the fields; others would come in as a group, to sweep the floor and garnish it with fresh rushes and sweet smelling herbs. Some would find there a little haven from the domestic noisiness of their home duties, and others might make a visit to lay flowers at the feet of a favourite saint's statue and to ask for a blessing. There were also the traditional divisions of labour and fund raising in which it was, for instance, the young men who brewed and sold the church ale at a social event, and the very young women who collected devotional offerings to maintain the candles burning before the statue of the Virgin Mary. Each group would elect its 'warden' who supervised the accounts and organised the works. We are left with a sense of the importance of the church in drawing together *every* person in the village community, and the pride with which they entered into their various commitments.

(For a more detailed study, try reading "The Voices of Morebath" by Eamon Duffy. Yale University Press 2001.)

*Dawlish parish priests in the 13th and 14th centuries*

In 1279 a vicar was appointed who served for what was in those days a very long period. His name was John de Sancto Jacobo. In his 32 years he must have got to know every soul in his care, and seen families develop, prosper and decline. Almost certainly much loved and revered, he would have supported many families through happy and sad times and guided them when crises took place. However, he was not perfect! He it was who allowed the statue of St. Gregory to become dilapidated and the subject of a reprimand by the Bishop on his visitation in 1301, although he had overseen the building of a new chancel that *was* praised. His successor David de Molton stayed here for another

27 years, so it seems that Dawlish Church had a period of nearly 60 years of steady and acceptable leadership.

After this, several very short appointments brings us to the fateful year of 1349. The terrible time of the *Black Death* seems remote to us now, but it came to us here in Dawlish and wreaked havoc among us. Every family was affected and some were totally exterminated. There was no remedy. Fervent prayers seemed to be unanswered. We can barely imagine the terror and anguish that swept through great swathes of the land. And the vicar, not surprisingly, was not spared, but was buried with the people with whom he had prayed. In that same year we had three new vicars who succumbed one after the other in a matter of months.

Throughout the land probably almost a third of the population perished, leaving an acute shortage of able workers in every walk of life. Manpower suddenly became a commodity in short supply, and workers were not slow to realise that they could bargain with their employers and landlords for better conditions and wages.

Dawlish and other hard hit communities gradually became able to reconstruct themselves and settle down, and to look ahead and entertain new ideas. Within 50 years St. Gregory's Parish Church embarked on the bold building venture which gave us our splendid *Tower* which was built at the west end of the Norman building. To understand the change in architecture we need to look back 200 years to that remarkable outburst of building fervour which provided a way of life for thousands of workers.

*The Age of Cathedral Building*

Beginning in the year 1114 the Saxon cathedral in Exeter was rebuilt in Norman style and dedicated to St.Peter in 1133. Less than 150 years later it was decided to adopt the new Gothic style with pointed arches and new load-bearing techniques which made bigger windows and greater height safely possible. The Gothic Lady Chapel was begun in 1275 and slowly the sanctuary, choir, crossing and nave were transformed with new stonework, and windows with 'Decorated' tracery. Much of the heavy Norman stone walling was removed, but the magnificent transept towers remain to mark the uniqueness of Exeter Cathedral.  The Gothic structural work was completed in the 1340s just in time before the scourge of the Black Death invaded our country in 1349.  After this time work on other Gothic cathedrals, still unfinished, was severely hampered, and in some cases was completed only with the inferior workmanship of poorly trained or inexperienced carpenters and stonemasons.  The great cathedral building epoch was at an end, and with it the ensured livelihood of thousands of remaining workers with diverse skills.  So they took to the roads!  For some, the artisans' Guilds who had trained them and guarded their interests, would be able to direct them to likely employers.  They took with them the tools of their trade and plenty of detailed knowledge as well as a desperate need for work.

Fortunately for them, a good number of land owners had prospered to the point where they wanted to build fine houses with private family chapels, or to finance the rebuilding of the parish churches within their lands.  Many chose to do this in the belief that such benefactions would stand them in good stead when they died and faced a judgemental God who might consign them to eternal damnation or to languish in purgatory.  (What a travesty of the Gospel of the just, forgiving and merciful God).

So round about 1400 when plans were made to build the west end tower of St. Gregory's parish church, the necessary workmen were around looking for jobs. There were quarrymen, carters, stonemasons and carpenters, and woodmen who made skilled use of trees in the landowners forests.

The tower is the oldest part of the present church.  West end towers are typical of churches in the south-west counties, and many are built of the warm red sandstone quarried around Exeter.  But why bother to have one?  The next chapter will let us think through this question.

# CHAPTER FIVE

## *A STRONG TOWER*

"The name of the LORD is a strong tower;
the righteous man runs into it and is safe."

Proverbs 18 v. 10

In ancient times a tower was a refuge, a stronghold. You could gain access only by a small, easily blocked door or by a ladder to an opening high above the ground. There were no vulnerable windows except very high up. In those days, as well as being places of safety, towers became emblems of status, power and prosperity. So is this why we have a church tower?

Certainly the site for St. Gregory's church was chosen well inland from the beach and the marsh where marauding invaders could land. Perhaps the earlier buildings *were* used as the place of refuge.

*Peace and prosperity*

But by about 1400 A.D. when our tower was built, the community was more settled and peaceful. The new tower had a fine west door and eventually, a window to give light inside the church through the tall tower arch opening into the nave. It was not very long before the well ordered agriculture and good grazing of the area brought enough wealth to the land owners to enable them to contribute handsomely towards the total rebuilding of the old Norman church in the same Perpendicular style as the tower. The walls of both would be in the same local red sandstone. We will come to that story later on.

For now, we have to ask: Why is the tower important, as it is no longer needed as a place of physical refuge or as a status symbol?

The short answer then and now is that it houses the BELLS.

*A communication centre*

We need to remember that there were no clocks as we know them today. Mediaeval people developed a delicate sense of the passage of time from the sun and moon, shadows and seasons and their state of hunger and weariness. *Co-ordination* of times for work in field or garden and marketplace, and for worship, could be achieved by the use of bells sounding from the church tower. Over the church south porch there was a large sundial (lost in the 1820s rebuilding). On fine days priest and sexton marked the hours of daylight pretty accurately......and they would make a good guess when it was raining!

The use of large bells to call the people to worship is a long-established Christian institution. Monasteries and abbeys had sounded the canonical 'Hours' night and day, and summoned the congregation to hear the Mass, for centuries. To call a whole town effectively to worship or work the bell or bells must be large and high up and able to give voice in all directions. So the tower was built tall (almost 80 ft) with louvred openings from the bell chamber at the top which let the bells ring out to the four quarters of the compass. Church and tower were a real nerve centre of the place.

*Built to last*

The next time you enter the church through the west door, pause and marvel at the rugged strength of the warm red stonework. Don't be misled by the newish mortar which was applied as part of the renovation work carried out (together with cleaning of the stone) in celebration of Queen Victoria's Diamond Jubilee in 1897.

Look up and appreciate the four-square massive structure, buttressed at each corner. It rises steadily, tapering very slightly, the vertical lines pleasingly balanced by two horizontal 'string courses' and the buff coloured protective capping stones set on the buttresses each time these diminish in thickness. This stone came from the quarries near Salcombe Regis in East Devon. It was shipped into Teignmouth and road-hauled to the building site. It was used also for the window frames of the bell-chamber, and for a plain parapet at the top. (The pinnacles and battlements on the main tower and the staircase turret, were added only in 1817, but using the same kind of stone).

## The view from the top

If you are fortunate enough to have permission and the strength to climb the spiral staircase (600 years old but kept in safe repair) you come out on to the lead covered roof of the tower. There you are rewarded with splendid views of the whole of Old Town and Dawlish Water settlements, (the original inner core of the parish), and the surrounding panorama of fields and hillsides. You get a wonderful sense of how the church and tower embrace and also represent the town.

If we were on a hilltop we would certainly be a landmark and probably the site of a beacon fire point for transmitting national and military news around the county, but our valley bottom position fits us well for serving the local community with some intimacy.

I am deeply moved when I stand on the tower roof and reflect on the fact that these bells just below my feet have for so long signalled the call to worship and told the whole parish of the most sacred moment in the Mass or the Eucharist when the Host was raised and shown to the people. It was thus for so many centuries, and I am sad because we have allowed this public proclamation to lapse. There was also the 'telling bell' that gave news of the passing of a loved one, counting out, or telling, the years of that life so that the whole parish shared in both the sorrow and the sober thanksgiving. Peals of bells have been rung out by teams of varying competence, but staunch loyalty, to celebrate marriages, or great national public events; to welcome in the new millennium....... and to wish Godspeed to those embarking on new ventures.

Our information about the earliest bells is woefully incomplete. This may be on account of the changes that were imposed in Reformation times. After the 'Prayer Book Rebellion' in 1549, the King's Privy Council ordered the removal of all but a single small bell from every church tower in Devon, since it was by bells that the people had been summoned to rebellion. I'm told too, on good authority, that bell metal and gun metal are virtually the same thing....and the king was short of guns!

## The recorded story of our bells

There must have been at least one bell when the tower was made, perhaps one that was previously rung from a porch or turret. The records that have come down to us speak of a peal of five tower bells which were re-cast at various dates. Bells are numbered in order of their pitch, the highest tone (and smallest bell) being called 'first'. Our fourth was re-cast at Kenn in 1614, the second by Pennington of Exeter in 1677, the first by Wroth of Exeter in 1735, and the third by Bayley in 1742. Then in 1784 all five were taken down and re-cast into a peal of six by Pennington of a subsequent generation, in Exeter.

Respect for the Monarchy lay behind the addition of two new bells in 1911 commemorating the coronation of King George the Fifth. This brought the 'ring' up to its present tally of eight fine bells, which includes a Tenor of 11 cwt. It is an attraction which draws visiting teams of ringers from many parts of the county. There have been differences of opinion over the choice of 'method' ringing or traditional 'change' ringing: a subject best left to the experts! Captains and team ringers come and go, and accidents happen, but tower ringing is a craft which should not be allowed to die. May there always be keen instructors and learners to carry it on.

Until 1984 the bells were rung from ground level within the tower and the congregation entered through the south porch. In that year a new ringers' gallery was made immediately below the bell-chamber. This facilitated better use of space at the west end of the building. The whole of the tower space is now much used, right up to the pole on the roof turret, where the flag of St. George (with the Diocesan badge) is flown for every Christian Festival and on Saints' days, and the Union flag on great national days. That the whole town appreciates the flags was made very clear when the pole was irreparably damaged in a storm at the end of the 20th century. The replacement cost was daunting and we hesitated.

"No problem" said the townspeople who in a gesture of common ownership contributed handsomely for putting it back.

## Superstitious magic or Christian message?

On the outside of the tower the upper string course carries our only examples of *'Grotesques'*, those strange carved figures that are seen on many old churches and cathedrals. We have eight of them: one on each corner of the main tower and another four on the external angles of the octagonal staircase turret on the south side. It would be too simplistic to dismiss them as relics of pre-Christian superstition and fear, put there by the sculptors to ward off malevolent spirits of the air. Mediaeval thought was rather more sophisticated than this.

It's difficult, but we can try to understand former ways of thinking in order to get some notion of the messages silently conveyed by these stony monsters. The amount of skilled labour expended on these carvings, which have no structural function, must mean that they are there for a serious purpose. (These grotesques are distinct from *'gargoyles'*, the carved heads which house chutes to clear rainwater from the roof).

We could try this approach:

Monsters which broke all the laws of nature were the expressions of lively minds at a time when the universe was seen as being made up of four 'elements', namely Earth, Air, Fire and Water. Fire and Water are fierce antagonists as are Earth and Air. It was thought that these opposites must be kept apart and held in balance, or chaos will return. Also Mediaeval man thought that all known living creatures belong strictly to Air or Earth or Water and must not cross the boundaries. Thus a bird belonged to Air, a lion to Earth and a fish to Water. How could you have a lion with wings and talons, or a fish with legs? Who knows what powers for good or evil such monstrous creatures could wield?

But the imaginative human mind has always delighted in playing with the possibilities! We reach beyond things as they are towards what *might* be. 600 years ago when our tower was being built a man would know that, even though he belongs to Earth, he is never-the-less keenly aware of his spiritual nature which, like a splendid free-flying bird, belongs to the realm of Air. He is dangerously straddling the boundary between Earth and Air. So he reaches out thoughtfully to grapple with the possibility that Earth and Air brought together could generate, not destruction, but a 'new creature'.

Perhaps the builders of our tower carved this adventurous idea in stone, literally trying out a new creation. They brought together the head and body of a lion, (king of the Earth beasts), and the wings and talons of the eagle, (the supreme monarch of the Air)......and there is a triumphant new creature! And four of them are up there reaching out from the corners of our fine tower!

Remember that while this building and carving was going on, the Church was seeking to teach that the apparent abyss dividing man's spiritual body from his physical, earthly, mortal one, had been bridged. The reconciliation between God and Man had been accomplished and made clear in the person of Our Lord Christ. Surely these carved new creatures on the tower are symbols of the Christian message that "when a man is in Christ there is a new creation". The physical and spiritual bodies *can* be joined together, and *can* work together, as God the Creator intended. This is the new man who has risen with Christ.

Mediaeval man was no fool; sometimes I feel as if today we lack his wisdom in some directions. He taught a great deal through his use of potent symbols which had, and still have, a powerful universal effect on us. Like this one, the 'impossible' new creature portrayed in stone, which yet conveys a great Christian message of truth and hope. And where did he display that symbol but on the top of the tower that reaches up into the sky to signify the meeting of heaven and earth?

# CHAPTER SIX

## *LETTING IN LIGHT*

Visitors to our church often say "How *light and airy* it is!" Today, the tall pillars, high roof and above all the large windows allow us to have this immediate reaction as we enter the building. If we think back to what the Norman building (of 1148 date) was like, with its heavy walls and pillars and tiny windows, we become aware that there have been great changes in architectural style. The leap from the oppressively dark interior relieved only by the flickering light of candles and wall torches, to the open lightness of the next St. Gregory's church building was dramatic indeed!. What had made this possible?

*Welcome to the Gothic era*

The introduction of the *pointed arch* was the key to the transition. Looking back to the cathedral-building era which began in the early 11th century, this art, together with the development of the ribbed stone ceiling vault, had enabled the cathedral masons to build safely to a hitherto unprecedented height, and to span much greater widths. Because they had discovered how to distribute the weight load in more efficient and safe ways without depending on massively thick and solid walls, they were able to use lighter stone work, and to *increase the size of the windows.* In addition, cathedrals and abbey churches included a novel set of windows high up above the pillars of the nave. This is called the *clerestory.* Its purpose, together with the large windows in the side walls, was to let into the building *as much light as possible.*

Apart from the convenience of a well-lit area, the advances in architecture which let in the light opened up a new world of appreciation of all the visual arts. Everyone, regardless of his status, came under the influence of *visible* things of beauty made by devoted people using carefully practised skills. These artists patiently made many treasures for the enrichment of the church and the worship that was offered in it. These included brightly coloured vestments and altar hangings, illuminated manuscripts, painted walls and ceilings, gold and silver Communion vessels and jewel studded altar and processional crosses. The carving of wood and stone was taken to new heights of achievement. The cathedrals with their huge window areas attracted artists in stained glass and a new world of *coloured* light was created. All this work carried strongly symbolic messages, for it was designed to portray the splendour of 'Jerusalem the Golden', the Heavenly City, suffused with the brilliance of the eternal light of God.

Whether it was actively taught or not, the worshipper could be caught up and immersed in an atmosphere which rendered him speechless and overwhelmed by these powerful symbols of the glory of God.

"Surely the Lord is in this place..........This is none other than the gate of heaven".

Genesis 28 vv 16-17

So said Jacob after his dream-vision, and so might the ordinary person feel when confronted with the dazzling effect of light of every colour of the rainbow. Surely God was shining on him, speaking to him, drawing him beyond his usual experience into the very presence of the Creator God and Father of us all?

This was all very well for the city dweller; country people would only rarely have the opportunity to visit a cathedral. But the notion of light as God-given, was deeply embedded in the mind of most parishioners in a community like the one that worshipped in St. Gregory's church in Dawlish. To let more light into the dark Norman building was surely an idea that would appeal to all; later on, the richly symbolic significance of light would exercise the minds of many lay and ordained people. But how could such changes be brought about in rural places?

*Light spills over into the Parish churches*

We have already met the numerous stone masons and other highly skilled craftsmen who became 'redundant' as work on the cathedrals drew to a close in the 14th and 15th centuries. At this time, following a slow recovery from the setback of the Black Death, there was renewed prosperity among land owners and traders, which resulted in the establishment of a distinctive class of wealthy citizens. These members of the 'Merchant' class were able to employ many travelling artisans to build their houses and family chapels, and they encouraged and endowed the rebuilding or renovation of their local parish churches. (See Chapter 4).

*A new building for St. Gregory's congregation*

There is preserved a record dated 1438 which tells us that Bishop Lacy of Exeter was at that time granting indulgences to all who would contribute to the fabric or give lights, ornaments or other necessities, for the church at Dawlish. We can assume then, that extensive work was being carried out on the St. Gregory's building. The style of the resulting place of worship strongly suggests that, apart from the tower, there was a complete rebuilding in the Perpendicular Gothic mode. But alas, detailed records have long been lost. We can also assume that because most of the lands of Dawlish were in the hands of the Dean and Chapter of Exeter Cathedral, they were the body who organised the raising of the new building and looked after the necessary finances and employment of the workforce.

Records may be lost but what we *have* inherited in the 21st century is a fine nave arcade of pillars and pointed arches which was so consistently appreciated and admired that it survived two major restorations 400 years after its first construction. It is well worth our detailed inspection.

Tall slender pillars draw the eyes upwards. The design of these is typical of the later Gothic period, called 'Perpendicular', for the obvious reason that the stonework of pillars and windows is characterised by strongly vertical lines. Pillars are no longer solidly round in cross-section, but made to look like clusters of columns or tree trunks. Not only did this artistically add to the theme of vertical lines, but it also reduced the weight of stone to be transported from the quarries, where rough stone sections could be shaped to a standard pattern before they were delivered to the building site. They could then be 'finished' on site and assembled one on top of another to form a column of the planned height.

Our pillars and arches are made from limestone from Beer quarry in East Devon, a beautiful white material which, when freshly quarried, can be worked and carved to intricate designs. Look up the pillars to find the carvings adorning the wider stones forming the capitals at the top. Here are stylised leaves, and garlands of intertwined branches. Some are recognizable as grapes and vine leaves and tendrils, some as oak leaves and acorns. Mediaeval sculptors liked to use natural plants and animals as motifs.

One capital shows a neat tribute to Bishop Oldham of Exeter who made a pun on his name and took the *owl* as his sign. (In the Oldham chantry chapel in the cathedral, carved owls stare at you from all directions!). In St. Gregory's church, start from the west end and count forward the pillars on the left till you reach the fifth one. There you will see an owl, and St.Peter's keys (for Exeter Cathedral), lurking among the foliage of the capital.

*In honour of Mary*

On the sixth pillar, (immediately behind the present pulpit), the capital bears a shield. It is somewhat damaged but you can make out a 'gothic' M surmounted by a crown. This was a well known sign for Mary crowned Queen of heaven and was often used in the days before the Reformation. Sometimes we forget that all parish churches in this country followed the edicts of the Pope in Rome until the second half of the 16th century. Here is a reminder of the strength of the veneration of Mary promoted so strongly by the Popes. It also suggests that this emblem of Mary the Holy Mother of God, may have been deliberately defaced by fanatical reformers. The survival of this feature is strong evidence for the antiquity of these pillars.

*A mystery figure*

In the much more recent (1981) upper narthex, made in part of the west end of the building, you can see 1438 capitals at close range. On the one on the north side you find a quaint little head peering out of some foliage. Who could this be? It is carefully carved by someone with a sense of humour. Look at the quizzical lift of the subject's left eyebrow. This is our only human figure portrayed in 15$^{th}$ century work. Could he be the master mason? Or is he a much loved parish priest of that time? Or an important donor whose wealth made it possible to build to such high standards? For the monetary outlay was not on a mean scale. Whoever he is, I think he is unlikely to be one of those popularly sought after 'green men'!

## Arches and Angels

Above the capitals we are watched over by ten beautiful angels. They hover just where the finely proportioned pointed arches soar upwards from the pillars to support the 'barrel' roof arching high above the nave. Those of us who worship here today are very familiar with these angels bearing shields. In some churches the shields are painted with the coats of arms of local families, especially of those who were generous donors to the building fund. Ours are plain; possibly the money ran out, or the colours were cleaned off later. From my point of view, I am glad the shields are not claimed by 'special' families, for as they are now, they speak silently of God's loving care for us all today, and for all who have ever been members of the extended Christian family in this place.

At the west end of the church, the (1981) construction of the screen dividing off the narthex areas, involved cutting two of the angels in half to accommodate the glass wall! The decision must have followed long and careful discussion, and I applaud the decision, and the care with which the work was carried out. Now we can examine these angels closely from the upper room.

I am very fond of these 'arch-angels', and you will find reference to all the many angels in our 21st century building in an appendix to this book. These lovely ones on the arcade are our oldest ones, and we give thanks for their preservation. For when the time came for yet another rebuilding of the church, our Georgian architects found that they too admired the nave arcade and were inspired to keep it intact.

*On re-building, and bridging the centuries*

It would seem that when the 1438 church was constructed, there was little attempt to incorporate parts of the old Norman building and its contents. We have no description of the old church, and can only imagine what it was like by our knowledge of surviving Norman churches in various parts of the country. The re-building process began with a dramatic 'clean sweep'. Would that we had records telling us what people thought about it all, and what were their feelings; probably there was both excitement and regret. But we are left with only fragments of stone to mark the continuity of our places of worship on this same site.

What we *have* in addition to the one Norman corbel stone, (see p. 19), is the strong likelihood that the many pieces of red sandstone to be spotted in the outside walls of the north and south aisles, are re-used bits of the old Norman walls. Building stone was as costly then as now, and there must have been plenty of rubble about. There were, or even are, probably not a few old houses near to the church which were strengthened and improved with the lovely red stone legally or illegally obtained!

What we *lost* was the old Font, most probably of Norman date and style. It would have been sited at the west end of the nave. Many carved and interesting Norman fonts were discarded all over the country at about this time; it was as if a new Gothic building demanded a 'modern' font, rather than that one of the most important items of furniture could be kept in service, to provide a meaningful link with baptised worshippers of previous centuries. (And what became of the old Altar stone?)

So we had a new font. An 'intelligent guess' has the new font made in the then currently popular octagonal configuration, and carved from the same stone as was used for the pillars and arches of the nave. (There will be further discussion of the font later in this book).

Whatever striking changes in the architectural style of the church building took place, the village and its people remained a familiar community from one century to another. Men and women often did spend the whole of their lives in the same locality and were buried in the graveyard of the church where they had been baptised, confirmed, married;  where they had come to  worship, and made their confession and received absolution.  Here they were cared for in times of thanksgiving and of sorrow and illness, and the priest brought them the sacrament of Extreme Unction as they were dying.  This pastoral care and instruction had been offered on that very site for over 500 years *without a break.*

It is this *continuity* which excites me and makes me search for physical links across the centuries as one building succeeds another.  It is true that the 'hallowed ground' is older than any of them, and when we walk there we can honour our forebears and know that we are indeed members of the same Christian family.

For the moment, let us reach back and try to enter into the 'feel' of the tremendous activity and noise involved in the replacement of one building with another.

# CHAPTER SEVEN

## *BUILDING AND FURNISHING A NEW HOUSE OF WORSHIP*

In 1438, all members of Dawlish families witnessed the planned demolition of their old church building. Then they saw the new building slowly rise on the same site. They watched the pillars and arches grow and take shape, the two side aisles marked out and new outer walls constructed. The place was a hive of activity for there were itinerant workers in considerable numbers. They probably found lodgings with local families, as the setting up of a special house for these workers would have been too expensive. Wagons laden with stone and timber were hauled to the site by teams of cart horses which needed watering and feeding while the cargo was off-loaded. On site a special group of men mixed mortar in accordance with carefully tried and tested formulae; the strength and durability of the whole building depended on their work. Somewhere close by, the carpenters would have needed plenty of space to 'dress' the timbers for the roof, while the woodcarvers were busy shaping the ceiling roof bosses.

The tithe barn, also known as the 'store house', to the east of the old church was still standing and in use. Its position determined the eastern limit of the church, and the chancel was shorter in length than it was to be later on. We have only later accounts of this 1438 building: they describe the wide nave as having five windows of large dimension on the north side (7ft by 5ft 4ins to the spring of the arch) and a window at the east end of the north aisle (8ft 6ins by 7ft 4ins). Presumably these were matched by windows on the south side, but the position of the south porch modified the pattern. The latter was an elegant structure which incorporated a spiral staircase giving access to the roof outside, and to the Rood loft within the building. It had carved decorative stonework and above the outer door was the all-important sundial. Perhaps there was also a Mass dial, a scratched pattern of lines around a hole into which the priest could put a moveable arm to indicate the likely time of the next celebration of the Mass.

The north and south walls were supported by buttresses which on the south side had niches for statues. An account was compiled by Mr. F. J. Carter from such Parish accounts as had survived to the 19th century. This is what he writes in his 'Notes on Old Dawlish' (Dawlish Museum Society publication No.1 1976):

"This church (1438) remained substantially the same until 1824. It was built of red stone in the Perpendicular style...... it was of a style peculiar to the West of England, and consisted of nave, chancel and two aisles with a western tower but, contrary to the practice in other parts of the country, the aisles and nave-chancel each had a separate roof of nearly equal height, thus showing three gables at the eastern end. This style of building, although giving a comparatively clear space inside the church, had the disadvantage of the two gutters between the roofs. These gutters were very liable to leakage and in Dawlish church they appear to have been always a source of trouble and constant expense.........entries in the parish accounts for these repairs cover a period of over two and a half centuries.........

"The roof was covered with flat stones known as shilling stones, which were brought from the quarry at Torre. These stones were also troublesome and we have the following entry in the parish accounts:

"1689 Paid to the hellier for mending the church roof when it was blown up with the wind: £1.5.0." (A hellier was a slater or tiler).

This last fragment of information refers to a building that was already 250 years old. When new it was a splendid place, full of light and colour and it served us for almost 400 years. There was the familiar sequence of damage and repair: in 1601 a tree trunk was 'squared' for propping up the wall of the church (!) but it was not until the beginning of the 19th century that the next re-building plans became inevitable.

*Why do we have a church building?*

This is a point at which we might spend some time thinking about the purpose of the building and how it was furnished to meet the needs of the people. In earlier chapters, we have seen that the many activities in and around the church building and churchyard were at the centre of everybody's devotional and social life. The community looked to the Church for instruction, comfort and, in conjunction with the secular courts, maintenance of law and order. (The town stocks were located in the churchyard which seems to have been the only large public space. We have them still, repaired and preserved). But of prime importance and at the heart of the purpose of the church building was its use as *the place for coming together to worship God.*

*Public worship and the meaning of Liturgy*

The Greek word from which we get this term was used of a *public duty of any kind*. Later it came to be used in English to denote all the prescribed public services of worship in the church which it was every parishioner's *duty* to attend. Often the term is applied to the Celebration of the Eucharist, the chief act of public worship, and, in a derived sense, to the written text of such services. To broaden our understanding and interpretation I can do no better than to quote from the work of that devoted explorer of the character and range of late Mediaeval English Catholicism, Eamon Duffy. In his 1992 book 'The Stripping of the Altars' he opens the first chapter with these words:

"Any study of late medieval religion must begin with the liturgy, for within that great seasonal cycle of fast and festival, of ritual observance and symbolic gesture, lay Christian men and women found the paradigms and stories which shaped their perception of the world and their place within it. Within the liturgy birth, copulation, death, journeying and homecoming, guilt and forgiveness, the blessing of homely things and the call to pass beyond them, were all located, tested and sanctioned. In the liturgy and in the sacramental celebrations which were its central moments, medieval people found the key to the meaning and purpose of their lives".

*Inside the 1438 church building: the Dedicated Furniture*

The first thing that people assembling for worship would see as they *entered* the building at its west end, was the baptismal font. Baptism was and is the sacrament by which a person *enters the Church*: it is an initiation, a recognition, and an opportunity for a welcome by those already committed to the Christian faith. Baptism may be 'on confession of faith' by adults, when, after penitential acknowledgement of misdoings and shortcomings, it signifies forgiveness and cleansing, and is symbolic of dying and rising with Christ to new life.

The administration of adult baptism suggests that the font was at one time of a design which allowed the candidate to stand up or kneel in the water, and to have water poured over his head. Some older churches still preserve such a large 'tub font'. In Italy you can visit places where the font is a pool below floor level, and was used for total immersion of adults, as is the practice within the Baptist and some other denominations today.

Infant baptism became increasingly popular in Parish Churches. Then, the confession of faith is made by parents and suitable Godparents who promise to teach the child and guide him towards 'confirmation' of his own beliefs as he becomes more mature. When Baptism was administered in this way, it was more convenient to raise the bowl of the font on a pillar, so that the child could be either totally immersed, or receive the water poured over his head or sprinkled on him "....in the name of the Father and of the Son and of the Holy Spirit".

I am led to wonder if infant baptism was firmly adopted as the more usual policy for the new 1438 church, and that the old Norman font was discarded because it was too heavy and cumbersome to be raised on a pillar.

There is some evidence that our 1438 church had both a pool and a pillar font, as both are shown on a plan of the building made by surveyors prior to the rebuilding in the 1820s. Later in this book there is a major chapter devoted to the Sacrament of Baptism, and also to a detailed description of our present Font.

*What you would see as you stood in the nave: dedicated artwork*

In the daylight streaming in through the wide and tall windows, especially those on the south side, it is likely that you would, in 1438, be struck by the *colour* with which the walls and ceiling and stonework were decorated. Wall surfaces were treated by plastering and then painted with pictures of Saints and Biblical characters. A wealthy village would have true frescoes applied to the plaster while it was still wet, making a more permanent picture; otherwise designs and figures were painted on to the dry walls with colours made from natural powdered stone or clay, lampblack or plant sources. When these faded, they could be replaced with different Saints or stories according to popular fashion. Almost certainly you would find St.Christopher, the patron saint of travellers, in a prominent position, often opposite the entrance door.

Dominating the scene in front of you as you faced east, was the chancel *screen*, shutting off much of your view of the High Altar. What you could not fail to see was the great Rood itself built high on top of the screen. This carved depiction of Christ crucified was to be the focus of worship for lay people in the nave. The figure of Christ was set between those of the Blessed Virgin Mary and of St. John 'the beloved disciple'. Votive (dedicated) candles would be lit around the Rood. The massive wooden beam on which it stood, also supported a floor structure making access safely possible for those who tended the lights and, in Lent, the veil with which the Rood was shrouded.

Below the Rood, the screen was probably a notable architectural feature, of intricately carved wood. Central doors opened into the *sanctuary* where stood the High Altar, and only the priest and his servers were allowed entrance. The screen was panelled to about waist height. During the Mass, this prevented the kneeling congregation from seeing details of what went on at the Altar, but you could just see the priest elevate the Host to show it to the people. He would then consume the consecrated bread on behalf of all present. While the service was in progress (in Latin) you could follow as far as you were able and join in the responses and acclamations that you had learned, and repeat the 'Our Father'.

Otherwise, here was the opportunity to study the wall paintings, salute the angels above the pillars and ask for their prayers, or to contemplate the Crucified Christ and so be led to examine yourself humbly. You could also think about the notable people whose images were painted or carved on the panels of the screen. Perhaps these were the four 'doctors of the Church' namely Augustine, Gregory, Ambrose and Jerome, symbols of the Church's teaching. Or, in a wide church like St. Gregory's, on the screen there would be room for all the Apostles, each bearing, on a sash or ribbon, a section of the Creed. Or there might well be the four Gospel writers, or a series of saints, including any that were of local significance. (I'm sorry to have to say that we do not know who was portrayed on St. Gregory's screen).

While at Mass you didn't stand or slouch against pillars or walls, but you were expected to kneel and pray meekly and quietly upon the floor. (The hard flagstones must have been a form of penance!). You were taught to rise when the Gospel was read; in every Mass a bell was rung to tell worshippers absorbed in their own prayers to look up because the moment of Consecration and Elevation was near. You would then kneel with both hands raised in adoration, to gaze on the Host (if you could get a glimpse) and to greet the Lord Christ with an 'elevation' prayer.

Both lay people and the Church authorities came to feel that this minimal lay participation in the Celebration of the Mass was inadequate, and during the 14th and 15th centuries books were produced to assist the devout laity to a better understanding and so to enter more fully into the ritual and symbolism of the service. Some of these were *private devotional books.* Lay people had for many years admired the devotional life of monks and nuns who so faithfully kept the daily cycle of prayers, psalms and readings known as the Hours. In addition to attending the parish Mass, some lay men and women liked to copy the monastic style of prayers at other times of the day. At this time in the 15th century, the ability to read was steadily gaining ground, and so was the production of books. Even before the advent of printing in the 1470s, there was a steady demand for hand written primers: books written in Latin or in English, or both, and often beautifully illustrated. From one of these you could learn to read, or translate or refresh your memory. Much of the content was for private prayer and to aid meditation on parts of the liturgy of the Church.

Ownership of a 'Book of Hours' was a precious privilege. You might very well take your book to the church and study it during the long Latin prayers and readings, and it could help you to a better understanding. In addition to selected Psalms, the Gospel readings set for the major Festivals, 'Our Father' and 'Hail Mary' and favourite hymns and prayers, there was usually the Litany of the Saints, and parts of the Office for the dead. There was also a range of morning prayers, devotions for use during the Mass, and prayers to the Virgin Mary and to Christ in his Passion. In the margins you might add your own thoughts, hopes or fears; or the names of your family and dates of births and deaths, much as later generations would do in the Family Bible.

Today the surviving personal Books of Hours help us to feel our way back into the kind of devotional life that was common among parishioners when the new church building came into use in 1438. These were the days before preaching and exposition of the Bible readings became a feature of public worship. And we must remember that heaven, hell and purgatory were anticipated as physical realities; judgement and doom and the devil were portrayed in lurid colours in wall paintings and later in stained glass. But as reading, and the possession of books, became more widespread, so did the ability to think and question and perhaps re-discover the kind and compassionate truth of the Gospel: word of a just, merciful and loving God whom we can trust.

As literacy, aided soon by the availability of printed books, became more widespread, it was imperative that the clergy should be able to increase their knowledge and develop their own thinking, and so help the people in their congregations to use their minds to sift truth from triviality, and to resist being diverted from sound teaching by misleading statements put about by the growing number of itinerant preachers, some of whose new ideas were stimulating and brought out the need for careful examination of long held attitudes and practices.

If a travelling preacher stood up in a public place to set out his ideas, there would be a ready audience. Probably he would stand at the crossroads where stood the 'waymarker' stone which was a common meeting point. Some of these ancient stones were retooled to make them into a cross, while others were put up already fashioned as a 'preaching cross'. It might be sited within the churchyard itself. In some villages the preaching cross was put there before the establishment of the first church on the site, and might then be incorporated in the building or graveyard.

The remaining stump of what was probably an old cross in Dawlish was moved to its present site just outside the eastern gate of our churchyard at some time in the 19$^{th}$ century. We do not know its history. It is fashioned from granite. This tells us that it was probably quarried on Dartmoor, (Dawlish local stone being of different kinds), and brought here for a special purpose. Whatever its history, such a stone would mark a well known public place where someone wanting to speak his mind felt that he could address the local people freely. A man with a message, especially if it included potential criticism of Church order or dogma, would make his stand here.

The coming of men of the preaching orders heralded changes which would rock the whole Church. The Dawlish congregation would not escape the effect of serious new thinking which was spreading by word of mouth, and increasingly through printed texts.

# CHAPTER EIGHT

## *CHANGEFUL TIMES IN THE CHURCH CATHOLIC*

For a hundred years after the new Dawlish church was built, priest and people continued to worship together, to care for each other and tend the building and the burial ground. This was still a largely agriculturally based community within the lands of the diocese of Exeter. Church lands were contributing to the success of the textile industry, for English wool and woollen cloth were much in demand. Monasteries and other landowners became rich but the benefits were sadly not generally shared in helpful practical ways with the dependent population. Instead, they were often used to embellish churches with monuments or stained glass windows, or chantry chapels making provision for prayers and Masses for the souls of their donors, who believed they could thus earn respite from the pains of purgatory and everlasting torment. Many items of artistic excellence were made, some of which survive for our admiration today, but how strangely distorted those supposedly Christian ideas seem to us now!

Latterly there was, in many parts of the country, a questioning of such doctrine and self-interested use of resources, as well as a growing unease over lax discipline within some of the monasteries. The wealth of some of these institutions did not go unnoticed. Among the clergy there were those whose sense of vocation and discipline seemed questionable and perhaps the people became aware of shortcomings in pastoral care and teaching. Many in the Church felt that reform and renewal were necessary, especially in response to the literature and learning now more widely accessible since the advent of printing (1470s onward). This unrest was already felt before the coming of all the political upheavals set in motion by the royal manoeuvrings that led to the break with papal authority.

This is not the place for a detailed analysis of the reasons for the changes which took place in Church and State during the reigns of the Tudor and Stuart Kings and Queens, so here I offer a fairly short reminder so that we can consider the practical consequences for our church building and the people in Dawlish. (I have a lot of sympathy with you if you choose to skip the next few pages!)

*The decades of turmoil and confusion*

King Henry VIII (1509 onwards) wanted money for his military exploits, and cast a greedy eye towards the riches of prosperous land owners including the abbeys and monasteries. The monasteries were steadily dismantled by royal command, (from 1536 onwards) and their assets seized by the Crown. This series of moves coincided with the difference of opinion between King and Pope over the validity of the King's marriage and his wish to re-marry in the hope of producing a male heir.

Angrily disappointed by the Pope's pronouncement that divorce would not be sanctioned, Henry then styled himself as head of the Catholic Church in England, claiming that he was a true son of the Catholic Church, but *not* of the Bishop of Rome. This title rapidly became modified to being 'Supreme Governor' rather than 'head', for obvious theological reasons, for *Christ is our only Head of the Church.* Our Queen is formally 'Supreme Governor' to this day in the 21$^{st}$ century. Henry, and subsequent monarchs, also wanted the royal coat of arms displayed prominently in every parish church, to signify that the reigning monarch had power over the organisation of the English Church.

The next king (Edward VI) enforced changes in forms of worship and ritual arrangements, now that the Church in England was no longer seen as necessarily conforming to papal rulings. Stone altars (which contained relics of saints) were removed and replaced with wooden communion tables. Roods were dismantled. A new Prayer Book, in English, was introduced and this led to armed revolt on the part of a number of parishes (the Prayer Book

Rebellion), and military intervention was accompanied by bloodshed and destruction, centred in Devon on Clyst St.Mary and Sampford Courtenay in 1549. We don't know what action Dawlish people took but they must have been well aware of the siege of Exeter which was part of that uprising. And they were subject, as elsewhere, to the enforced Inspections and confiscations of their manuscript Latin Mass books and Psalters, rich vestments and processional crosses. St. Gregory's lost a silver cross, silver incense boat, censer and cruets, together with a green velvet cope. Even the bells were seized. (Bell metal was useful because it was of the same composition as gun metal!)

Remember too, that all these rich items were sacred things which the people themselves had helped to provide for their local church, by their own money-raising efforts. As now, fund-raising was a vital activity binding the parishioners together in a meaningful and good natured family. We can imagine the anger and distress among our own Dawlish people at the despoliation of their beautiful church, and the confiscation of its furnishings for which they had worked so hard and willingly.

Nevertheless, there were good things that were introduced as well as those which caused distress. Our Dawlish records for this time period are scanty, but we may assume that our experiences were similar to those in places where written evidence survives. Under Edward VI, we were allowed to receive both consecrated bread *and* wine and thus to be *partakers* with the priest instead of being devout *spectators.* The new Communion Table was repositioned so that we could gather round it.

In 1552 a new Prayer Book had been imposed which allowed for Morning and Evening Prayer to be said in the nave among the people. We could use Psalms sung in a rhymed metrical version. Four part harmonies were composed for tunes set in the old psalters, and the singing might be accompanied by music for viols and wind instruments. These practices were short-lived for they were to be forbidden by the next monarch.

*Yet another upheaval*

When Mary Tudor came to the throne in 1553, she reinstated the Roman liturgy (in Latin) and encouraged the bringing back of the Rood and the use of splendid vestments. We are perhaps not surprised to learn that in many country villages much like Dawlish, some of the precious sacred Communion vessels and vestments which the people had treasured, had been hidden so that they were 'not there' for surrender to the royal authorities during the reigns of Henry VIII and Edward VI. In Mary's time such jealously guarded items suddenly re-appeared from their places of concealment, as did portions of the dismantled Rood and its accompanying figures. What confusion and distress must have been aroused in the hearts and minds of the lay people of Dawlish! *How* were we to worship, and *what* were we to believe, when even our vicar and our bishop seemed to change their minds as one royal proclamation followed another and destroyed all sense of stability and familiarity? But surely it made us all think long and hard!

*Reform was coming again, and this time for a long stay*

Queen Mary died in 1558, and her successor Queen Elizabeth I firmly embraced the reformed Church of England, and imposed a standard English liturgy upon her loyal subjects. All over Devon, the very last parish Mass in the Latin Roman mode was celebrated on or about Advent Sunday 1558. The diocese of Exeter began to enforce the Elizabethan settlement with great strictness. The revised English Prayer Book was to be used exclusively, and many former rituals suppressed. Within three years, William Marwood (the last Dawlish vicar to serve under the papal practices) was succeeded by Hugh Trevor, who must have laboured long and hard to restore quietness and confidence among his parishioners.

Hopefully, in Dawlish throughout these times of change, priest and people supported each other, although there were inevitably matters which provoked regret and a sense of loss.

Among these was the severe simplification of the priestly vestments and altar dressings. (The special altars where prayers and masses were said for the souls of the dead had long since been removed). Many of the devotional activities such as the provision and tending of the many candles, and the care of the remaining vestments, which were carried out by close-knit groups of lay people, were curtailed. Sadly, with the loss of these widely distributed and valued personal responsibilities, there must have been quite a lot of fragmentation of the old socially coherent community. An individual man or woman or child might well lose the sense of being an essential member of the worshipping congregation, or indeed of the village.

## A community in danger of losing its cohesion

Divisive forces were at work even though outwardly there appeared to be a period of settling down, accepting, and then embracing, the new ways with good will. But the growing next generation had no chance to enjoy many of the old village 'red letter days' based on festivals of the saints, when everybody had prepared for, and joined in, the dancing and fun of the Holyday after attending the appropriate Mass.

Weekly attendance at church was enforced by the state but the church building was no longer the awesome and colourful place which had previously inspired its worshippers. If you like, the 'magic' had been taken away. In some ways, this was a necessary move against superstition and too much reliance on the outward, physical, features of organised worship. Yet there were many who had used the symbolism at the heart of ritual high drama, to pass through and beyond the tangible things to reach a profound level in their worship of a God of kingly majesty who was in the same breath a loving Saviour. Such perceptive people would not cease to worship when these aids were denied them, but there would be others who, when the building became colourless and ordinary, were deprived of a dimly understood but powerfully *felt*, inspiration or awesome urge to join with the Psalmist and "kneel before the Lord our Maker" in confidence and with joy. Something special had gone from their lives.

*Drama and simplicity in worship enter into sad opposition*

There was great controversy over the place of ritual high drama in worship. While, as we have noted, some people found its symbolism a powerful aid, others wanted bare simplicity of language and action, and a return to the practices of the very early Church as they are recorded in the New Testament in the Epistles and the Acts of the Apostles.

In the decades ahead, the holding of extreme views would lead to the sadness of intolerance and eventual violence. Adherents of the 'Old Religion' (under papal ways) would be persecuted, and at the opposite end of the scale, overzealous Puritans (who called for a stern simplicity) would wreak havoc upon many of the remaining Mediaeval artistic treasures in church buildings. Stained glass and statues and paintings that had survived earlier attempts to remove them, would later on fall victim to ferocious iconoclasm ('image destruction'). Church buildings would be seized and used as battle stations or barracks during the Civil Wars and the thoroughly unsettling period of the Commonwealth led by Oliver Cromwell (1642- 1660).

*How did this affect our Dawlish Church and building?*

No, Dawlish has no tales of horses being stabled in the nave! But as well as the changes in ornamentation of altar and vestments made at the start of Elizabeth's reign, others followed as the Puritan-led movement towards extreme simplicity gathered momentum. At the peak time of its influence, in all probability the interior walls of our church were whitewashed to cover up the pictures of saints, and any statues we still had, were removed from their niches and smashed. As for stained glass windows, those which depicted saints were either irretrievably destroyed or just the heads and halos were knocked out. The Rood and rood loft were taken away, as were the altar hangings. Other furnishings of the sanctuary were greatly changed. At the east end where the altar had stood against the wall, backed by a carved or painted reredos, the wall was now covered with great boards on which were painted the Ten Commandments and Our Lord's Prayer and other texts. Weekly attendance at church was enforced by the State and fines were imposed upon defaulters who could not give adequate reason for the absence of themselves or their families.

*The royal dream of a uniform State Church fades*

It seemed that the religious Settlement achieved by Queen Elizabeth in which a single State Religion was established, could not last. Its hope for unity in the future was best expressed in the publication in 1611, during the reign of King James 1, of the first Authorised Version of the Bible in English. In the production of this translation, Puritan scholars and divines played an equal part with those of the more cautious Anglican Church. Yet all too soon after this achievement, opinions on discipline and conformity in worship became polarized.

*Dissent and the struggle for freedom in worship and practice*

The 17$^{th}$ century was a time when individual thought and belief reached a new level of confidence. It was based on the spread of teaching by educated and dedicated people who valued the ability of a great many otherwise 'ordinary' citizens, to read and ponder what they were taught by Church and State. Devon people had already demonstrated their readiness to question decisions made by those in authority, and had only too readily used armed force on occasion. We continued to pay attention, and to debate rather more peacefully many matters of concern over how the church was organised and to what degree it was subject to the monarchy and political manoevrings. Above all, was it ministering faithfully to the pastoral needs of its people?

The complex history of the non-conformist Churches dates from this stirring of conscience and the courage to express and try to justify differing views. Gradually this led to the formation of groups of believers who wanted either to reform the practices of the established Church, or to have the freedom to worship in other ways. These groups were mistrusted in high places and their members suffered deprivation and sometimes persecution in the early years of the 17$^{th}$ century. The year 1620 saw the Pilgrim Fathers seeking religious freedom by the risky emigration to the New World; papal 'non-conformists', and members of the new dissenting movements, were now being denied participation in local and national government. But new thinking could not be suppressed, and the steadily growing polarization of ideals and loyalties over matters of State and Church led eventually to the Civil War, and the deposition and execution of King Charles I after he had tried to rule without co-operating with the people through parliament. Then followed the restless time of the Commonwealth under Oliver Cromwell. The tragedy was that these years were a time of aroused public conscience and desire for freedom in daily life and in worship. No-one doubted the initial religious fervour of Oliver Cromwell and the Puritans, or the sincerity with which the Independents, Congregationalists and other non-conforming groups set out their Declarations of Faith and Practice during the later Commonwealth years. These were years of both boldness and grave disquiet which divided faithful Christians.

*The Act of Uniformity and the Great Ejectment*

In 1660 the Monarchy was restored. After years of hurtful strife and wastage of manpower and funds, the prior concern of King Charles the Second, was to bring back social, legal and religious stability to the whole country. One measure was designed to re-emphasise the status of the Church of England as subject to the monarch and also to centralised and strict discipline. So the *Act of Uniformity* of 1662 was devised and became legally binding. This Act laid a heavy hand on all the dissenting factions, including groups of Papal adherents, and also the new 'Free Churches' whose members were devoutly and boldly seeking new, more flexible, ways to worship Our God together.

Here we must ask "Was our own Diocese of Exeter involved in these disciplinary measures?" The answer is "Yes". Not to any great extent in Dawlish itself, but in a not very far away parish there was disruption and suffering.  Here is the story:

## *The Dissenters' Pit in Bradley Manor Woods*

After the restoration of the Monarchy in 1660, the Church of England set about establishing its authority regarding the pattern of worship that was to prevail in every Parish Church. The Book of Common Prayer was revised and approved in the new 1662 version, and an Act of Uniformity was passed by Parliament in the same year.  All ministers were required to give assent publicly to 'the Book'. Thenceforth it was illegal for any parish priest to alter, omit or add anything to the prescribed Liturgy. This included both words and actions.

Within the company of priests, were some who, following what they believed was their God-given freedom to determine the manner of worship, held to their convictions with courage, and took the path of God-fearing dissent. Such a priest was deprived of his living (he was *'ejected')* and he and his followers were subject to ridicule and hatred and actual persecution. They were 'hounded out' and the Law forbade them to meet within the parish boundary.

In the Parish of Wolborough (by Newton Abbot), the dissenting priest and his sympathisers had to meet for worship *outside* the parish bounds, and they did so in a disused quarry deep within Bradley Woods. They made many perilous and secret journeys under cover of darkness, sworn to secrecy as to their meeting place. The place is hard to find even in broad daylight!

Remember that these people were Christians who agreed with the essential doctrines of the Church of England but refused to be constrained by its discipline and practice, especially in matters of ceremony. No-one could doubt their sincerity in the search for what they felt were alternative  and equally worthy ways to come together to worship the God and Father of us all, and to seek together, under the guidance of the Holy Spirit, to know the will of God in things spiritual and practical.

It was not until 27 years later that the Toleration Act was approved by Parliament in 1689. This granted 'freedom of worship' to the dissenters, and permission to open chapels within the parish boundary. Wolborough's dissenting priest, The Reverend William Yeo M.A., became the minister of the first non-conformist chapel which was built in Wolborough Street in Newton Abbot. There is a rather fine commemorative tablet set in the lych gate of Wolborough parish church telling the story of a brave man. From time to time members from nonconformist Churches all over the southwest hold a service in Bradley Pit remembering those very difficult times. In 1962, the 300$^{th}$ anniversary of the Great Ejectment, this act of worship was addressed by the Bishop of Exeter as a gesture of ecumenical goodwill.

And in Dawlish? Our records do not tell of the violent eviction of any of our priests. St. Gregory's Parish Church building remained the focal point of meeting and worship for the majority of Dawlish families, and the continuity of pastoral care and administration of the sacraments was maintained. Like the great stones of the nave arcade, these pillars of faith and order stood firm. Our sister nonconformist churches were opened one by one in the town. There was, gradually, a growing acceptance and respect for those who wanted to worship God together in ways that were superficially different. However hard we try to understand the reasons for denominational fragmentation within the Church, we are left lamenting our inability to practise 'diversity within unity'.

*Caring for the Parish Church Building*

One cannot be surprised to know that during these times of change and enforced expenditure on new Prayer Books and furnishings, not much money was left for maintaining the actual building! This degenerated slowly, and there were continual problems with the leaking and storm damaged roof. The troublesome 'shilling stone' roof had to be replaced with sturdy slate. Surviving records tell that in 1601 funds had to be found for the "squaring and setting up of a tree to stay the church".

Obviously the local woodmen knew their craft, for the church was not only 'stayed' then, but it lasted for another 200 years! Then, despite the rugged strength of the pillars within, the outer walls and roof of this beloved building fell into serious disrepair. At the end of the 18$^{th}$ century, plans for a major reconstruction were obviously needed, and by this time, major re-developments in society were taking place too.

*Dawlish people enter a new phase in their life together*

Social and economic change began to move at an ever increasing rate during the 1700s, and these, together with the resultant increase in the population of Dawlish, led to the firm decision to rebuild and enlarge the church. We must follow these changes in the next chapter.

# CHAPTER NINE

## LIFE IN GEORGIAN DAWLISH

*Discovery and Invention lead towards Economic Revolution*

  The years between the Restoration of the Monarchy in 1660, and the middle of the 18$^{th}$ century, saw English life begin a big turn-around from an economy that was essentially agrarian and rural, to one that was industrial and urban. These changes were slowly gathering momentum for some decades before the Industrial Revolution 'took off' after about 1750.

  Dawlish at this time was still relatively isolated; the prime necessity for the expansion of trade and employment was the provision of roads capable of carrying wheeled traffic. We had only rough track roads, and these were regularly maintained for only a short way beyond the village. The building of 'main' roads and the organisation of their upkeep was the task of the new Turnpike Trusts from 1730 onwards on a national scale, but it was not until 1753 that the newly formed Exeter Trust began to feel its way towards the outlying towns and villages. Newton Abbot was reached by 1765 but rural south Devon including Dawlish waited till 1823.

  To travel to Exeter from Dawlish you needed to use a horse, a lift on a carrier's cart, or 'shanks's pony'. You could go, equally slowly and unpredictably, by boat. Until the better roads were made, Dawlish was used to being locally self-sufficient. Messages came by mounted mail-carriers until the road system was good enough to bear the horse-drawn Mail Coach (personal mail and official business letters), and the Stage Coach for passengers, which called at the London Inn. This inn was one of the first hotels to be built (about 1800), after Dawlish Strand began to be used as a resort. It stood at the foot of the steep and curving hill down into the village, which was a real challenge for the horse teams and heavy coaches. Much later, Dawlish Urban District Council made a compulsory purchase of the considerably altered site for a very desirable road widening scheme. (The Midland Bank was built on the remnant of the hotel site in 1926).

So, from being a rather isolated village whose inhabitants were used to being locally self-sufficient, Dawlish was growing into a more complex small town which increasingly traded with the surrounding areas. It steadily developed its structure as a part of a wider district community whose people shared common hopes for prosperity and peaceful living and care for all its inhabitants. The Parish Church continued to be the hub of local organisation.

*The Dawlish Vestry*

The Parish Church played an important part in the co-ordination of village activities and in the keeping of law and order, increasingly so as the jurisdiction of the old manor courts declined. The *parish meeting* was, at its beginning, a gathering of *all* the people and has been described as the 'parliament of the parish'. It met in the church after Evening Prayer, usually in the room (the Vestry) where the priest went to put on the liturgically appropriate vestments for conducting worship. The people who met together to transact the business of the parish became known also as 'The Vestry'. The meeting was chaired by the vicar by virtue of his office. At first it was open to everybody, but gradually its work and decision making became divided up and delegated to groups of those who were willing and competent to carry out special responsibilities. Not surprisingly, these were prominent members of the local community.

The Vestry had the authority to elect Churchwardens and a list of parishioners from which some would be chosen to be officers with special responsibilities. Elections were held at specified times of the year, usually at the great Festivals of Easter or Advent Sunday. As well as organising care of the building and the churchyard and the finances, church officers carried out the work of constables, identifying miscreants and hearing particular complaints. Punishments for minor offences were within their powers too. The use of the parish stocks in the churchyard was not banned until 1837! The Vestry, through its appointed Overseers, was also expected to organise the maintenance of local trackways and bridges, these matters being parish responsibility until 1835. The other never-ending and major concern was for the unfortunates in society for whom there was no comprehensive scheme of relief.

*Problems of poverty*

The latter half of the 17$^{th}$ century had seen the end of the smallholdings of many rural families as land was 'enclosed' and made part of larger estates, worked on a different system. Many able-bodied men and women found themselves without either income or habitation as 'tied cottages' were withdrawn. There were also many soldiers discharged from military duties when the monarchy was restored and foreign expeditions disbanded. The State took some responsibility for its redundant soldiery by organising compulsory manual work for the strong and healthy in an attempt to lessen the risk of crime.

For the rest, the women and children in families without a breadwinner, and the aged and sick without relatives to support them, these unfortunate people became the responsibility of the parish. They were known in legal documents as 'the impotent poor', and the law required that the parish support them by voluntary alms and other fund-raising activities. Chief among the latter was the implementation of the 1601 Poor Relief Act which allowed churchwardens and Overseers of the Poor to assess the rateable value of every dwelling in the parish and to levy a tax on all owners of property worth over £10. This was known as the Poor Rate. The Dawlish Poor Fund was distributed by the Vestry, and applicants for relief were carefully scrutinised.

To be reduced to dire poverty was not uncommon, and the process of appealing for parish relief could be a demeaning experience. Yet it was a safety net that could tide a family over, after tragedy struck them, until some kind of income was re-established. There was also the problem of migrant beggars and illegitimate children whose call on a particular parish for support could be hotly disputed. Each parish, understandably, gave priority to its own resident families and required others to return to their place of origin.

For young people in the village, training and efficiency became increasingly important, and the learning of a trade or skill through a legally binding apprenticeship was a good route to an economically viable lifestyle, and a recognised place in the village community. The drawing up and execution of documents for sealing an apprenticeship were another of the responsibilities of the Vestry. This system made provision for many destitute children who did not have a family tradition to follow.

We shall find many references to problems of poverty as we move into the next century and beyond: it doesn't go away!

For our present purpose which is to tell the story of Dawlish and its Parish Church of St. Gregory the Great, it is right to include reference to the important and wide-ranging duties carried out by the Church as it functioned as the central village institution. The Vestry had wide-ranging powers and its use by higher administrative authorities for the collection and distribution of the monies raised by the various and growing number of taxes meant that it became able to control rules or by-laws in *civil* matters. It was a force to be reckoned with!

*What about the ecclesiastical concerns?*

Having thought about the very practical work of the Church as a 'town-based' institution, we turn again to the subject of the worship and pastoral care being offered by the Church in Dawlish.

In this 18th century we had only three Vicars: Humphry (that is how he spelled it) Harvey, who served for 40 years to 1729 when he died in the year when an epidemic caused the death of 60 Dawlish people. He was followed by Thomas Prowse who stayed till 1789. This was an astonishing 60 years, and I assume that he died here 'in harness'. William Ralfe was here for a more modest 18 years, taking us into the 19th century.

Towards the end of his time, Humphry Harvey paid attention to the sorry state of the church floor. There were ancient memorial stones laid in the aisles and, on the floor of the tiny space used as the chancel, one which commemorated an earlier vicar, "Philippus Skynner MCCCCLVII" (1457). These stones were said to be defaced by the action of many footsteps. In 1727 the church accounts record a payment of 11s. for the carriage of "Perbick stone", and another of £1.12s.8p to a Mr Hartwell, to pave the church. I wonder how much of the floor was graced with such expensive Purbeck stone: perhaps just the chancel and aisles. The monuments are lost now. (It is possible that some of this Purbeck stone was re-used to make the doorway into the new Ringers' Chamber half way up the tower, in 1984. The shiny black stone door jambs are out of harmony with the red walls of the spiral staircase and the paler steps).

Thomas Prowse, who lived in the old vicarage in Weech Road, seems to have bought up land extending down to Dawlish Water, to extend the vicarage garden to ¾ of an acre in 1748. (There were subsequent additions until it covered 3 acres in 1869). Mr. Prowse had his personal bridge over the Water which he crossed on each of the many times he walked to the church.

These long ministries in St. Gregory's Church seem to suggest that public worship and personal pastoral care continued to the satisfaction of the people and the diocesan authorities. However, contemporary writers tell of a decline in the depth and seriousness with which many people approached church worship. Attendance later in the century seemed to become a matter of conformity to fashion, and social standing and propriety. (Read Jane Austen!). Much depended on the attitude of the local gentry: an ideal estate owner would take seriously the support of a suitable incumbent. Together they would be involved in the proper maintenance of both church fabric and well-delivered and genuine acts of worship and pastoral care. I like to think that towards the end of the 1700s our Dawlish Church *was* strong enough and sufficiently devout to tackle in all seriousness the matter of the growing population and the need to increase the seating capacity within the church.

## Pews, Preaching and Population

By now there had been benches, and then enclosed 'box' pews, in the nave of the church for many years. Those families who could afford to do so paid an annual rental which secured the exclusive right to occupy a designated pew. Sadly it would seem that class distinction had become a factor in the allocation of pews. Pew rents were not discontinued until 1841.

Services were lengthy, and 'personalised' high-sided box pews were made more comfortable by cushions and warmers in cold weather. No church heating, but a wrapped pre-heated brick to put your feet on, or a hot potato inside your muff made a lot of difference.

For in these times, *preaching* had become a regular feature of the main act of worship, perhaps threatening to overshadow the importance of administering and receiving Holy Communion. Sermons were delivered from the 1738 pulpit which was a plain wooden panelled structure with a domed canopy and set to one side of the central aisle. Sermons could be very long indeed, and some parish churches, (though not ours), have preserved the tell-tale hourglass on the pulpit ledge which might, at the whim of the preacher, be turned over to begin the second hour! Small wonder that the high-sided box pew became popular for its ability to keep out draughts and hide a multitude of minor sins!

## Dawlish appears on the Map

On the outside of the church tower, the newest of a series of clocks (made in 1715 for £12) marked the time for all to see. (This clock mechanism is on display in Dawlish Museum. I think it is a great pity that we have not continued to have a church clock on our tower). The number of folk who *did* look at that latest clock regularly was about to increase rapidly, for towards the end of the 18th century, seaside towns began to look very attractive, particularly to wealthy people who were prevented from going to France and beyond by the Napoleonic wars. Now that road travel was more comfortably possible, Dawlish welcomed a number of visitors who stayed to become new residents, and who built high quality houses for themselves, and also set up premises for the necessary tradesmen who followed in their wake.

Soon the very unpredictable lower parts of Dawlish Water were re-channelled and the marshy banks drained and landscaped to make the "Lawn". Good housing went up in several places, and improved roads joined the Old Town around the church to the newly established 'Strands' overlooking the stream and lawn. There was building on the river terraces which became High Street and Plantation Terrace, and on the seafront near where the fishermen and their families lived. As the demand for building land increased, plots higher up the east and west cliffs were sold to affluent newcomers or to trades people who had 'made good'.

We were no longer an isolated village, but had become a small town. At the turn of the century the 1801 figures showed a population of 1590, and this would double in the next 30 years. In the church, new residents began to find that there were no vacant pews for them to rent. So clearly something had to be done to accommodate them and the next generation. Would the answer be to build capacious galleries?

*Galleries and Music.*

There was already a gallery in the church building, extending half way across the west wall. It housed a pipe organ whose bellows would have been worked by hand, in the same way as those powering the blacksmith's furnace down the road. Certainly an equally responsible task for a boy who had to be trustworthy, for he had it in his (possibly mischievous) power to let the instrument fade out in a series of discordant groans! Repairs to the organ feature in the parish accounts as far back as 1618 when "a new skynne of leather (was) bought to repair the organ". The supple leather (often lambskin) used in parts of the instrument could well have been attacked by the proverbially hungry church mice so common in a country church! This west gallery could have housed other instrumentalists, though the record of the purchase in 1800 of "a clarionet and a bass viol" probably refers to the addition of further 'stops' to the organ. Was there a choir up there too? (Almost certainly there was).

Congregational singing of *hymns* as well as psalms during Divine worship was becoming generally acceptable, not only in nonconformist Chapel worship, but also in such Parish Churches as tended towards an evangelical Anglicanism. The 18$^{th}$ century has been called the 'Century of Divine Songs', for nonconformist writers such as Isaac Watts ("When I survey the wondrous Cross"), Philip Doddridge ("Hark the glad sound! The Saviour comes"), and many other writers, were producing a wealth of memorable hymns for ordinary people to sing. These became immensely popular as expressions of faith, commitment, praise and reverent devotion.

The *nonconformist* style of worship with preaching and much singing, appealed particularly strongly to families of poor and lower middle class standing. Sadly, for many of these good people, the formality of the Parish Church rituals and the persistence of class distinction, led them to feel that the Anglican community was 'cold', and less welcoming and caring than it might have been. John Wesley strove hard to remedy this perception from within the Anglican system in which he was ordained priest, but finally he began to train and ordain ministers according to a 'Method' and so was inaugurated the Methodist Church. Likewise, in the Congregational Church, members were able to feel they were indeed an integral and responsible part of a worshipping group, for they took an active part in regular Church Meetings in which, "under the guidance of the Holy Spirit", they took decisions *together* about worship and leadership, the care of those in need, and the day to day practical affairs of their Church.

Charles and John Wesley, and other hymn writers of those times, saw the power of *song* as a means of awakening people to the relevance of the Gospel in their lives. "Sing unto the Lord a new song" was a call that was obeyed in the publication of new devotional poetry set to music. These compositions had universal appeal because they were rhythmical and easily memorised. Like the ever popular folk songs of work and merrymaking and social tradition, hymn singing 'caught on' and indeed a number of hymns were written or happily set to old folk melodies.

Hymnbooks were now being introduced of which an early one was John Wesley's 1737 work. It included metrical psalms, translations of Greek and German hymns, six of the poems of George Herbert, a number of those of Isaac Watts and, of course, many of the compositions of John's brother Charles Wesley. This was at a time of renewed religious awakening which drew, into the nonconformist fellowships particularly, numerous converts and lapsed believers. There was a fresh appraisal of social concerns which inspired many members of *all* denominations to address the growing evils that arose as workers migrated to the cities and found themselves sucked into a world of poverty and squalor and inhumane working conditions.

Perhaps this seems a long way from Dawlish, but the singing of hymns caught on here too. It did not remain the province of the 'Free Churches' but became universally accepted as a worthy part of Anglican worship too. It is to Anglican sources (Bishop Ken) that we trace such wonderful hymns as:

"Awake my soul and with the sun thy daily stage of duty run. Shake off dull sloth and joyful rise to pay thy morning sacrifice".

"Glory to thee my God this night, for all the blessings of the light"

"Praise God from whom all blessings flow......"

The story of hymnody is an interesting subject in itself, but at this period in the story of St. Gregory's Church it tells us that the extreme Puritan aversion to accompanied singing had become a thing of the past. Everyone present in church was now encouraged to "...come before his presence with a song", like the Psalmist.

And obviously we did!

*Our Growing Population: Where will the Children sit?*

There was an increasing number of children who were cared for at the expense of the parish. They lived in various houses, often poorly maintained. One of these was in what is now Brunswick Place. In 1796 the Vestry agreed to extend it and in 1797 appointed Jane Parr as the overseer at a salary of 2s 6d a week. (This house was destroyed during the great flood of 1810). The children would have been taken to the parish church each Sunday under supervision. With the establishment of the National Parochial Schools in Old Town Street in 1819 many more children of ordinary families were *required* to attend Sunday worship, so the need for extra seating became urgent. If some seating for children from the Poor houses was located in our west end musicians' gallery, it would surely have soon become inadequate. There would be regrets over the loss of some other gallery seating by the unauthorised destruction recorded in the following letter addressed to the Vestry:

"...was there not an ancient gallery which belonged to the parishioners at large, over the south wing of the chancel, capable of holding 50 persons? And was it not a few years ago taken down by Mr. H...... because he had a pew under it and for his more convenient sitting therein, and was not such gallery and part of the screen under it so destroyed without a Licence or Faculty first obtained for that purpose?"

The congregation was very ready to put its feelings into writing! The Devon County Records Office holds a clutch of such hand-written letters covering 20 years of serious comments and complaints about pew rents and allocations, and lively arguments for and against the suggestion that more galleries should be built over the north and south aisles. "Galleries would make the church too dark" was a frequent comment. (The existence of the west gallery had already made it necessary to insert two huge skylights in the roof over the north aisle. We have pictorial evidence of this feature, dated 1750). These letters make comical reading today, except that sad undercurrents of class distinction and power seeking can easily be read between the lines. Vestry meetings must have been lively and we should admire the Vicar, Dr. J. D. Perkins (1807 onwards) for his patience and wisely firm hands on the reins. I imagine that the very word 'gallery' must have dampened his spirits on many an occasion!

The matter of the galleries would be resolved only after the Surveyor's report in 1819 which in effect, condemned the 1438 church and made rebuilding an essential and urgent matter. In accepting the report, and setting the work in hand, the Vestry confirmed the opinions and desires of those who saw the need to provide a sound and worthy place of worship, and one more able to serve the needs of the *growing and changing* town.

*The Changing Town: From Parish Vestry to Local Boards*

We know that by the turn of the century, the setting up of secular Boards, (institutions to organise and oversee such basic needs as health, education, roads, water and sanitation and poor relief) was well advanced. This meant that Parish Vestry officers were now able gradually to hand over some of their former responsibilities to these bodies whose structure and economics would provide, from public funds, payment of their officers and employees on a regular basis.

Although the Church continued to have its own separate *ecclesiastical* discipline and funding, its members clearly were *not* abandoning involvement in town life. For the office-holding members of the Vestry were, because of their personal standing in the town, prominent and influential in the elected secular Boards.

Church and town were still intertwined in providing for the well-being of all parish residents.

Everyone was involved in the matter of the condemned church building, and the plans for its renewal. There was no questioning of the expectation, on the part of Exeter Diocese and the Dawlish people, that continuity of Divine Worship, and the teaching and supportive ministries of the Church, would be maintained.

So we turn now to the story of this major event in the life of the Parish Church of St.Gregory in Dawlish.

# CHAPTER TEN

## *RAISING THE ROOF*

"Your ancient ruins shall be rebuilt; you shall raise up the foundations of many generations.......

Isaiah 58 v 12

To rebuild the church was a bold and expensive venture which put the Vestry and congregation into debt for many years. With Georgian confidence and pride they set about finding and employing an architect who was sympathetic to their specified needs, and with whom they would work for the next few busy and changeful years from 1823 to 1825.

The architect employed to draw up plans and to undertake the rebuilding work was Andrew Patey of Exeter. Happily, his admiration for the late Mediaeval arcade of pillars and arches was such that he saw fit to preserve them in his overall design. The red stone tower would also continue to be the main feature of the west end of the building. He was an architect who sought to combine features which he felt to be good in the old church with what was necessary for the changing needs of the day. I like to think that the continuity of a major part of the fabric was pleasing to those who experienced the tremendous upheaval that was to take place.

Mr Patey was asked to make provision for galleries on the west, north and south walls. This instruction raised a problem of the first magnitude. In order to give enough headroom for the people occupying the seating underneath the galleries, the roof would need to be three feet higher than in the old building. To satisfy this requirement, *and* to conserve the arcade, was indeed a test of his ingenuity. (How would you tackle it?) Here is a clue from the preserved records:

In 1823 a petition was lodged for a Faculty (the obligatory document from the Diocesan Board giving permission to carry out the work) "for the enlargement of the Parish Church of Dawlish because of population increase". This Faculty was granted and includes the following instructions:

*"...to take down the whole of the present galleries, to take off all the roof, to take down the arches and pillars; and all such parts of the walls of the church as required to be extended to be taken down to their foundations, and the remaining walls to be pulled down as low as the bottom of the present windows......"*

Phew! And that was only stage one, the necessary, and apparently destructive part of the undertaking, which would in due course make possible the constructive phase in which the stated aims would be cleverly realised. The pillars and arches would be re-assembled, as we shall see later.

*Surviving the Adventure of Reconstruction*

The Reverend John David Perkins became Vicar of Dawlish in 1807. He was a well educated man, having been awarded a Doctorate in Divinity, and bringing many gifts to his calling as the incumbent of St. Gregory's Church benefice. He must have chaired many long and involved meetings at which crucial decisions were taken about the future of the crumbling building, and the huge financial burden to be shouldered if rebuilding was to take place. Any doubts about the necessity for this were wiped out when a stone pinnacle collapsed on to and through the roof during Divine Worship in 1821. Mercifully no-one was hurt. The roof was already shored up with tree trunks!

Plans for the first of two substantial monetary loans were in hand so that the demolition work could begin in 1823. Dr Perkins had many important functions in the town; he was a Justice of the Peace and chairman of influential financial committees, but as Vicar his prime concern was to pilot the Church through three years of upheaval. His pastoral duties must continue without a break even without a church building. Where could they go?

By now schools were being established in Dawlish, and in 1819 and 1820 the National Parochial School and an Infants' department occupied good stone buildings in Old Town Street, paid for by the Hoare family of Luscombe. The teaching of religion according to the principles of the Church of England was required and the elected School Committee was chaired by the Vicar. There would probably therefore have been no objection raised to the request that the school premises be made available for public worship and other church meetings during the years of rebuilding. So the school room was dedicated, and pews or benches brought from the old church. And there we met for worship for the next three years. Presumably the school continued on weekdays.

The whole town was actively involved in a continuous sequence of fund-raising events which must have provided a good deal of social life for a worthy cause. And a walk to watch the builders' progress must have been both interesting and pleasant.

*What was destroyed?*

The plan to enlarge the east end of the church involved encroachment on land where the old tithe barn had stood, behind Church house. This barn, described by F.J.Carter in his Notes on Old Dawlish (1936), as "a cob-walled roomy building with a thatched roof", was demolished: its storage functions continued in another barn in the Stonelands Estate until tithing was abolished in 1836. £100 was paid to a Mrs Churchill who had been, we suppose, the custodian of that part of church land and who had a house there. The east lych-gate was removed, and also an adjoining house for which Mr. James Hexter was paid £60. The loss of these structures made room for the limited extension of the chancel and the building of a new vestry to its east.

With the reconstruction of all the windows, much old stonework was lost, together with nearly all the old stained glass. How much of the latter there was is not recorded. All we know is that subsequently, the *new* east (chancel) window had its five lights...

"fitted with stained glass old and new, some of which in gaudy colours...... there are several figures of bishops, saints etc. in the

Romish style and dress, among them an archbishop with an abbot kneeling before him. Two pieces also of several minute figures apparently relating to the history of Moses and the Israelites...of foreign manufacture and bearing the date 1583".

(Extract from the Rev. James Davidson's book, 1846).

The old church had a south 'tower' towards the eastern end of the south wall. It had a sundial above the door, (and possibly also a Mass dial with a hand showing the time of the next mass), and an unusual semi-octagonal turret housing a spiral staircase which used to give access to the rood loft (long since removed) inside the church, and to the roof through an external door. Sadly, this richly carved feature was taken down, probably to give room for the making of a small south transept. It seems that some of the carving *was* saved, for Davidson writes: "The entry to the south transept has an elegant little ancient doorway formed by a pointed arch.... the mouldings on the sides ornamented with knots of foliage and the like..."

The old south-facing wall had been strengthened with stone buttresses which had niches for statues, but all of these carvings had crumbled beyond recognition by 1803. Perhaps they had been defaced by over-zealous Puritans? The wall was topped with pinnacles and battlements (similar to those which have adorned the west end tower since 1817). All this was to come down but be replaced later, for how we loved such ornamentation then!

*Down and up again.*

If you look at the bottoms of the nave pillars as we have them today you will see that extra stone has been added *underneath* the ornamented section that would have been at ground level in the old church. Our Georgian builders took the whole of the fabric right down to the foundations, and started to build it all up again. Pillars, arches, roof timbers and all: it was amazingly careful, skilful work, carried out with great devotion. Every section of arch and pillar was marked and numbered as it was removed, ready for accurate re-assembly. Roof timbers were taken down and inspected and repaired, or replaced where necessary.

What a chance to clean the soot-begrimed stones! Now we know why the pillars are so white that people today have difficulty in believing that the arcade is nearly 600 years old. The soot from thousands of candles and clouds of incense would have gone on settling on the stones and in the rafters, turning the stone greyish black, and the building dark. Every piece had to be scrubbed and chiselled clean to enable the white Beer stone to shine as it did when first used. You can still see the chisel marks today. New supplies of Beer stone were brought in, shaped to match the pillar segments, and laid on the old foundations. Then the old columns were re-assembled *on top* of the three feet of new work, thus achieving the required height. You can see that this was how they did it, by the position of the shaped stone of the former base section of the original pillar, which is now at the level of the top of the present pews. An ingenious solution!

The side walls of the aisles had been taken down only to the bottom of the windows, making it possible to think that some of the Perpendicular window stonework may have been cleaned and re-used. The red walls were replaced with rather rough mixed stone like many another house and wall in the Dawlish area. The 'finish' was irrelevant because it would all be masked with external plastering which they called 'Roman cement'. (Yes, the Romans discovered and used this as building material before the Christian era began, and they brought the technology to Britain).

*The new east end of the building*

In 1438 the east wall of the church was situated where we now have the chancel arch. There was a recess some five feet deep, where the altar stood. The screen was at the level of the next pillar from the east, the first bay east of the screen being the chancel. Documents exist showing north and south 'wings' as part of the chancel: these were just the eastern ends of their respective aisles. The north wing served as the vestry.

1823 saw the east wall rebuilt on new foundations farther east so that the sanctuary could be enlarged in depth. The new five-light window was inserted above the altar. Below the window a carved stone *reredos* was installed. This is a decorative panel visible above and behind an altar; ours here in St. Gregory's bears symbols of the Passion, which are displayed above the four arches of the design.   (This reredos is now in the Lady Chapel).

The plans also provided for small north and south transepts (12ft by 11ft) jutting out from the next bay on the nave side of where the screen had been. A transept is a part of the building which opens out from the nave, in a 'north' or 'south' direction. (Literally, they 'cross the hedge', in this case the line of the original nave side wall).  Our once rectangular church had  now become cross-shaped.  (You may notice that today, the entrances to the transepts from the nave occupy the length of *two* bays of the nave arcade).

There was no choir seating in the chancel, for this space was for the altar, raised one step above the nave, and was more correctly called the sanctuary. A new vestry was built beyond the east wall, with access to the sanctuary through a small door in the wall and the leftmost of the four panels of the carved reredos. The north wing of the sanctuary, which was previously used as the vestry, was now free to house the pipe organ for a while; later this instrument would be put back into the west gallery.

*The new roof*

Having erected the pillars-and-arches arcade, the walls and their new buttresses, the transepts and the enlarged chancel, the roof could now be re-assembled and made sound. This was a very welcome stage in the re-building. All was taking shape again.

Typical of West country design, the nave and two aisles each have a  'wagon' or 'barrel-shaped roof' made with closely set, braced rafters and finished with a plaster ceiling and wooden ribs having carved bosses at the intersection points. There was scope here for some more foliage designs. We don't know who carved these. A careful study using binoculars discovers modest leaf motifs which tell of someone's many hours of patient work. I can imagine him enjoying the quiet labour which gave us these unobtrusive decorations. Maybe they were even saved from the former roof and are mediaeval in date. Notice that the three long roofs persisted together with the gutters in between, which continue to give trouble in the form of leakages to this very day!

## Heavy woodwork

Now that work on the interior could go ahead protected from the weather, the insertion of galleries began. They started with the west one across the whole width of the nave. Over the next 12 years further galleries would be added until by 1836 the nave was dominated by three huge galleries: those on the north and south walls extending along the whole length of both north and south aisles of the nave *and* over the new transepts.

They provided seating upstairs on three sides of the building. So that the windows would not suffer damage, a space of two feet was left between them and the back of the wood work. This allowed rather more light to filter in, but the overall effect must have been to darken the interior most undesirably. But the galleries were there to solve the problem of insufficient seating for the greatly increased population of Dawlish. At the end of the rebuilding and refurnishing, it is said that the Parish Church of St. Gregory in Dawlish could seat 1500 people. I've wondered, with other recorders, if it ever actually did so. There are suggestions that the school children and parishioners found some of the gallery seating very unsatisfactory. (After all that trouble!)

## More heavy woodwork: the story of the pulpit

In 1814 a petition had been granted which allowed for the moving of the pulpit from its old position (north of centre as now), to the central aisle, a position which would enable the large congregation to hear more easily. This pulpit had replaced the 1783 one, and was of massive proportions. It was to be supported on pillars so that people would be able freely to pass and re-pass under it! Presumably this was to allow them access to the altar rail to receive the Elements during Holy Communion. This re-ordering of the furniture suggests strongly that the emphasis in worship had shifted away from the prime importance of the Sacrament of Holy Communion, to a point where *preaching* had acquired an over-riding significance.

This lay-out of the building was maintained in the 1823 plan for rebuilding. Old photographs and records tell of a three-deck structure. I am told that the Parson would sit in the middle desk and the Parish Clerk below him. In front of the latter was a reading desk. During Divine Worship, the Parson and Clerk would read alternate verses of the Psalms, and the Clerk would make the responses in the lesser litanies at Morning and Evening Prayer. When the time came for a sermon, the Parson would ascend to the upper preaching rostrum. Curved stairs led to the lofty place where the preacher was indeed 'six feet above contradiction'. Placed in the central aisle the pulpit dominated the view eastwards and almost completely obscured the altar.

Heavy box pews at floor level, and rented seats under, and probably also in, parts of the ponderous galleries over the aisles and transepts, housed those who could afford the seat rents; in other parts of the gallery seating was 'free', provided at parish expense for anyone to use. In the nave there was a notice which informed those entering the building "All seats on this side are free" (!) Extra seats in the west gallery (courtesy of Mr.Hoare) were for the school children.

Given these features, (asked for by the Vestry), we can, with difficulty and perhaps with amusement, understand the high pulpit from which the preacher could be seen and heard by occupants of the box pews *and* all the galleries. And *he* could see what was going on in the depths of the box pews!

*Furnishing the Sanctuary*

'Way back in 1301, the report on the Visitation by Bishop Stapledon (still preserved in Exeter Cathedral archives) tells us that we had, among other sacred items "a good High Altar......two Chalices, gilded within and without......a processional Cross; and a leaden vessel for Holy Water". We don't know what happened to these precious things during the many changes and confiscations which took place during the years of the Reformation and the Commonwealth. Later on, in 1675, we acquired a Paten and Chalice made in that year, and presented by the 'Church

Wardengs' (what quaint spelling!) These continued in use in the new church in 1825 and are still in our possession.

A new Communion Table and chairs were commissioned and set in the still smallish sanctuary behind the pulpit. This Table was placed in front of the stone reredos, and it served as the High Altar, though without any link with the ancient practice of housing the relics of saints. It was raised up by one step from the floor level of the nave. The stonework behind it (i.e. the reredos) had...... "perpendicular tracery and a cornice of foliage above. In the panel on the north side the door opens to the vestry" (Davidson 1846). A later recorder, Beatrix Cresswell (Notes on churches in the Kenn Deanery, 1912), describing the reredos when it was re-positioned in the south aisle in what is now the Lady Chapel, says: "It is of old Gothic type ...... with the Creed etc. painted on it". The 'et ceteras' were likely to have been the Ten Commandments and Our Lord's Prayer.

All traces of the old screen, dividing the nave from the small chancel, seem to have gone by now, and communicants would have knelt at a rail at the altar step, having carefully negotiated the passage under or round the pulpit furniture. It seems clear that whatever was the personal practice of the vicar, in these years his congregation only received the Elements at Holy Communion on a few occasions each year. The 1662 edition of the Prayer Book, (then in use), stipulates that "...every parishioner shall communicate at least three times in the year, of which Easter to be one." We may note that since then, each time of religious revival has aimed at increasing the frequency with which people were invited to be partakers of Bread and Wine in Holy Communion. This trend would feature importantly in the story of St. Gregory's Church in Dawlish during the next fifty years.

*The Re-opening of the New Building*

This finally took place in 1825 with all due ceremony, but there was still a heavy debt load which would not be cleared until some twenty years later.

# CHAPTER ELEVEN

## THE RESTLESS YEARS OF THE EARLY NINETEENTH CENTURY

"...... (he) laid the foundations of the house of God in Jerusalem; and from that time until now it has been under construction, and it is not yet finished".

Ezra 5 v 16.

After the restored building was re-opened for worship in 1825, Dawlish people had high hopes that the building would be all they had wished for. But before long, to the dismay of many, it became obvious that this was not so. The seating arrangements still gave grounds for complaint. The retention of the many high-sided box pews in the nave was unfortunate, as these took up a great deal of space that would have been better used in providing more ground floor open pews, for Dawlish was still attracting many more permanent residents.

Dr. J. D. Perkins was still our Vicar, and he offered to revive the practice of holding a third service of worship for a while. As we have seen, the provision of more galleries was soon put in hand (completed in 1836), but even these proved to be unsatisfactory and were probably not used to their full capacity. And there were other, more profound reasons for steadily growing dissatisfaction. These we shall try to understand shortly. The fact remains that within 50 years, there was strong pressure from many serious and well meaning critics, to undertake yet *another* series of alterations and improvements to our building.

*Dawlish Parishioners' Undaunted Energy*

But for the time being, much energy went towards eliminating the heavy burden of debt. Parishioners and friends had every reason to be pleased with their efforts, for the books were successfully balanced within twenty years. Well done!

And it would seem that Dawlish parishioners did not sit back idly when this milestone was passed. They set about building a fine Vestry Hall in the centre of the town (in Lansdowne Place). This answered a need for rooms where both the Church Vestry, and the newly appointed secular local Boards (such as Health, Education, and Poor Law administration) could hold their several meetings. It was maintained with public money contributed in taxes. Increasingly used by the Town Boards, Registration and Rates Officers and the Judiciary, it became known and used as the Town Hall, until the Manor House was acquired for this after 1945, when the Vestry hall was sold. It is now the Baptist Church.

*The Industrial Revolution is Unstoppable!*

If the next few pages read like a history book, please be patient! When I was at school, I struggled hard to find any real interest in $19^{th}$ century politics, the expansion of world trade, and empire-building. Nobody inspired me to imagine *myself* growing up or working in those times. Sixty years later I know that in writing this book I have consciously set out to enter into the lives of Dawlish people, even before the establishment of St. Gregory's Church, and to travel with them "through all the changing scenes of life......" It is a journey that has brought me much of interest and pleasure and I make no apology for inviting my readers now, to try to get the feel of how the great Industrial Revolution affected the lives of everybody in villages, towns and in the expanding cities. Alec R. Vidler writes in the Preface to his contribution to the Penguin History of the Church (Volume Five: The Church in an Age of Revolution, 1789 to the present day):

"I wish I had been able to say more about the ordinary life of Christian people in parishes and congregations which has gone on steadily from generation to generation, and without which there would be no church history worth mentioning".

(Parishes like Dawlish, perhaps?)

So we will take a look at the origins and feel the increasing momentum of the Industrial Revolution.

Britain's plentiful supplies of coal and iron, and the ingenuity of her scientists and inventors, led to the development of ways of generating and harnessing *power which could be controlled.* No longer were we dependent on manpower or unpredictable wind and water power to drive machinery. The use of steam for this purpose took the Industrial Revolution to ever greater heights of productivity. Its use in pumping water made mining safer. It hurried up the transport, not only of raw materials to better-powered factories and workshops, but also the distribution of manufactured goods, and *the movements of people.*

Dawlish was now no longer an isolated small town of little consequence; it too was carried inevitably into the era of discovery and technical development. In 1846 the South Devon Railway reached Dawlish and our people began to travel to Exeter on trains using Brunel's short-lived Atmospheric system, and then steam-hauled locomotives. There they could find work, and take goods to sell. They could go shopping, and join in wider social and intellectual pursuits. We have already seen how the railway brought people and fashionable prosperity to Dawlish.

It was not easy for leaders in the Dawlish community to ensure that novelty was beneficial to the majority of the people. And the Church had to grapple with the impact that the expansion of knowledge had on belief and behaviour. Was the Church alert and ready to respond to new challenges, and to provide help where there was need? During the first quarter of the 19th century there were so many important inventions and developments which, when applied in the workplace in both town and country, inevitably brought new, and not always welcome, changes in life patterns. There was growing competition for jobs, and the hardships that ensued for those who were marginalised or exploited in the process, began to kindle a series of dramatic social and political struggles which were on a nationwide scale. These ultimately led to the introduction of many much needed reform measures. And yes, this *was* relevant to those living and working in Dawlish.

Unrest was widespread in *country areas,* including Dawlish, where employment was jeopardised by the introduction of the new mechanised farming methods. The land owners obtained the legal right to keep the price of corn (and their profits) high even though they could manage with fewer labourers. There were other reasons why the cost of bread and other dependent foods did not come down, but spiralled upwards. One was that Parliament had banned the import of cheaper foreign wheat, with the result that prices remained so high that rural poverty again became common among those who had been thrown out of regular employment. In Dawlish, poverty and hardship in some families, was a constant burden which had to be addressed by the local community. It did so through the Parish Vestry, until this responsibility was transferred to a District Union based in Newton Abbot in 1836.

The Parish Vestry Minutes give some vivid glimpses into the (literally) immobilising poverty of some parishioners who applied for Parish aid back in 1831:

Parish Vestry Minutes of 12$^{th}$ July 1831.
   Gilly, Anne: child to have a pair of shoes.........6 shillings
   Taylor, Maria: for her son, towards jacket and trowsers and a pair of shoes (so that he could be decently enough dressed to apply for a job)............6 shillings.
   Bowden, Joseph: in need, being ill.........5 shillings. (to be repaid to the parish if Mr. Hoare pays him full wages).
   Taylor, Mary: Money towards the cost of a shrimp net. (She promises to repay the parish as soon as possible).
   Carsie, Ann: Her girl aged 10 to be put out (i.e. sent into service) without delay, in order to support her widowed mother.

(The influx of wealthy residents provided steady employment and training, together with bed and board for quite a few girls, who then contributed to the upkeep of the rest of their families).

Money was also provided for women to care for the lone elderly and sick, and for 'someone to sit with them all night'.

These were the years when Turnpike roads were still under construction, and we have this entry in the Minutes:
February 21 1832: Letter from the Surveyor of Highways: "Many labourers wanted, to work on road-making and repairs. Does the Parish Vestry agree it is better for the poor to be thus engaged rather than being thrown on the Parish Poor Rates?"
Of course the Vestry agreed with the proposal!

*Treating the symptoms rather than the disease*

In the absence of fair negotiation procedures by which to address the heart of the problem of increased poverty in places like Dawlish, the unavoidable local result was the proliferation of *poor*-houses for the destitute. Then the town was ordered to provide *work*-houses for, at first, the more able-bodied who had lost their source of income. (Later on the workhouses sheltered the old and the infirm who had no-one else to care for them). Prison-like, they were dreaded and regarded generally as the final degradation of a person's confident independence. Dawlish district was served by the Newton Abbot Workhouse whose original building later became the hospital there. It was built of stone and expected to last!

Slowly, the public outcry over high food prices, (voiced through fairer Parliamentary procedure), secured the repeal of the Corn Laws from 1846 onwards, but it would be many decades before the 'disgrace' attached to Workhouse institutions was replaced with public support and compassion for the needy.

*The Shift from Rural to Urban Living*

Country towns like Dawlish were beautiful places in which to live, and the move to seek a better and more reliable income in the industrial cities was often the result of circumstance, rather than of choice, for many families who made the change. A 'living' wage was increasingly hard to come by in the country. As we have seen, families who had occupied cottages 'tied' to their employment on large estates, might find themselves without income and, in addition, with nowhere to live. The prospect of work and housing to be had for the asking, in the industrial towns, led many a disillusioned man to see that it was his *duty* to take that path, in order to provide for his family. We can begin to understand why this kind of personal upheaval led to major social changes throughout the land.

It was more efficient to concentrate powered machinery and manpower in large factories close together in the rapidly growing industrial towns and cities, so the availability of work and housing became focused there. Financial power shifted from the landed gentry to the successful mill owners. The latter were the entrepreneurs of the day, a new, energetic class of men, many of whom seized the opportunity to gain great wealth for themselves, and for the shareholders whose money had enabled the factories and industries to be established.

*Wealth and Greed, and Poverty and Ill-health*

Conditions of work were determined by the factory owners' desire for profit, but this was too often at the expense of the wellbeing of their employees. The work potential of children was cruelly exploited, and their need for education neglected. Because the only way to get to work was to walk, all the housing provided for factory workers and their families was in tightly crowded proximity to the mills. With the development of steam power, factory chimneys poured out smoke and smuts all day and often all night as 24-hour shift working was introduced. Indeed all was not well for the ordinary family, for whom in the cities particularly, the scourges of malnutrition and dirty air, and of epidemic fatal illness had come terrifyingly close at hand.

This was all the more sad because the many wonderful inventions and discoveries of this period held such promise of a more interesting life, and prosperity for many people. But the benefits were, to say the least of it, out of reach of the majority of families. It would be true to say that in the textile factories men, women and children were being used to *keep the machines running*, regardless of the dangers arising from sheer exhaustion during the long periods of work. Moving parts of machinery were often not protected, and accidents to children and untrained or careless workers became far too common. Profit for the mill owners was everything. Much the same was true over conditions of work in the mining industry. Who would speak with compassion and strength for the needs of the ordinary man? How sad it is that the selfish pursuit of wealth should cast such a shadow over the wonderful achievements of scientists and inventors in this amazingly fertile age!

*Searching for Remedies*

We can look back now and give thanks for men and women of a lively conscience, who brought these ills of a changed kind of society into the limelight through literature, preaching, and in publicly performed good works in prisons, factories and workhouses. Bold spokesmen and women arose who were aware of the growing dissatisfaction over the limited way in which people were represented in Parliament. Their efforts to find a better way led finally to the passing of the Great Reform Bill in 1832, which began to restructure the method by which people were given an effective voice. The Trade Unions had been recognised at last in 1825, the same year that saw the opening of the restored church of St. Gregory in Dawlish.

It would be another eight years before the Factory Act of 1833 began to limit the use of child labour. We remember the forceful Christian spokesman Lord Shaftesbury, in this context. William Wilberforce and a group of fellow Christian 'Evangelicals' devoted themselves above all, to the abolition of the slave trade. Slavery was to be abolished throughout the British Empire in 1834. Gradually, other kinds of 'slavery' such as the industrial exploitation and misuse of vulnerable families, began to be replaced by more humane practices.

*Some Further Christian Responses*

Our Dawlish congregations must have been acutely aware of what was going on around them at home and in the nation at large. We have seen the local efforts to relieve hardship, and surely pressure was exerted through the permitted spokespersons and in the fledgling public press?

Among the first to act to improve the lot of factory workers were Quaker mill owners whose example was followed soon by other conscientious Christian employers. And we should not forget the Sunday School movement which arose, in the first place, to answer the needs of children who were employed for a full working week, to have some kind of basic education in their limited free time, on Sundays.

*The need for more Churches*

During these years of heart searching and reform, many new Anglican and nonconformist churches came into being because so many *city* dwellers were without a nearby church where they could meet for worship and the social support and comfort that they so needed. Funding for the establishment of these came from government sources and from private sponsors. This was an era of *new* church buildings and the chance for architectural experiment. The Nonconformists were severely practical, and typically built quite a plain, but capacious galleried church *and* a large church hall where Sunday School, youth club, adult education and leisure activities could take place. Anglicans too, were aware of the need for bringing people together into community activities which fostered a sense of belonging: something which so many had lost when they moved away from strong local village traditions.

*Dawlish joins in the movement for new church building*

We have seen that in Dawlish too, changes had come about which altered the size of the town, and the needs of its population. The social focus was shifting from the Old Town around St. Gregory's church down to the Lawn and the many fashionable houses being built nearer to the sea and up the east and west cliff roads. It was decided that a sister church, or 'chapel of ease', was needed in addition to the long-established main Parish Church. It would provide easier access for people living in the newer residential part of town, and I am told that it was felt to be desirable for the servants in the big houses to be able to attend Evensong nearby. (I expect *they* enjoyed meeting up with their sweethearts too!). It would also help to solve the seating problems still troubling those who wished to attend St. Gregory's church. Importantly, the venture was seen by many as an 'outreach' project to attract and serve a new generation of families. So the new church was built on the south side of the Lawn in 1849-51 and dedicated by Bishop Henry Phillpots on the 3rd of April 1851. The leaders and people of the Diocese, and of St. Gregory's were indeed concerned and forward-looking.

*Welcome to the sister Church of St. Mark*

The new St. Mark's Church building had at first just the nave and sanctuary. The walls of this chapel were of Torbay limestone, which was a popular choice for important new buildings in the town; this was matched by the Methodist and the new Congregational chapels built durably in stone in 1860 and 1870, which also fronted the Lawn. St. Mark's had many friends and supporters who continued to adorn and furnish its interior. A side aisle, pulpit and vestry were added in 1883, and a two manual pipe organ in 1886. There was a single bell to call the worshippers together, often tolled by Mr. Jack Batten, and a clock sounded the hours of day and night. A carillon was installed in the turret, on which hymn tunes were played to the passing public on Sunday mornings. It was the gift of a Mr. Gray in memory of his mother. (This carillon was given to the United Reformed Church in 1975 when St. Mark's building was dismantled, and it continued to sound for many years from the opposite side of the Lawn). In 1902 the west gallery in St. Mark's was removed and a new west window installed. The importance of the *sanctuary* was additionally highlighted by the provision of a richly decorated reredos for the High Altar in 1911. This feature, in mosaic and opus sectile work, depicted the Ascension of our Lord. (There is a detailed account of this art form on p. 138, where I write about the examples in the St. Gregory's building).

Those who remember worshipping in St. Mark's Church tell me it was a happy experience. They were understandably distressed when in the early 1970s, with major building repairs pending, it was decided that Dawlish could not maintain two churches, and the congregation was asked to join again with that of the mother Church of St. Gregory. It must have been a sad day in 1975, when after 120 years, a worthy building was demolished and the site sold for development. Happily, the name is preserved in St. Mark's flats, and we do not forget this part of the story of the Church of England in Dawlish. For 'St. Mark's' architectural style was of great significance. The design of that building in 1850 was greatly influenced by the new thinking (or re-thinking) about worship, which was sweeping through the whole country.

*Rethinking the ways in which we are helped to worship God*

This stirring-up process is what we know as the *High Church movement,* led by John Keble and Henry Newman in 1833 from Oxford, (hence the 'Oxford Movement'). To understand just what was involved, we need to look carefully at the ordering of worship in St. Gregory's church as it was shortly before, and again after, the 1825 re-building.

Our records confirm that we had a nave furnished with high-sided box pews, which, together with the huge centrally placed pulpit, obscured any easy sight of The Lord's Table. Over the side aisles and small transepts and right across the west end were heavy timber galleries obscuring much of the daylight. The whole place was depressingly dark and as soberly forbidding as were, perhaps, some of the very lengthy sermons delivered from the top deck of the pulpit. Perhaps I am painting too gloomy a picture, but the surviving photograph certainly encourages remarks of this kind!

It is difficult to avoid coming to the conclusion that in late Georgian and early Victorian times the most eagerly awaited (and heeded) item in a service of worship was the *sermon*. We have already noted that attendance at Holy Communion was *required* on only three occasions during the year. In other words, the building had almost become a 'preaching station', (or in polite terms, an 'auditory church'). Sadly, church-going had become something of a social ritual, with firmly entrenched class division playing its part where seating and greeting were concerned. In worship, the sermon seems to have taken pride of place over the lay members' participation in the Celebration of the Sacrament of Holy Communion. In practice too, the Sacrament of Baptism was often not being administered as prescribed in the Prayer Book, (after the last Lesson in Morning or Evening Prayer), but often in a semi-private family gathering separate from the main services of public worship. It seems that the opportunity for *all* members to receive Holy Communion, to renew their own Baptismal vows regularly, and to welcome the newly baptised members into the fellowship of the church, was not thought to be very important.

We have to ask whether Sunday worship in these almost *non-sacramental* forms was adequate fare for the congregation in its worship together, and for the personal spiritual growth of its members. The Catechism in the Book of Common Prayer, in use then, sets out the prime importance of the Sacraments of Baptism and The Lord's Supper, or Holy Communion, which are described as "necessary to salvation":

"What meanest thou by this word *Sacrament?*

"I mean an outward and visible sign of an inward and spiritual grace given unto us, and ordained by Christ himself, as a means whereby we receive the same......"

I believe we starve ourselves of the Grace of God, if we neglect the regular and frequent opportunity to receive the benefits of the Sacraments. *God's* action is potent here without words.

But *teaching* about the Sacraments and the Faith must also take place in the building up of members of the Church.

*Nourishing the members of the Church*

It had become the practice to say the Offices of Matins and Evensong as the main public acts of worship on Sundays. These had been renamed in the Book of Common Prayer as Morning and Evening Prayer (to reassure those who were oversensitive to anything that smacked of popery and monastic ways). But in the Prayer Book there was no set provision for a *sermon* in either of these services. The Prayer book does, however, specify that after the second Lesson of Evensong "The Curate of every Parish shall openly in the church instruct and examine ......Children of his Parish ......in the Catechism".  We must assume that this was done in St.Gregory's church and in St.Mark's too, where it was easy for the (very young) servants to attend Evensong when their duties were over for the day.  It was only at a Celebration of Holy Communion that a sermon was *required.*  So, for a conscientious parish priest who desired to instruct and inspire all his people regularly, the main opportunity to do so was at the time when his flock was assembled for Morning and Evening Prayer. So, at the end of the set Liturgy, there would be a time for further prayers and a sermon.  Hence the notices, displayed or spoken, which announced "Morning/Evening Prayer *with Sermon*".

At a time when public oratory had assumed great popularity and importance in the fields of politics and social issues, the words of a gifted preacher could carry great weight with his congregation. However, there must have been a good deal of variation in the style and content of the preaching, for the highly educated divine was not always a good communicator, and the gifted orator might not be equipped to bring the richly deep messages of Scriptures alive and relevant to his flock. Happily, the 'ordinary' dedicated parish priest (if there was ever such a man!), would expound the Scriptures to his people week after week, to the best of his ability, and in constant awareness of his sacred calling.  And if there was in some places rather humdrum preaching, from others many fine sermons found their way into print, and are still available today for our edification. Publication of sermons has continued ever since. A borrowed sermon can be effective if used by a 'preacher' who can make it relevant to the particular congregation (whose members he knows personally), at the time when it is delivered. The concept of 'in service training' is by no means new, and priest and people can benefit from sharing the wisdom and careful thinking of a variety of minds. Especially was this so at a time like the early 19$^{th}$ century, when the world was changing very quickly indeed.

*"Feed My Sheep"    The Gospel according to John 21 v 17*

As we consider further the shepherding of our own local congregation in the Parish Church of St. Gregory, it is necessary to ask: Did the content of the acts of worship inspire the flock in their personal devotion, and foster a desire to deepen their understanding, and to see the relevance of the Gospel in all aspects of life and work?  We can be sure that it did for some thoughtful people, but we are also told that many of those attending had drifted into unthinking apathy, even nodding off during the sermon despite the forceful rhetoric (!). Had the worship of Almighty God become trivialised?  Were some vital elements being too frequently left out?

*A low period in the life of the Church of England*

All-in-all the Established Church at that time had, sadly, become an object of ridicule among some public writers and cartoonists.  Not only was there growing apathy among members, inadequacies within worship and teaching in local parishes, but also there were gross inequalities among the bishops and clergy in respect of income, housing and the chance of preferment to better 'livings'. Seriously, as for most of us from time to time, there was a need for revival within the Church. We were being called back to the prime tasks of making possible *the dignified worship of Almighty God "in spirit and in truth", of making the Gospel available, attractive and relevant to everybody, of 'feeding' and spiritually extending believers, and of having genuine loving care for one another and for all God's children.*

How easy it can be to criticise from a distance! We must remember in humility that this *was* the very period in which the pioneer Missionary movement sent dedicated men and women to the far corners of the earth to spread the Gospel, as exploration, empire building and trading gathered momentum...... and it *was* also a time of fervent re-thinking among theologians and those who were concerned with liturgical matters.

*Seeds of Revival*

The questions raised by the Oxford movement and its subsequent ramifications drew attention to the increasing neglect of valuable *symbols* incorporated in church buildings and furnishings, and the many treasures preserved in the liturgical instructions in the 1662 Prayer Book. Chief among the underused provisions for regular worship together, was "The Order for the administration of The Lord's Supper or Holy Communion".

Those who were influenced by the Oxford Movement sought to increase emphasis on the centrality of *sacramental* worship: to move the central focus away from the pulpit and back to the Altar, the Holy Table. It is there, in the Sacrament of Holy Communion, that we are most poignantly aware that God is present in our midst in His Son, the One who shares our humanity to the full, and who, by loving us unto death, frees us from the despair of feeling that we have no identity, no value and no hope. Our Lord Christ, our Redeemer, invites us to become joined with Him in His risen life, so that we, Our Father's treasured sons and daughters, may "Go in peace to love and serve the Lord".

Here in Dawlish we were fortunate in our leaders who were open to the feeling that we too were in need of revival, and that to emphasise again the primacy of the Sacraments in the ordering of worship, would be our way forward. In 1850, St. Mark's church was designed in a way that reflected these attitudes which had been maturing with careful devotion. The Holy Table was central in worship, and so was raised to be in full view of the people. When the pulpit was made it was set off-centre, to the north side, and the lectern (a fine Eagle, I'm told) to the south. The Ministry of the Word in the reading of the Bible and in preaching, was rightly prominent, but not exclusively central in importance.

It seems that we had here in Dawlish, a most fortunate chance to experience both 'High Church' design, (St. Mark's) with the focus on the Communion Table and Font and therefore on the Sacraments, and on the other hand, the Preaching-centred furnishing as portrayed in the St. Gregory's building. I think this opportunity probably played an important part in the long discussions which led up to the major re-ordering of the eastern end of St. Gregory's Church building. When the time came to take a practical decision, everyone took a deep breath and made a leap of faith, for great were the changes that were proposed. They were most carefully considered, then approved...... and finally realised. The east end of the building was to be strikingly extended, and within it, the Altar/Communion Table was to be so placed and elevated, that it, and what it represents, would draw and focus our attention when we gather together to worship the Lord our God.

*Enthusiastic support for the new venture*

By the time the foundation stone of the new extension work was laid on the 27th of May 1874 by Mr. P. R. Hoare of Luscombe, our lay Rector, his own handsome financial donation was being supplemented by many other gifts from members and supporters. Over two thirds of the costs anticipated were in hand, and as in previous times of repair, renovation and re-building, fund raising was carried on with great zeal.

In the next chapter we will look at some of the thinking behind the planned additions, and note the carefully chosen materials used in carrying out the accepted designs.

# CHAPTER TWELVE

## *IS THERE AN IDEAL HOUSE OF WORSHIP?*

Some of the Victorian church architects were over-heavily influenced by the 'High Church' movement. In addition to the emphasis on sacramental worship, they clung to the notion that there was a specifically Christian church architecture, and that it reached near perfection in a complex $13^{th}$ century Gothic style. In their thinking, every church building should have a nave, a spacious chancel and a sanctuary, three parts together being a symbol of the Holy Trinity. Many pre-Reformation buildings had only a simple nave (where lay people gathered) and a chancel (where the priest officiated). We shall try to understand the term 'chancel' shortly. Bear with me for the moment.

At about this time, (early $19^{th}$ century), major structural repairs became necessary for the survival of many ancient churches, and sadly, *some* architects moved in, ostensibly to 'restore' these buildings, but instead of simply conserving them, they tried to make them conform to 'the best Gothic style'. This was 'achieved' in some cases by making what now seem to be quite inappropriate alterations. Sometimes there was the tragic loss of many features which told the story of how a particular village church had developed, and served the local people over many centuries in a style which reflected distinctive local needs and resources.

Such relevant visible and tangible features, when understood in the light of the history of their time and place, are valuable in keeping alive a sense of *continuity*. They emphasise the fact that the worshipping congregation of today is an integral part of an unbroken chain of believers in *this place.* People had a real sense of belonging together in the history of a particular place. This is less true in modern times, when we all seem to move about so much that we do not really know where we belong. Does this loss of information about our 'roots' trigger today's interest in family ancestry, and in television programmes such as "Who do you think you are?"

Here in St. Gregory's church we have enough in the way of older fabric and records to link us up, in a recognisable way, with our past. We are fortunate to have retained the splendid 15th century pillars and arches, and the even older tower. They remind us repeatedly of the devotion and efforts, in money and labour, that were contributed in order to have a worthy and awe-inspiring house of worship here, on *this* ground which has been regarded as a sacred place since before written records were made. And, yes, we had here until the later 19th century, a building which was basically an ordinary nave and a simple chancel. Did we need to make changes? Have they subsequently helped us to worship, and to attract other seekers to learn about the Christian faith?

In writing this book, I have tried to set down, in story mode, as much of our past as is easily accessible. The tale is far from complete, but enough can be told to alert us to the dynamic, and by no means unchallenged, changes which have taken place *here.* Happily, all this speaks of an institution which is not only alive and adaptable, but which also *treasures the received wisdom and experience and artistry of the past,* as it looks ahead to new ventures under the guidance of the Holy Spirit. It is right that we change some things in order to gain the interest and loyalty of each new generation. Right also, that we encourage each other to experience and consider thoughtfully, ways of worship which have been valued by people of former times.

Clearly, all the available history of Christian worship in Dawlish would have been reviewed during the lengthy time of discussion and planning which led to the decision in the 1870s to extend and refurbish *this* parish church.

*What changes to our building were now felt to be necessary?*

Here are quotations from a contemporary newspaper, (the Exeter Gazette), dated 28 May 1874:

"……yesterday was laid the memorial stone of a new chancel to the (Dawlish) parish church which is undergoing restoration…… The church has been badly in need of restoration for a considerable time. In the first place it has always been without a chancel, and in the second place the old seating was very high, narrow, and inconvenient. Besides this, several parts of the building were in a somewhat dilapidated condition. The flooring was bad, the ventilation defective, and, in short, a thorough restoration has become almost a matter of urgency……

"……The old and unsightly pews will be replaced by low and more agreeable seats; the flooring will be new; arrangements will be made for warming and lighting the church, and besides this there is the new chancel, organ chamber, vestry and chancel aisle, which will not only…… increase the accommodation, but will greatly improve the appearance of the building.

"The western gallery has been removed, but in our opinion the work of restoration will not be complete until the north and south galleries have shared a similar fate."

(They were finally dismantled in 1897, leaving us with the light and open plan that we enjoy today).

*A look at the overall extension plan*

The major feature of the enlargement plan was to be the new and spacious chancel. It would be 43 feet long and 22 feet wide, and correspondingly high, the roof supported by open and robust pitch pine rafters. There was also the provision of an organ chamber on the north side to house the organ which would be near to the newly located choir (see below). Adjacent to this was a two-storey vestry furnished for robing, and for the storage of vestments and choir robes, altar furnishings, registers and calendars and Communion vessels.

The new south aisle area was planned as an integral part of the building. It is south of the chancel and east of the transept, and it became the Lady Chapel a little later on. The former small north and south transepts were to be taken down and rebuilt, to extend north and south from *two* arches of the nave arcade instead of only one. Extra seating was thus made available in these larger transepts and in the east south aisle.

Building materials were carefully specified: all the new outer walls to be faced with limestone from quarries at Chudleigh, with Bath stone 'dressings', and "Blue Lias mortar to be used".

The architect employed for the detailed technical and artistic planning of all the work was Mr. Piers St. Aubyn, a well known and experienced London man. The builders were Messrs. Diment and Stevens of Bristol.

*Clearing the site for the new Chancel and Transepts*

The old east wall, including the five bay east window, and the 5ft recess in the former chancel area where the Altar had stood, were taken down, as were the old vestry and the walls of the one-bay transepts. The parts of the north and south galleries over the transepts came down in the process. We had already lost the south 'tower' and its carvings and spiral staircase to the roof. And fashions had changed, so that it was decided that the fancy battlements and pinnacles all round the tops of the walls outside, should be removed, together with all the rough-cast plaster. The revealing of the variegated stonework of the north and south walls of the nave (1825 work), was welcomed. And now the new work could take shape.

Such major changes in the layout of the building beg for some explanation.

*What is a chancel?*

We have kept some words, now unfamiliar to many, to describe different parts of a church interior. These words tell us stories from the past. The term 'chancel' is derived from a Latin word meaning 'trellis', or 'crossbars', and was used at first to designate the part of the building east of the screen or trellis-work. This area was regarded as the holy place, which housed the Altar whereon "Christ our Passover is sacrificed for us". In times before the Reformation, only the priest and deacons and servers were allowed to enter it. (Something like the Holy-of-holies in the Jewish Temple, where entry by an ordinary person was forbidden).

Then there was a very significant change, for with the Reformation came the moves by which the Altar was seen, *not* as a place of literal re-enactment of the sacrifice of Our Lord, but as the Holy Table to which *we are all invited.* We may all come to enter into the New Covenant that our Lord Christ makes with believers: we are to join Him in His risen life. We *do* have access to the Table of the Lord. So the screens as barriers were removed, but the sanctity of the Holy Table and its symbolism, reminding us of the Presence of Our Lord with us, is emphasised by the physical elevation of the Table at the east end of the chancel space.

Only the area in which the Table stands is now properly known as the *Sanctuary,* the place where reverence and dignity are called for on the part of believers at worship. It is there that, being penitent, forgiven and made welcome, we kneel to receive by grace, our healing and nourishment from the Lord's Table. This action symbolises our recognition and acceptance of the enduring Covenant between God and ourselves: we who are his people, and precious in his sight. Through our Lord Christ and with him, we are entering the promised new life and eternal joy.

The rest of the now large chancel space has taken on additional functions. Many see it as the approach path to the Table, an echo of the 'going up to the Temple in Jerusalem'. From the nave, we, the communicants, are invited to ascend three steps as we enter the chancel, passing through the open, boldly constructed chancel arch. Perhaps for some this is helpful as it can symbolise a rising level or focus of devotion. For all who approach the Table, it is part of the dignity appropriate when we worship our most holy God.

*The inauguration of parish church choirs*

The High church movement did a great deal to foster the notion that 'the arts', when used with true dedication to the service of God, could contribute much to the richness and beauty of worship. This applies to music as well as to the visual arts.

Formerly, hymn-singing in St.Gregory's was led by an amateur group of loyal singers and instrumentalists up in the west gallery. Now, with the plan for a spacious chancel, the move was made to give room there, in special choir-stalls, for a robed choir of men and boys carefully trained under the discipline of an able organist and choirmaster. The choir-stalls were to face each other from the two sides of the chancel, not only so that there could be antiphonal singing of Psalms, (as in monastic and, later on, in cathedral practice), but also ensuring that the Table was in full view from the nave. This arrangement became the model for many parish churches, and St. Gregory's chancel was furnished in this tradition. Choir members wore black cassocks until 1950, when it was discovered that because long ago we had a royal association with King Edward the Confessor, they were entitled to wear *red,* as they do to this day.

The *Chancel* is now seen to comprise the *Sanctuary* and the *Choir*. In the west end of the choir nearer to the congregation, there were to be oak prayer desks matching the choir-stalls. Many acts of worship, especially Morning and Evening Prayer, would be led by a priest from this position, as would the first parts of the celebration of Holy Communion.

Before we consider the alterations in the nave, spare a thought for what was involved in unifying the old and the new parts of the enlarged building.

*Blending the old and the new: the Chancel Arch.*

The architect had the task of joining the new structures to the old, in an harmonious design. The chancel arch represents a triumph of imaginative planning expressed in fine stonework. We have here a blending of the workmanship of masons from the fifteenth century with that of their successors in the nineteenth. Both groups used relatively local stone from south west England. The old pillars are of Beer stone from east Devon, the adjacent new chancel arch supports are of Bath stone, adorned with columns of polished Dartmoor granite and carved capitals of Bath stone. Little, but carefully thought out, touches can be very pleasing: these capitals are set a foot higher than those on the old pillars so that there is no conflict between the ancient hand carvings and the modern ones which are machine carved. The interval of over four hundred years is bridged by the way in which these pillars are built touching each other, to become unified structures, one on each side. Ironically, the blending is so good that it is easy to miss the significance of the survival of the symbol for Mary crowned Queen of Heaven. It is carved on the 15th century capital on the left (north) side. This was a revered motif in the years before the Reformation, and frequently destroyed thereafter, as an undesirable 'popish' feature. But because we too honour Mary, *we* can treasure it now as a sign of our Christian kinship across the centuries:    "… for all of you are one in Christ Jesus." (Galatians 3 v 28).

The lofty moulded arch itself is of a type of Bath stone. The requirement is specific: "Doulting stone from Mr. Charles Tasker's quarry at Ilminster". This stone is used also for the side arches opening from the chancel into the organ chamber and into the south east aisle or Lady Chapel.

The floor of the chancel was raised above that of the nave by three steps. From Dorset, a very popular and hard-wearing dark stone containing many visible fossil shells, was brought for making these steps and the others leading up to the altar. This is Purbeck 'marble', and it is also used for the step into the Lady Chapel and in front of the Table there.

*The building which we inherited in 1875*

The improvements to the *nave* were considerable. Old 'box' pews had been replaced by lower, open seating made of durable pitch pine. In the enlarged transepts too, pews were installed. These have all been regularly polished ever since, with waxes and 'elbow grease' applied by loving and willing hands. Moveable chairs were given for use in the south-east aisle (later the Lady Chapel).

The floor of the nave was raised by 12 inches to allow for under-floor heating pipes, and conduits for gas or, (later on), electricity for lighting systems. The Exeter Gazette reporter writes: "Under the organ chamber is situated a vault for the heating apparatus which is by Haden of Trowbridge". Maybe this scheme both warmed us and improved the air circulation and helped to remedy the defective ventilation complained of in former days. Re-flooring in the nave took the form of red quarry tiles in all the aisles, and new wood planking beneath the pews. The central pulpit was dismantled so that all could see into the Chancel: I wonder what happened to the valuable, well matured timbers?

Now we have an idea of the main shape and lay-out of the 1875 building. This was but the beginning of the process of furnishing it and providing for orderly acts of worship.

*The House of Worship: the importance of coming together*

We began this chapter by asking "Is there an ideal house of worship?" We could equally well ask "Why has there been a church building in Dawlish for a thousand years?" The answer is surely that Christians know that in addition to private devotion at home or wherever we may be, we need to come together to worship our most Holy God. A committed believer is welcomed as a member of the world-wide Christian family; we are invited to be the cherished *children* of God. It is good that members of a family keep in touch with each other; when we come together to worship God, our loving Creator, we *meet each other too. We belong together, and we need each other.*

Together, our learning from sacred writings is enriched, and we gain strength and support from each other, and become more aware of the presence and the voice of the Lord. The wondering disciples *came together* on the evening of the first Easter Day, and "Jesus came and stood among them and said, 'Peace be with you'". (John 20 v 19). They were "…all together in one place" (Acts 2 v 1) when the Holy Spirit came upon them at Pentecost. It is as if God wants or even commands us to come together; he seems to do things when we are together that he does not choose to do when we are alone.

Beyond our being part of the familiar *local* congregation, we are worshipping the God of *all* times and places. Knowing this, and as we offer prayers for those whom we do not and cannot know individually, we may achieve awareness of the fact that we are a part of something far greater than ourselves. Our near horizons are not an impassable barrier, but a challenge to explore farther afield.  God is there too.

St. Gregory's Church, Dawlish
south-west view — St Mark's Day 2007

S - Sedilia.
RW - Raphael Window

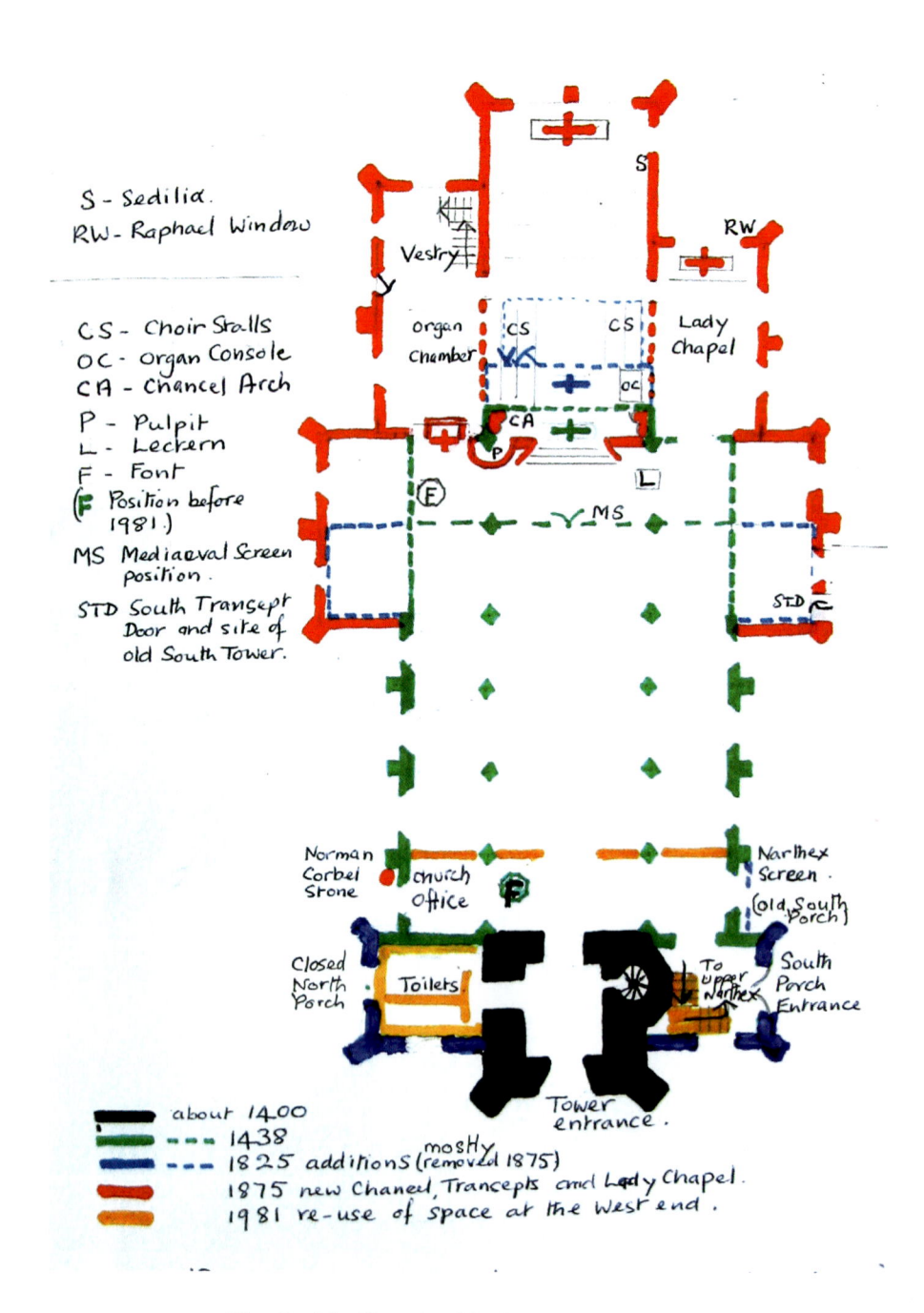

CS - Choir Stalls
OC - Organ Console
CA - Chancel Arch
P - Pulpit
L - Lectern
F - Font
(F Position before 1981.)
MS Mediaeval Screen position.
STD South Transept Door and site of old South Tower.

- about 1400
- --- 1438
- --- 1825 additions (mostly removed 1875)
- 1875 new Chancel, Transepts and Lady Chapel.
- 1981 re-use of space at the west end.

The Parish Church of St Gregory, Dawlish

Norman Corbel Stone - St Gregory's, Dawlish  FC

The Norman Corbel Table at St Mary & St David, Kilpeck, Herefordshire

The 1400 A.D. Tower, after cleaning and repointing in 1897 to mark Queen Victoria's Diamond Jubilee. (the author abseiling)  PH

On top of the Tower — the Flag Keeper Miss Diane Coombes  MKB

4

View of Town from Tower    MKB

View of Graveyard from Tower    MKB

One of the 1438 capitals  F C

The Nave Arcade and barrel roof seen from the Narthex  F C

RMQ

The Dissenters' Pit in Bradley Wood, Newton Abbot, where Nonconformists met in secret beyond the town boundary from 1662 to 1689. 300 years after the 'Great Ejectment,' this 1962 scene is of a commemorative service during which the gathered people were addressed by leaders of the Congregational Church and the Anglican Bishop of Exeter, Dr. Robert Mortimer, giving thanks for the growth of mutual recognition and the establishment of freedom of style of worship.

The old Church and Tower from 1438 (north aspect)

South view of St Gregory's immediately after the rebuilding of 1823-25 (increased height), but before the restoration and rebuilding of 1873-75

St Mark's (daughter church)
The Reverend Christopher Robin

St Gregory's nave in 1850 before the building of the present chancel and transepts showing the original pulpit, box pews and galleries.
*Note that the pulpit obscures the altar (see pages 99-100)*

Is this *your* holiday memory?

**Dawlish Sea Front:** Steam Special visits us in 2006

The New Chancel — Easter Sunday 2000   MKB
The Easter Garden and the rough crosses carried by the children
in their presentation

In the Sanctuary : the High Altar in festival colours

The north wall of the Sanctuary : the Prophets revered

13

The Font  F C

the Pulpit  F C

# The Patron Saints

St Gregory the Great     F C

St Michael     F C

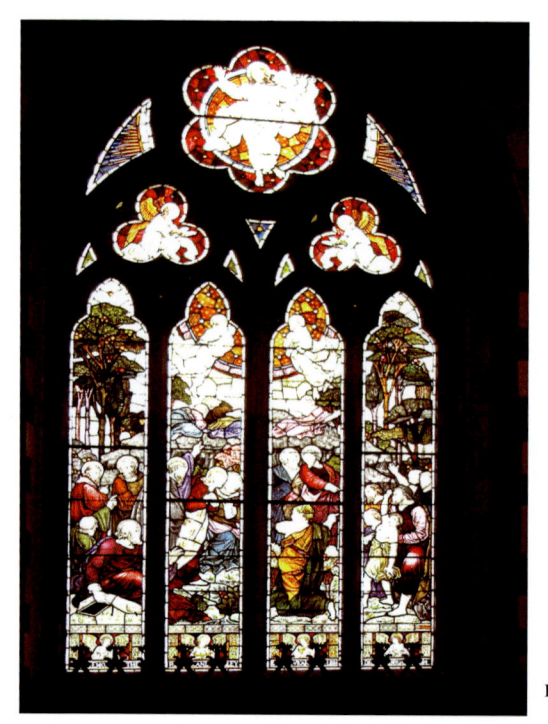

F C

The Lady Chapel Altar and Raphael's "Transfiguration" window     F C

The ancient Cross stump  F C

Lady Chapel exterior and Cross stump  F C

Palm Sunday Procession - 2000  MKB

Palm Sunday — entering the West Door  MKB

Making Music for the Lord : Organist and Choirmaster George Elliott at the organ console

Easter Eve 2000
"The Lord is risen:" "He is risen indeed"
Alleluia

MKB

*Using the enlarged House of Worship*

The time honoured way to meet our need to worship, *and* to be together, has been to provide a building which is large enough, and suitably designed and furnished for the purpose. This is a building that is *different;* a visitor, on coming in for the first time, may often be seen to pause and take a deep breath, and then quietly begin to look around appreciatively. People will mention the great height, the clean light pillars, the central aisle up which we can walk and have our attention drawn, without conscious effort, towards the chancel and right up to the Altar and the east window telling the story of Our Lord being with us. The 1875 chancel in St. Gregory's church, (mirroring the plan of the St. Mark's building), emphasises the importance of the Altar, used as the Lord's Table, as a focal point in worship. This is especially the case when the full liturgy of Holy Communion is celebrated, but it is also an obvious reminder of the presence of Our Lord when we meet for any other act of worship or for any public event.

*The doors of the building are open to all*

Public worship is an opportunity for believers, and for all those who are searching for meaning in their lives, to share a time of bringing the joys and sorrows of daily life into a wider context. We are helped to reflect on the eternal mysteries of God, and of our own existence. Which of us can bear to do this without a sense of awe? We need a building and a liturgy which inspire this sense.

Our 1875 building, though most importantly recognised as a place of worship, would continue to be a meeting place for many activities open to everyone. It had become a fine auditorium, and would host many concerts and recitals, as well as lectures. Dawlish was proud of its church building, and the people would continue to be generous in their giving for its furnishing and upkeep. Attendance at Sunday worship would remain a focal point of the week for a large part of the town population.

*The Call to Worship*

In 1875, the call to worship was broadcast to all the townspeople by the ringing of our fine peal of six bells. After a period of 'change-ringing', the pattern would alter, often to the sounding of a single bell, so that those approaching knew they had but a few minutes to complete their journey on time. As they entered the building they would perhaps hear organ music coming from the west gallery, until the choir entered from the vestry in the north aisle. These trained boys and men were robed in black (red after 1950) cassocks and white surplices. They solemnly processed through the chancel archway and took their places in the new choir stalls. Then the Vicar, The Reverend Orlando Manley, suitably robed, and his Curate and perhaps candle-bearers, entered the chancel; each of these groups would be led by a *Crucifer,* an assistant bearing a processional cross. All was done with great dignity, as the congregation stood in silence.

Morning Prayer was well attended, and the Vicar would call upon the people to remember, in the presence of God, that we fall short of the blameless life which would be our proper response to his all-embracing glory and holiness. True repentance is urged, so that we can be ready to receive forgiveness, and be restored. Then we will be able to continue:

"......to render thanks for the great benefits that we have received at his hands,
    to set forth his most worthy praise,
    to hear his most holy Word,
    and to ask those things which are requisite and necessary,
        as well for the body as the soul."

from The Book of Common Prayer.<br>(1662 wording, in use in 1875)

This version is still authorised and used today in the 21$^{st}$ century whenever Morning and Evening Prayer in this traditional form, are offered in public or private worship.

The opening of the new chancel in St. Gregory's in 1875 heralded a number of changes to the interior appearance and furnishing and music of the house of worship. The congregation needed to give due thanks for the *continuity of what really matters in our Church life and worship.* The same is true for us today in the 21$^{st}$ century.

*What does **not** change*

The eternal message of salvation is unchanging.

We have a priceless heritage in the wisdom and learning and devotional riches that have come to us in the Bible and the Book of Common Prayer. When following the pattern set out in the latter, (gently modified but basically unchanged in Common Worship), we are led to hear the Good News, and to make the *essential* response of believers, in our worship. This Liturgy, ("our bounden duty"), is set out in such a way that priest and people are together drawn nearer to the presence of God, to whom it is all addressed as worship. It contains and expounds all that is necessary for us to hear and, if we will, to respond to God's offer of salvation: the hope that gives meaning and significance to our present lives.

To follow the liturgical pattern in worship is fitting for all times and seasons. It is a discipline that has carried priests and people of St. Gregory's Church, unruffled at heart, through all the upheavals of re-building, re-decoration, conflicts over vestments and furniture, hymnbooks and financial demands. It is part of the rich heritage that we, as faithful stewards, are called to pass on to those who will succeed the present generation.

We have followed the changing styles of Dawlish Parish churches down the centuries, and we can be quite sure that we have not finished yet! Throughout this process, the fundamental objectives remain constant: the church building is here *because of our desire to worship God, to deepen our faith and understanding,* and to do so *together.*

## Priests, People and Furniture

Our *priests* are fellow members with us; they have been called and ordained to special forms of service in the Care of Souls, and in the Ministry of the Word and Sacraments. In the House of Worship, there is provision of furnishings that are helpful for the carrying out of their privileged duties.

And to this House, all of us *the people*, come to worship God together. True worship leads us on to invite others to come too. The doors are open to all.

So we have in the church building:

> Space and seating for people of *all* ages and abilities: children, committed members, visitors and all seekers after truth and comfort.
>
> The Lectern and Pulpit, from where the Scriptures are read and the Gospel is preached (the Ministry of the Word),
>
> The Font (for administration of the sacrament of Baptism),
>
> The Holy Table (to which we are invited to partake of the Sacrament of Holy Communion).

In the next section of this book, we will look in detail at a great deal of what has come into the building as furnishing and adornment. So much of it is meant to help us to worship, to understand our Faith more fully and to extend and enrich our thinking and feeling. Some features can help to focus our attention as we take part in services of worship. Most important of all are those items which are used in our participation in the Ministry of the Word, and in the administration of the Sacraments of Baptism and Holy Communion.

# PART TWO

*Understanding the Christian Faith through the furnishing and adornment of the building*

# CHAPTER THIRTEEN

## *THE MINISTRY OF THE WORD*

As you sit in the nave pews, facing forwards, you will be aware that prominent in front of the north side (left) of the chancel arch, is the fine Victorian stone pulpit. To the right side of the arch is the lectern. These two important structures are used regularly in the part of the liturgy called the Ministry of the Word.

*Reading the Bible during Public Worship: the Lectern*

The brass lectern was given in 1889, "to the Glory of God and in memory of Charlotte Dick". It is a fine, ornamental, and reliably steady reading stand. It doesn't have an eagle to symbolise the Gospel carried on wings, to the four corners of the earth, but the Bible is read aloud from it week after week, to all who will hear.

Sometimes we take for granted the fact that we hear the Bible read to us in our own language. Take a look back to the times when it was available only in Latin, and read aloud only by an *ordained man*. Then give thanks for the courageous work of those who, despite deprivation, persecution and martyrdom, have enabled us to have our present day ready access to its contents.

For now we have the Bible in English, the result of scholarly and painstaking translation from the original Hebrew and Greek and the early Latin texts. In 1875, the King James Authorised Version (1611) was in use in Dawlish, and much treasured. Since then, many linguists have devoted years of labour to give us versions in modern English, more easily followed by those who are unfamiliar with the beautiful literary style of the Authorised Version of the Bible. Modern translations benefit from continuing scholarship, and from translators' access to an additional number of ancient, carefully authenticated texts. These studies help to bring the writings in the Bible to us more clearly and accurately, and help us to see them as relevant to people of every age.

Today, we must not forget the privilege we have, of holding our own personal copies of the Scriptures, nor that, as *lay members, men or women,* we are now invited to read the Bible out loud, to the assembled congregation during Divine Worship.

*The preaching of the Word: the Pulpit*

Much thought went into the well executed design of the pulpit. It was given, during the re-building work, by the widow of the Reverend John Rashdall who was Vicar of Dawlish 1864-1869. Supported on a base of clustered polished granite shafts, the sides had niches for statues (added finally in 1902), and lots of carving of locally occurring natural plant life.

True to traditional church use of sculpture, these statues are *reminders* to help us think carefully about the whole story of God being with his people. History and the law, worship, prophecy and fulfilment, the establishment of the Church, martyrdom, preaching and the spreading of the Gospel......they are all there in these nine figures, each with an identifying motif. The figures were carved by E.T.Rogers of Exeter. Here is the list:

From the north side:

MOSES......with the TABLETS of the LAW.

DAVID......King of Israel and artist of poetic song. He carries his HARP, and is CROWNED.

ELIJAH......A PROPHET proclaiming what he sees happening to the Chosen People. Or is he seeing the fiery chariot coming to take him to God?

ISAIAH......leans on a SAW. The writings of a 2nd century Jewish Christian suggest to us that Isaiah was martyred by being sawn asunder.

JOHN the BAPTIST......in CAMEL HAIR COAT, carrying a staff with a PENNANT (proclaiming the coming of Christ).

PETER......with KEYS and BOOK.

STEPHEN......carries a MARTYR'S PALM and PILE OF STONES.

PHILIP......is reading from a SCROLL (with the Ethiopian). Notice the CHARIOT WHEEL behind.

PAUL......with the SWORD of the SPIRIT and a BOOK, reminding us of his Letters to Churches, and, of course, the Word of God.

Those who preach from this pulpit stand on a firm tradition. To be called upon to preach the Word is a privilege and responsibility, which is why a sermon is prefaced by the affirmation that it is offered "In the Name of the Father, the Son and the Holy Spirit". In many churches, including St. Gregory's, you will find a Crucifix on the wall behind the pulpit. What is portrayed there is at the heart of the Gospel, and is a remedy for any shortcomings on the part of the preacher...or the listeners.

*Theories, Proofs and Understanding the Bible*

When the lectern and pulpit were installed in our newly opened building, the Victorian world was embroiled in the process of adapting current thinking and understanding to the rapid flow of discovery, and the application of fresh technology. We had come into an era of 'experimental' or 'scientific' method. This approach, it was supposed, could lead us beyond tentative *theories* about our surroundings, to *facts* which could be *proved*.

Scientific and statistical evidence became all-important. The results of direct observation and measurement, with bold experimentation and deduction, made us look again at much of what had been assumed to be true, but which had never been questioned or tested. We were about to be disturbed.

Some of what was discovered, and apparently safely established as fact, produced shock waves of surprise and often consternation. There were many new items of knowledge which would alter the way we lived, and what we believed. Some were to have an enormous and unsettling impact on the way in which the Biblical account of God creating the earth in *six days* was viewed. Geologists were now telling us that the process of bringing the earth to its present form had taken *billions of years,* and were bringing convincing evidence to substantiate that claim.

Here in Dawlish, as elsewhere, what is stated in the Bible in so many words, had been accepted as *literal* truth for many centuries, almost without question. With advances in general education and knowledge of the material world, this attitude towards the Scriptures was being challenged. What could we trust to be *'reliable knowledge',* in what is given us in our Holy Bible?

*Unrolling fresh understanding*

During this period of growing uncertainty about the most enlightened way to receive what was written in the Bible, the great natural scientist Charles Darwin was earnestly pondering the significance of what he had carefully observed and recorded during his extensive voyages, and the conclusions he had drawn from his evidence. His thinking matured into the form of a detailed and comprehensive volume: "On the Origin of Species by Natural Selection". He knew that its publication would invite extreme hostility, particularly on the part of conservative elements within the Church. Courageously, he finally made his work public in 1859, and then painfully weathered the ensuing storms which rolled across both the secular and ecclesiastical worlds.

We refer to the work of this remarkable man and his contemporary scientists, as embodying the idea of *Evolution.* This term means *'unrolling'*, or *'spreading out'*, and it is eloquent of an understanding of the way the earth, *once formed*, developed and was gradually populated with living things of increasing complexity and variation. (and don't forget that *we* are part of this process *which is still going on).* All this pre-supposed the passage of the billions of years which geologists said had elapsed since the earth was formed. An exciting panorama of on-going, burgeoning development, (and some attempts on the part of excited scientists, to show ways by which it could happen), was being spread out before our eyes; how would all this be received by the critics and the general public?

Now that newspapers, tracts and magazines were available in Dawlish, such topics led to vigorous discussion. This was a time when serious, informed conversation had become possible as a result of better education and the greater variety of interests among local residents. The attempts to address such matters had a far-reaching effect on all Christians. They led to many questions about how to 'read' the Bible. Take the accounts of the creation of the universe that we have in the Book of Genesis: are the details given there to be taken as historical facts, or are they more helpfully read as wise attempts to teach, in story form, some fundamental truths which are otherwise not easily conveyed?

What about the rest of the Scriptures? Surely it was right in that 'Age of Revolution' in society and in the Church, for scholars in the fields of literature, history, archaeology, language studies and the niceties of translation, and of course Church history and theology, to continue to direct their expertise towards a fuller understanding of the Bible?

George Rawson (who lived from 1807 till 1889) wrote a hymn celebrating our freedom to go on seeking enlightenment:

> "We limit not the truth of God
> To our poor reach of mind,
> By notions of our day and sect,
> Crude, partial, and confined:
> No, let a new and better hope,
> Within our hearts be stirred:
> *The Lord hath yet more light and truth*
> *To break forth from His word."*

The words in italics were used by Pastor John Robinson as he took leave of those who left his church in Leyden to sail with the Pilgrim Fathers to America in 1620, to seek greater freedom in worship, and in the study of the Bible.

The words were also an appropriate call to churchgoers in Victorian times, some of whom were afraid and worried because of new scholarship and daring thinking. For others, there was excitement about this expansion of man's ability to know about, and to some extent manipulate, his environment. Such enquiring minds found fresh energy to go on searching for a fuller truth, to reassess their present life situations and to try to plan ahead.

I have a lot of sympathy for the clergy and congregations in those years of thoughtful turmoil arising from new knowledge and its impact on former ways of thinking. In Dawlish, as elsewhere, in these Victorian times, our vicars, together with the nonconformist ministers, had been trained in the belief that the Bible texts were *literally* true. The new approaches in the light of scientific advances must have thrust them into energy-draining study and discussion, and made sermon writing something of a nightmare, as they could anticipate lively criticism. Edward Fursden 1846-, John Rashdall, 1864- and Orlando Manley, 1869- were in the thick of the controversies. Their confidence and their credibility in the eyes of the Dawlish people, must have resided in their resolute and faithful conduct of Divine Worship as set out in the Book of Common Prayer, and in the ongoing pastoral care of their loyal but puzzled flock.

*The Limitations of Scientific Knowledge*

Among their congregations there were the serious minded persons who rightly addressed the question: *"Are there not many things that we experience and believe, which lie beyond the sphere of scientific proof?"*

Priest and people would have to find a way through the supposed dilemma of having to choose to trust *either* science *or* religious belief. It was false confusion, for scientific knowledge of the physical universe could not possibly address tremendous religious questions such as *why* rather than *how* we came to be here at all, and, *what* is the meaning of our personal existence: *when* did it begin, and does it end when we pass through a physical death? For these are questions in a different category altogether; they are mysteries that lie beyond any physical discovery. Here is a quotation from the St. Gregory's Parish Magazine of May 2006, on this very subject. It helps to summarise and ease the perceived dilemma:

"*Creationism*.......is the belief that the origin of the world and all that is in it occurred *literally* in accordance with the accounts in the first chapters of Genesis—six literal days. In other words, it treats Genesis as if it were a scientific account. This is a real misreading of the purpose of Scripture, which, here, gives a lovely insight into God's creative relationship with all things, set out in a pictorial, poetic way, that calls for our response in faith, as stewards of his bounty, children of his love.

"*Evolution*......is a scientific hypothesis, increasingly validated by increasing knowledge, to explain the way that living creatures reacted to their environment, adapted to it, and, over millennia, evolved into new species. It makes no claims about origins, much less about Creation, and the Church does not see any conflict between evolution as a theory, and God's role in creating and sustaining all things.

"......you could almost say that theology asserts *that* God created all things — and evolution (and other sciences) elucidate *how* they work. And, properly understood, science unveils much that should prompt us to be thankful for the increased vision of the glory of it all, increase our awe before its Creator, and inspire us to seek ever more deeply to understand the meaning of such glory and wonder.

"......one does well to keep the word 'create' solely for God's action: all action by man, however marvellous, is subordinate to that, (for) all our action is with and within, what God has already created".

The Reverend Canon Colin R. Evans.  May 2006.

*The Bible records Man's Search for Enlightenment*

The search for enlightenment on the path towards the profound truths that lie beyond the reach of material discoveries, is at the heart of all religions and all sacred writings. So we look for signs of this search in our reading of the Bible.

The Bible incorporates the works of many authors and contains many kinds of literature in memorable and beautiful poetry and careful prose.  In it we have, preserved for our use and instruction, a history of the Semitic people who began to believe in One God. We can follow the development of their trust, thought and prophecy about the involvement of God in the wellbeing and maturation of the human race. And as Christians, we read with sadness and bewilderment, of their rejection of Jesus as the one who would fulfil their hope for the Promised One (the 'Messiah' in Hebrew, the 'Christ' in Greek). As Christians, we treasure and embrace above all, the story of Jesus our Lord Christ, who *is* our Promised Saviour.

The Bible describes the birth of the Church. We read of the evangelistic fervour of the Apostles endowed with the Holy Spirit at Pentecost, and the careful instruction of members of new Church communities as the Christian faith spread to other areas.

The riches of the Bible are endless, and the more we study the whole of it, using all our faculties, and remaining open to unfettered thinking and feeling, the closer we may come to receiving the Bible as a collective *affirmation of God as Creator of "all that is, seen and unseen", and of this same God's enduring and loving covenanted relationship with mankind,* from the time when man first began to search for the meaning of his longings and questionings about what lay beyond his immediate sensory experiences.

"This is the Word of the Lord"

\*\*\*\*\*\*\*\*\*\*\*\*\*\*\*\*\*\*\*\*\*\*\*\*\*\*\*\*\*\*\*\*\*\*\*\*\*\*\*\*\*\*\*\*\*\*\*\*

We have thought about the lectern and the reading of the Bible; and the pulpit where preaching based on the Scriptures is delivered to the people. Now we turn to the Sacrament of Baptism, and the Font which is as essential a structure in the house of worship as is the Table round which we gather for Holy Communion.

# CHAPTER FOURTEEN

## *THE SACRAMENT OF BAPTISM*

In a number of places in earlier chapters in this book, mention has been made of the Font, and of different ways in which the Sacrament of Baptism has been administered. In this chapter we will think first about the Sacrament itself, and then follow the story of how it was offered in this Parish.

*What is the Sacrament of Baptism?*

Baptism is primarily an act of God. We are bidden to make use of water, an outward, physical sign, to convey the *reality* of the inward spiritual grace of God poured upon us at the beginning of our life in the Christian faith. When we receive this Sacrament, this 'effectual sign', we enter the company of all who believe in Our Lord Christ and in His power to redeem us from human shortcomings and sinfulness, and give us new and eternal life as children of God.

We know that a number of eastern religions and mystery cults used symbolic rites involving water, to seal membership of their organisations, but Christian Baptism is of wider and deeper significance. John the Baptist used water to seal an act of *repentance:* a change of heart, a need and a desire on the part of his disciples to change the direction of their lives. And Jesus came for baptism at the hands of John, to stand beside us in our human need for renewal. It was *then* that a sign was given to Jesus, which tells us that in receiving Baptism by the outward sign of water, we must be open and ready, as was Our Lord, to receive the Holy Spirit of God Himself. We are accepted as God's children. His Spirit seals us in that relationship and lovingly directs us and strengthens us in our new life. Those who are baptised as infants will personally accept this at their *Confirmation.*

"...no-one can enter the kingdom of God without being born of water and Spirit".   John 3 v 5

*The Water of Baptism*

We marvel at the rich symbolism of *this* use of water:

...To cleanse and heal our human nature;
...To signify our passage with Our Lord Christ through death to new life;
...and, as new beings, to show our readiness, like Jesus at His baptism, to receive the Holy Spirit.
...With all this is included the giving of a new name, *a Christian name*, by which we are identified as individuals and yet are joined together with Christ and all His people.

In the early days of the Church, agreement was reached over a formula for the words to be used whenever Baptism was administered. This was in accordance with the commission Our Lord gave to his disciples:

"Go ......and make disciples of all nations, baptizing them in the name of the Father and of the Son and of the Holy Spirit......"
   Matthew 28 v 19

This form: " I baptize you
   in the name of the Father
   and of the Son
   and of the Holy Spirit."

is used throughout the world today, whenever baptismal water is poured or sprinkled on the candidate or when total immersion in pool, river or sea is carried out.

Baptism marks entry into the fellowship of believers, so the font or pool containing the water to be used, would usually be situated at the west end of a church *where the people come in.* The font would be the first thing to be seen, and many would use the sight to remind themselves of their own baptism.

Where did the water come from, and how was it prepared? Church authority required that it be blessed, signifying that it was set apart for holy use, but did this alter the water in any way? Or is it ordinary water, used to convey truth symbolically, and is it not *ourselves* who are changed as we receive Baptism?

We should try to get an insight into the minds of those who wanted to believe that water consecrated for baptism had special powers of healing. Many centuries ago, when there was little understanding of the causes of disease and a lamentable paucity of remedies apart from some useful herbal wisdom, belief in the healing power of certain *waters* led to the veneration of wells and streams. The Celtic West country is full of stories of such places. We saw how, when guidance about them was sought, Pope Gregory advised Augustine to teach that the holiness of such treasured sites could be honoured even more by making them holy *Christian* centres.

*The siting of St.Gregory's Church*

Many of these revered water sources did indeed become the places where the earliest churches were constructed, and it is possible that St. Gregory's church in Dawlish is one of them. For the ground where the west end of the present building stands is drained by a stream issuing from a spring. It is marked on the Ordnance Survey two and a half inch map, and behind the old yew tree by the west door there is a very suggestive dip in the ground like a stream bed, running down to the mill leat beyond the north gate. Flooding by the west door after heavy rain is not unknown.

I suppose we shall never know with certainty whether or not this stream water was used for baptisms. Whether from this spring or from a nearby well, water was brought into the church, placed in a vessel known as a Font, (from the Latin word for a spring), and ritually blessed, setting it apart for special uses.

The consecration of the water was a complicated ritual involving the addition of (consecrated) salt and oil. It took place usually once a year, at Easter, and the water was then kept in the covered font for the rest of the year. So any ordinary villager might be forgiven for supposing that these dramatic procedures *charged the water with extra-special powers.* They understood that it was *set aside for holy use,* but the line between this and *powerful magic* was a fine one. The temptation to steal some for magical rites and desperately needed attempts at bodily healing could be hard to resist. The church regarded such theft as a serious offence, and took measures to prevent it.

*Guarding the Consecrated Water*

In Dawlish, we are back in the time of our Norman church building. In 1236 the Archbishop of Canterbury, Edmund Rich, made an order to the effect that fonts were to be kept locked under seal, so that the hallowed water could not be stolen and used in magic. Our own Bishop of Exeter, Peter Quivil, in 1287 declared that each church in his diocese should have a stone font, well sealed. We had already conformed to this ruling, for at the Visitation of St. Gregory's Church by the Bishop in 1281, among the items of equipment listed, is "a font with a lock". I like to think that the font in Dawlish church then was handsomely and boldly carved in the grand Norman style, but alas, there remains no record describing this piece of sacred furniture in which nearly every person in the parish would have been baptised.

*Other uses of Consecrated Water*

While its chief use was for Baptism, water was also consecrated to become Holy Water for sprinkling in the houses of the villagers on Sundays, and on the assembled congregation at the beginning of the Mass. By the time we had a Norman church building, there was almost certainly a 'stoup' (a carved stone basin) containing Holy Water, at the entrance. As you came into church you would dip the finger and make the sign of the cross on yourself. These were the rituals set under the authority of the Popes of Rome, and which were practised here until the Reformation in the 16th century.

*Baptising the Children*

Long before Christianity came again to this country and eventually to Dawlish, the children of believing parents throughout Christendom were being brought for Baptism. Every child had to have one or more sponsors (Godparents) whose task it was to see that the child received Christian instruction, and was brought for confirmation of the vows undertaken on his behalf, when he was old enough to make his own commitment. Baptism in infancy is only the beginning of his growing in the faith, but he is already a member of the Church.

The move away from baptism in a tub-like font or a pool in which an adult or child could stand to have water poured over him, was a result of a change in the way infant baptism was carried out. The move was towards total immersion of the very young child. Perhaps that is why we in St. Gregory's Church discarded our probably heavy and deep Norman font, and chose instead, a lighter bowl raised on a pillar. This would be so much easier for the priest!

So when the new church was built in 1438, we seem to have thrown out the old font and ordered a new one in a style matching the new church architecture. The Gothic building was so different in style and illumination from its dark predecessor, that, like many other parishes, we made a 'clean sweep' of many earlier features, apart from the tower which was itself relatively new. So a tangible link with previous generations of baptised parishioners was lost, but there was no diminution in the importance of the font to the people. This was reflected in their choice of an appropriate successor to the old font.

*Eight-sided novelty*

The new font resembled those in many parish churches built at about this time. An octagonal bowl was one of several possible shapes, and this was chosen for the new St. Gregory's font. It is interesting to ask "Why eight?" The number eight was an accepted symbol of *salvation* and *new birth*. If we find this puzzling, it is because it is not easy to recapture Mediaeval ways of thought, although it can be very interesting to try to do so. For parishioners in those days, teaching encouraged them to think of the *eight* souls *saved from destruction* by entering the ark and riding the flood waters; also that God made the earth in six days, rested on the seventh day, so that the *eighth* day is the day of *new beginnings* when the cycle of creation and life begins all over again. So an *eight-sided* font embodies these rich patterns of thought.

*Saving the soul from destruction (?)*

In those days there was enormous emphasis laid on the dangers of dying unbaptised, when it was believed you would be subject to the torments of the Devil, suffer in Purgatory, and might even be consigned to eternal damnation. The elaborate liturgy of baptism included exorcism in the form of prayers asking for the restraint of the powers of evil, the putting of grains of salt in the candidate's mouth (to purify and preserve), and anointing with special oil. All this came before the actual Baptism with water, and the pronouncement of the Trinitarian formula. After this came the anointing with 'Chrism', a consecrated olive oil with added balsam, and then a white robe or a veil was put on and a lighted candle given to an adult; a baby had a white cloth bound to the forehead to cover the oil of anointing. This cloth was to be returned to the priest when the mother came for her 'churching' (or Thanksgiving) when the child was six weeks old.

Under the authority of the Pope in Rome, the Church, through the parish priest, had enormous power over the lives and beliefs of the people. After the Reformation there was much new thinking by priest and people which eventually led towards a more helpful understanding. Our need for salvation is as great as ever, but not from the terrors of Purgatory and Hell. It is to do with our being saved from the perception of life, and ourselves, as having no meaning or value. In our personal lives we need to be saved from our wandering away from the truth that *all* persons are made by God in His own image. For so many of the ills of the world stem from our failure to see *ourselves* and *others* as valued and loved and essential members of God's wonderful creation.

At Baptism we are given a Christian name to identify us, and to signify a new beginning of life with God-given meaning.

We are received into the family of believers. Every time we, as members of that family, renew our baptismal vows (at Easter, and when witnessing the baptism of others), we confirm our acceptance of forgiveness for wrongdoing, and for what we have left *un*done. We recover our closeness to God and receive again the power of his Holy Spirit, to raise us to new life.

*Making the Font*

Rather unromantically, octagonal fonts like ours were made to order from the mason's yard, and constructed in three pieces: bowl, pillar and base. Each piece had a drainage channel bored centrally. The whole font would be assembled in the church for which it was designed: it was rather like putting together a child's stacking toy! By 1400, masons had given up making fonts from expensive lead and imported marble, and granite was too hard to carve easily. They returned to the use of 'freestone', as the more workable limestones were called. Like the nave arcade of pillars and arches and angels, which has survived for us to enjoy today, our new font was made of Beer stone. This stone is easily carved when freshly quarried, and lends itself to elaborate designs. (You can visit the quarries at Beer, in East Devon, in the summer months, and enjoy a guided tour of the workings which go back to Roman times).

In about 1438, then, we acquired a 'state of the art' font. But the font we see today in the 21$^{st}$ century cannot be said to be the original one, at least not in its entirety. It is my belief that the bowl itself is 15$^{th}$ century work, as are the eight angels on the underside. These parts are carved out of one piece of stone. The eight side panels were probably left plain at first. Of one thing we are assured: there was a wooden (oak?) cover with a stout iron crossbar made to engage with staples let into the stonework and sealed with lead. Heavy padlocks would secure it so that theft of Holy Water was impossible. How do we know this?

If you take a very careful look at the bowl itself (the pillar and base are much younger), in really good light, you can see where it has been mended. The obligation to lock the font was gradually dispensed with, and had ended by the time of Elizabeth the First. Many churches then discarded the locking mechanisms, and the staples were wrenched out, often causing a lot of damage to the stonework, or even splitting the bowl. In the St. Gregory's font there are tell-tale lines showing where the bowl itself, and the rim on the two opposite sides, have been repaired. New stone has been inserted to 'make good' the damage. Those who carried out the repairs did an extremely good job, but we don't know exactly when this was done.

*Further history of our Font*

The next traceable information comes in the preserved plan of the building made just before the restoration in 1823-5. It shows the font located at the west end of the nave, and beside it is drawn a small pool. This suggests that since early times, baptism may have been performed with the candidate standing or kneeling in the pool while water was poured or sprinkled over him. The pillar font would be used for baptising infants by total immersion, or by pouring water on his head three times while the Trinitarian formula was being spoken. There is a cautionary instruction in the Book of Common Prayer, which says that the priest, after he has named the child and consulted the parents… "if they shall certify him that the Child may well endure it… he shall dip it in the water discreetly and warily……but if they certify that the child is weak, it shall suffice to pour water upon it".

There was a step at the west side of the St. Gregory's font, which had disappeared by the time the 1875 restoration took place.

In 1846, the Reverend John Davidson writes: "the font is a small and elegant octagonal stone basin, the sides made into pannels" (his spelling) "...with a moulding of foliage below, resting on an octagonal shaft carved in trefoil headed panels". Now this poses a problem: he describes *foliage* in place of the *angels* seen now on the underside of the bowl. Are we talking about the same font? Or, was Mr. Davidson unable to bend down and observe accurately during his brief visit?

It is stated by the press report (March 1875), that, ten years before the opening of the eastern extension of the church, a new font was presented by a Miss Lavis. It would be logical to suppose that the old font was discarded or destroyed, but evidently it was 'stored' until the 1873-1875 changes. The same press report says enigmatically: "During its progress (that of the restoration) a fine old font was found in a small tool-house, close to one of the gates of the churchyard, the pedestal and base thereof having been underground". Minutes of the committee which planned the eastern extension to the church include a comment made on March 9 1875: "The old font (is) wanted by both the Earl of Devon and Mr.Hoare!" Sadly I cannot trace what actually happened. My guess is that someone, at zero hour, felt strongly that the old font should not leave the building for which it had been made and dedicated over 400 years before, and that an agreement was reached. It's just possible that the new pillar and base was used to support the old bowl: a happy resolution to satisfy everybody. I have to say I cannot substantiate this, though I like the idea! On the other hand, neither can I trace any Faculties (permission documents) for changing or re-dedicating the font.

Church Wardens' records of the Contracts for the restoration work (1872-8) include the following:
"Re foundations:
A proper well to be formed under the font- 3feet deep and 2ft diameter, with proper cover stone.

"Re font: Provide and fix new steps for the font, to be of Limestone, neatly sanded.

"Re carpenters:

    Provide a font *cover* and Poorboxes, of wainscot oak, with such ornamental wrot-iron work as may be required......"
(This suggests that the font already in place would continue to be used, but it was to be 'refurbished').

The contract directions continue:
"Re plumbers:

    Line the font with 8lbs of milled lead in one piece dressed down over the top and furnished with a margin round the bowl. The lead to be sand polished.

    Provide and fix to the font a $1^1/_2$ inch strong lead waste pipe to the wall below, provided with a waste plug and chain of brass".

I assume that for 'wall below', we may read 'floor', and that the pipe led down into the newly lined well. The holy water would then flow out into the spring draining the well, and so back into the natural earth. By now, it was the practice to put fresh water into the font and to bless it, at each Ministration of Baptism.

    My reverend friend, (well-informed and experienced in matters ecclesiastical, and in the art of carving), suggests to me that we might expect a font bowl of this age to have a deeper profile inside, (i.e. vertical side walls), whereas this one has a hemispherical shape. I still think that it *is* 500 years old, and that this detail doesn't necessarily rule out such antiquity. Over the details of the carvings on the outside vertical panels of the bowl, his expert advice is accepted without question. We can turn to these features now.

*The Carvings on the Bowl of the Font*

    The eight outside panels offer a wonderful chance for a set of carvings which symbolically illustrate vital beliefs, and can be used as teaching aids. They highlight the basis of our faith and how it has been shown to us.

Like the church itself, the font is carefully orientated to the four cardinal points of the compass. The four panels which show the essential features of our Christian Faith, face out to the north, south, east and west arms of the cross-shaped building.

*The North side* of the church is in shadow. For centuries it was associated with the devil and the dark, unfathomable, seemingly cruel (to us) aspects of creation. Our need for faith and hope is great indeed, so here is carved the triumphant *empty Cross*, the supreme symbol of *victory over the powers of darkness.*

We find the symbols of the holy Trinity occupying the other main directions. These speak about three aspects of the One God made known to us: God the Father, God the Son, and God the Holy Spirit.

Turning to the *West side* first, God the Father Almighty is indicated, rather unusually, by a six-pointed star surrounding the Greek *Alpha and Omega.* If this seems obscure at first, remember that the letters stand for *The Beginning, and the End*, and we turn our thoughts to *God the Creator,* and *God the Judge at the end of time.* God the Father Creator is an image most parishioners can grasp with positive and (hopefully) warm understanding, but God as Judge has been in the past, a truly formidable figure. The west end of the church used to be where the Day of Judgement was depicted, often in lurid colours in stained glass or wall paintings: God the Judge dividing the sheep from the goats and consigning the latter to the gaping jaws of hell!

Today, in our revulsion at this harsh picture, perhaps we have swung too far from the truth that God *is* indeed our judge, and we are not yet perfect. But surely we know that He is a *Just Judge* whose nature is always to have mercy. We do not need to be afraid. 'Alpha-and-Omega' includes the whole alphabet, and it speaks of a God who embraces all things, who *is* all things, and yet who made us to be his children whom he loves dearly. This awe-inspiring symbol appears again on the green liturgical altar frontal, and on the wall behind the altar.

Now for the six-pointed star. I learn that this is a very ancient symbol and it was not adopted as that of the Jewish faith until the 3$^{rd}$ century A.D. Some people think the double triangle referred to the union of the male and female principles to make the earth fertile. It isn't a big step from that, to seeing it as another way to express the completeness of God. When used to show God the Father Almighty, the six points can refer to His attributes of:

Power, Wisdom and Majesty, and Love, Mercy and Justice.

My readers will probably be relieved to know that the other symbols are much more straightforward!

On the *East side* is the Sacred Monogram of *God the Son*. The first three letters of the name Jesus, in Greek: I H S. These letters can be used to head words which convey the purpose of God in His coming among us as a Man: in Latin we can have

Iesus Hominum Salvator (Jesus the Saviour of mankind).

Or we may dedicate ourselves to a life 'In His Service'.

This symbol faces east and points us towards the altar. It is there that, in each Celebration of Holy Communion, we meet with Our Lord Christ and partake of His life, and His salvation.

On the *South side* is the symbol of *God the Holy Spirit*. The descending dove representing this aspect of God is familiar from many works of art. It is firmly based on the Biblical account of the baptism of Jesus, in the Gospel of Matthew Ch.3 v.16. And where do we find it on the font but on the south facing side, the direction from which the greatest possible amount of light streams into the building?

"Come Holy Ghost our souls inspire and lighten with celestial fire"

*"Four for the Gospel makers": How the Faith came down to us*

The other four panels call us to remember, and give thanks for, the Gospel writers or Evangelists. They are shown with their names on 'sashes', and as the four living creatures around the throne of God, as described in The Revelation to John Ch.4 v.6. These emblems are present again on the wall behind the altar. On the font carvings, Matthew takes the form of a man (or an angel?), Mark is the lion, Luke the bull and John the eagle.

Notice that the names on the sashes are in *English.* This is the clue to the time when these carvings were added to the old font. My reverend friend surmises that if they had been put there in Mediaeval days, the names would be in *Latin.* Also, as one who loves carvings, and enjoys his own handiwork, he tells me that these examples are machine-tooled, whereas 400 years ago all such works would be hand-carved. It is because of these observations that I made the suggestion that the panels were left plain when the new font was made in the 15$^{th}$ century, and were carved only relatively recently.

*Symbols carved in stone and wood*

We have followed the sometimes violent swings from the high rituals of worship under papal authority, to the extremes of the Puritan period when ornamentation of any kind was to be deprecated. In Dawlish in the 19$^{th}$ century, the rival attitudes were exemplified by the highly ornamented interior furnishings of St. Mark's (the result of serious re-appraisal of the high value of symbols and ritual), and the plainness of those in St.Gregory's. The new chancel, added to St. Gregory's in 1875 was clearly in the 'High Church' style reflecting the renewed focus on the Sacraments and on liturgical ritual and ceremonial. This included a return to an appreciation of the visual arts as being aids to worship. Carvings and colour were allowed to return. So at this stage, we acquire the detailed carvings on the pulpit and font.

On the font, the plain panels were lavishly carved with the symbols we have studied, and other carving on its pillar was retooled. I am quite sure that the subject matter and the style of the panel carvings are copied from long-established patterns, but the technique of their execution is clearly more recent. Also the newly donated pulpit was designed to include figure statuary which was completed in 1902.

This is perhaps a good place at which to attempt an answer to the riddle of the change in the dedication of the Parish Church in Dawlish. In about 1870 the dedication to St. Gregory was changed to become one to St. Michael. It seems reasonable to think that this was because of persistent fears that the move in the direction of a more 'ceremonial' liturgy, an increased sense of dignity in worship, and an appreciation of the continuity of the Church, were all signs that would lead back to 'popery'. And to be members of a parish Church dedicated to *Pope Gregory* could have become a matter for angry concern. Hence the change to a Patron Saint who was known by all to have an untarnished reputation! (The original dedication was restored in 1923).

Loyalty to St. Michael explains the acceptance in 1902, of a statuette of him slaying Satan, which is set in a carved recess on the sixth pillar of the north arcade. Michael, which means 'Who is like God?' is described as the protector of Israel and leader of the armies of God, and is best known as the slayer of the dragon Satan. (The Revelation to John Ch.12 vv.7-9).

So it was as the 'Parish Church of St.Michael', that the extended and embellished building was re-opened for worship, and the new chancel dedicated in March 1875. The Vicar at the time was The Reverend Orlando Manley for whose devotion and hard work throughout this demanding period we can wholeheartedly give thanks to God. After his death in 1884, he was buried in the centre of the churchyard, and a fine polished granite gravestone marks his resting place. His ministry for fifteen eventful years was commemorated by the gift of the Raphael window in the Lady Chapel. Deo gratias!

# CHAPTER FIFTEEN

## *FURNISHING THE SANCTUARY*

Three of the four essential items of 'furniture' in the House of Worship have now received our attention. These are the *lectern* where the Holy Bible is read, the *pulpit* where exposition of the Scriptures, and other kinds of preaching are delivered, and the *Font* for the administration of Baptism, the first of the two necessary Sacraments. Now we turn to the Sacrament of The Lord's Supper, or Holy Communion, for the administration of which a *Table* is required.

*The Holy Table within the Sanctuary*

The oak table made for the 1825 re-building, was used in the new 1875 Sanctuary. It is raised up above the sanctuary floor by more steps so that it is fully visible by the congregation, and is a focus for worship. On the Table, at all times except when there is a celebration of Holy Communion, there stands the 'empty Cross' telling us that Christ is risen from the dead and is here with us now and for ever. We know and honour him as the 'Light of the World', and mark this by lighting candles on and around the Table during public worship. Communicants come to kneel on the first step, at the brass rail which has been lovingly polished by many generations of 'holy dusters'.

To give thanks and to hear the words of the Institution of The Lord's Supper in the Eucharistic Prayer, and to receive Bread and Wine at the Table of the Lord, is the climax of the full liturgical act of worship. In 1875 we would hear, (from the Book of Common Prayer), these words of invitation:

"Ye that do truly and earnestly repent you of your sins, and are in love and charity with your neighbours, and intend to lead a new life following the commandments of God......Draw near with faith, and take this holy Sacrament to your comfort......"

During the years after the building of the new chancel, much was done to adorn the whole area of the sanctuary, and to encourage our feelings of awe. Wonder and awe are our proper response as we come to worship the most Holy God. He came to us in Our Lord Christ, and he it is who invites us to his Holy Table, to join in his sacrificial and risen life.

The use of the word Altar, was shunned at the time of the establishment of the Church of England, but this has been the subject of a great deal of theological discussion since then. Both terms, Altar and Holy Table, have a solemn dignity that reminds us of the supreme Sacrifice made once by Our Lord, for us all, and of His feeding us so that "we may evermore dwell in Him, and He in us". In the Book of Common Prayer we find "The Lord's Table", or "the Holy Table" as approved names.

## Going up to meet Our Lord at the Holy Table

As the stained glass was put in place in the new chancel windows, the journey up the steps towards the Table became illuminated with glorious coloured light, and the 'approach' took on an additional splendour within which a truly penitent guest can feel both humble and inspired with thankfulness and joy.

## Opus Sectile treasures

The new *east* wall behind the Table and below the window, is adorned with a copy of a representation of The Last Supper. The original picture is a fresco at the convent of St. Onofrio, in Florence. It was thought to be the work of Raphael, but more recently believed to be that of a pupil of Pietro Vanucci Perugino who in turn taught Raphael. It was rediscovered in Florence in 1845, and our copy here is thought to be the first of its kind. One of the interesting features of the fresco is that the name of each apostle was placed under his figure. These have been changed from Italian into more familiar English forms in our version.

This picture is not a wall painting, nor a canvas, but a fine example of *opus sectile* work. This technique makes use of crushed, powdered and carefully baked coloured glass, and gives a different visual effect. The tiny fragments of glass reflect the light in random fashion which imparts a lustre or sheen to the work. With the wide range of colours at his disposal, the artist can 'paint' components of a picture which are then assembled on an opaque backing. In addition to 'The Last Supper' we have another such work, 'The Adoration of the Magi', behind the altar in the Lady Chapel. In both pictures, details are highlighted by using pieces of gilded glass for haloes, crowns and gold braiding on kingly robes. This effect is most striking at night when the east windows are darkened and candlelight catches the goldwork.

The crafting of these treasures was carried out by one James Powell at the Whitefriars Glass Foundry in London.

'The Last Supper' was installed in December 1878, and 'The Adoration of the Magi' in 1914. There were other similar pictures in St. Mark's church. I learn from Sheelagh Wurr of Warminster in Wiltshire, that there is, in the Parish Church of St. John there, a fine collection of similar works by James Powell. A further set is in the church of St. John the Baptist, Clayton, Bradford. Those were made in 1914-1920. The latter ones were designed by Gaetano Meo, a minor member of the Pre-Raphaelite Brotherhood. They were installed in the Clayton Church by a Mr. Harrison Benn, a local mill owner. Mr. Benn spent his later years in Holcombe Hall and died there in 1921. He worshipped at St. Gregory's, and as he was a keen musician, he may have sung in the choir and played the organ from time to time. His admiration for the *opus sectile work* here and at St. Mark's may well have defined the nature of his thanksgiving gift to his much loved Church in Clayton. Such work was popular towards the end of the 19th and the beginning of the 20th centuries.

"...the Holy Spirit......who has spoken through the Prophets"

The furnishers of the new chancel gladly saluted the Prophets. On the *north* wall we have opus sectile representations of Isaiah, Jeremiah, Ezekiel and Daniel (1899). These are not portraits of course, but like so many features of the building, they are symbols: reminders that may engage our imagination and lead us into a deeper understanding and experience of how the Holy Spirit spoke and still speaks through these Men of Vision.

The homage due to them is evident in the surrounding decoration, the liberal use of mosaic gold and flourishing grapevines.

*A 'hark back' to earlier church buildings*

On the *south* wall we have a touch of 19th century nostalgia for the 13th century, in the stonework representing a carved 'piscina', and sedilia (seats). The *piscina* was the basin where the priest cleansed his hands during the Mass, and where the sacred vessels were washed afterwards, the water draining away into sacred ground. In the Latin of ancient Rome, a 'piscina' was a *fish* pond, a pool or a trough, and it is thought that early Christians in Rome may have used some such basin, in the meeting house, for ritual cleansing as liturgical practices developed. The *fish symbol*, used by early Christians to identify one another, has come back into widespread use today. (Some of us find these associations both interesting, and a powerful way of bridging the ages between the first Christians communities and our own.).

We know that in our new sanctuary of 1875, this 'piscina' is an architectural indulgence because there is no drainage hole! The plain surface there is used as a shelf for the candle snuffer and tapers for tending the candles on the Table. Nearby stands a *Credence table* on which are placed the bread, wine and water to be used in the Celebration of Holy Communion. Water and a towel are there too for the ritual cleansing of the priest's hands and the sacred vessels after use. (The name, meaning *trust or faith,* was at one time used for the side table where food was tasted before it was pronounced fit for the lord of the manor's plate)!

*Sedilia* were seats for the clergy within the sanctuary, often at different levels indicating the status of the occupants! Carved canopies overhung these recessed wall seats which were often separated by pillars of polished ornamental stone, as they are indeed in our own copies. Their presence in the new St. Gregory's chancel seems to have been a backward glance to the 'ideal' 13th century provision. They are still used as seats for the servers and clergy when the Holy Table is in use during the Celebration of Holy Communion.

*The patterned tiles*

The raised floors of the choir and sanctuary, and the walls around the altar table gave scope for the Victorians to indulge their liking for coloured and patterned tiles. They were following older and widespread traditions which had made mosaic floors and inlaid tiles carry messages both sacred and mysterious, or secular, such as heraldic badge pieces. Our floor is made with good, straightforward and not very interesting pieces, crafted by the firm of Godwin of Hereford. To make these high quality encaustic tiles, the basic tile material is inlaid with different coloured clays to make the required design, and each piece is fired as a whole item. Brown and wasp-yellow, red and dark blue, they were then laid like carpet pieces to make a shiny patterned finish.

Wall tiles low down in the sanctuary were less successful in their appeal: these are different in style and manufacturing technique and seem to me to be an odd misfit in colour too. They have since been covered up and uncovered according to taste. There are among us, people who really do like them!

Some people today regard the sanctuary walls as over-decorated, and it is true that there are no blank spaces! Yet, apart from those pinkish tiles low down, every feature is symbolic in character. To study these can be rewarding. We may start with the east wall (leaving the description of the window for another chapter).To the right and left of the depiction of the Last Supper are the winged creatures, emblems of the four Gospel writers: the man/angel for Matthew, a lion for Mark, a bull for Luke and the eagle for John. Search further and you will find the Greek letters Alpha and Omega, and will remember the words of the LORD in the Revelation to John: "I am the Alpha and the Omega, the first and the last, the beginning and the end"   Revelation 22 v 12. Also on the east wall are portrayed ears of corn, and grapes "ripe unto harvest" to remind us of the bread and wine from the Table.

All these are set out in mosaic and opus sectile panels delineated with highlights of gold, and the background to it all is a tangle of rampant passion flowers whose branches and tendrils wind their way everywhere. We have even been given both white/blue flowers *and* a red variety! Much has been written about the symbolism of these striking flowers. The use of flowers and foliage has been popular since early mediaeval times, and some say this brings additional life to stone and metal and woodwork. This attractive idea is carried further by the busy needleworkers and embroiderers who craft banners and kneelers, vestments and altar frontals. This is an art form which has recently become very popular again. But that is a wide subject that is best left to the experts and devotees of these works.

*The Liturgical Colours*

The Sanctuary is often a colourful place with daylight streaming in through east and south facing stained glass windows, and highlighting the polished brass Altar Cross and candlesticks, and the precious silver communion Paten and Chalice. Our Puritan forefathers seemed to see many dangers surrounding the use of rich decoration and coloured vestments. In later years we are finding that the use of colour and splendour can lift us up into the glory and majesty of God, as we worship him.

We have seen fit to embrace a return to the use of a meaningful colour scheme for the vestments worn by the priest, and applied to other objects used during the Celebration of Holy Communion. There is a special colour assigned to each part of the Christian year. The altar frontal drape continues to show the appropriate colour for the duration of the season in progress. Sacristan Olive Gill has contributed this description of the colours and their significance:

"*Purple* for Advent and Lent. A time of preparation before the great festivals of Christmas and Easter.

*White* for Feast Days, e.g. Christmas and the days after it; Easter and all the days following it, until Ascension Day and Trinity Sunday; and for Saints' Days (unless they are Martyrs).

*Red* for Martyrs. Also for the week before Easter (Holy Week) to signify the Blood shed by Jesus on the Cross. On Good Friday the frontals are removed to emphasise the starkness of the day in contrast to the glory and celebration of Easter.

*Red* is also used for Pentecost (Whitsun), and for Confirmation, as a reminder of the Coming of the Holy Spirit as described in the Acts of the Apostles Chapter 2: "Tongues of Fire".

*Green* is used between Epiphany and Lent showing the growth of the Ministry of Christ and his Disciples. Also it is used after Trinity Sunday until Advent Sunday, showing the growth and spread of the Church.

*Purple* and *Black* vestments were formerly always used for funerals but now it is more usual to use *White* as a thanksgiving for a person's life."

Here in St. Gregory's church our splendid 'white' frontal is laced with *gold and crimson;* we have in our care a rich collection of frontals and vestments, some of which came from the now closed St. Mark's church. They are kept in good repair by a gifted needleworker called Rosemary whose quiet labours are not often sufficiently appreciated.

*Preparing the Building for Worship*

There are many such tasks involved in making all things ready for our coming together to worship God in a dignified and reverent manner. We should remember that these very practical things are faithfully carried out by churchwardens and other officers, sacristans, musicians, cleaners and polishers, flower arrangers and sidesmen and women ......and many other members of our congregation. It is very easy to forget the faithful contributions of those who offer transport to the elderly or infirm so that these members can still come to church; those who launder and iron linen for the Holy Table, and others who refresh the many cassocks and surplices used by choir and clergy.

These details and the general maintenance of the whole building are important in that they make it a worthy place of meeting and worship. They are also intended to free us from the distractions of cold and avoidable discomfort, so that worshippers may turn to the things that are of greatest importance, and can be more freely receptive to teaching and inspiration offered in the Liturgy and in music and visual art.

The donation of stained glass windows, and other art work has been an age-old tradition within the Church. Since the Reformation, this giving is no longer associated with earning relief from time to be spent in 'purgatory', but at its best, is now a sign of thanksgiving for people who have enriched us, and a way to beautify the place of worship. In the next chapter you will find descriptions of the windows of the chancel, transepts, the Lady Chapel, nave and tower.

# CHAPTER SIXTEEN

## *THE INSPIRATION OF LIGHT and COLOUR*

We have seen that in Mediaeval times, the church building was a source of colourful wonder to the people who came together regularly for worship and instruction and pastoral care. Later there were times when colourful art was attacked as if it was a distraction from serious contemplation. But far from dulling the physical senses, surely the rituals of worship, and the surrounding settings, should help minds and hearts to become *illuminated* and *enriched*. Slowly we came to recognise again that, far from being intrusive or encouraging idolatry, light and colour streaming into our building and especially into the sanctuary, could inspire people and help them to be aware of being in the presence of our great and glorious God. Such wonders can help us to 'think beyond' ordinary things, and to reach out towards what seems awesome and mysterious, and yet is touching and enfolding us.

As we enjoy colour and light and begin to ponder their origin and meaning, we can appreciate them as marvellous signs pointing to the glory of God, and as messages from God to man, telling us of his loving care for the world. A world favoured from the outset by the Creator God's tremendous word "Let there be light". And God speaks to us powerfully in colour: remember that the first recorded *sign* of his covenant with us his people, was the *rainbow.*   Genesis 1 v 3 and 9 v 13

*A gap in our known history*

In the 1875 reorganisation we lost our only remaining older stained glass, namely the former east window. Perhaps it was too frail to preserve. We know almost nothing about any ancient coloured glass which might have survived in this church from before the Reformation. It would be surprising if during the 100 years between the 1438 rebuilding and the beginnings of the

Reformation, there had *not* been wealthy parishioners wishing to make donations in the form of stained glass windows. The tradition to do so (for whatever reason) was strong.

*Making stained glass*

The stained glass of those earlier times was crafted from 'pot metal', so called because the special metallic salts which infused the glass with various wonderfully rich colours, were added to the molten glass in the melting pot. There were only a few methods by which the pot metal could be laid out to form flat pieces relatively free of blemish and irregularity, and the size of the resulting usable bits was limited. So they had to be joined together with pliable lead channel strips to make a design or picture. Later techniques included the art of painting flat pieces of glass before they were finally re-fired. There was much bold experimentation on the part of master glaziers who sought ways of increasing the range of available colours. They discovered that the use of silver salts gave a brilliant yellow-orange effect, and very popular indeed were the resulting golden angelic hair and kingly crowns.

By the time we engaged the services of our Victorian glaziers, there were novel methods drawn from several countries and traditions, by which the artists could 'draw' detailed pictures in glass. However, they needed to take into account the fact that a large stained glass window is too flexible to withstand the pressure and suction forces involved in storm and temperature variation. So it is strengthened with frames and crossbars inserted into the stonework. If you are sorry that this gets in the way of the pictures, be glad as well that Perpendicular Gothic architecture gave us these large windows, letting in so much light.

*A thoughtful walk round to look at our windows*

Our *nave* windows are filled with tinted 'Cathedral glass' by Messrs.Lavers and Barrand of London, leaving us free to enjoy brightness with reduced glare, and to focus on the Table and the east window in the sanctuary. But do notice the delicate strips of colour which give a pleasant finish to the glasswork in these plain windows, and take a moment to appreciate the satisfying proportions of the basic stonework and tracery. The designers in the Gothic era had a fine sense of the rightness of their creations, and our re-builders have respected and copied their work.

Within the new *chancel* and enlarged *transepts,* there was a rare opportunity to design and install a series of stained glass windows. That chance was eagerly grasped, and it was agreed that a matching set illustrating memorable and instructive scenes from the earthly ministry of Our Lord, would be appropriate. Prospective donors were happy to comply, and we now have a set of Victorian windows of a high standard of workmanship; the glass colours are strong and in many ways they are a link by which we can pay tribute to gifted glaziers of the $14^{th}$ and $15^{th}$ centuries. (I shall leave description of the east window until the end of this chapter, as it is a very special aid to worship).

*The North Transept Glass*

Here we have two memorial windows donated by Mrs Ware of 'Irene', Dawlish, in thanksgiving for her parents, Mr. G. and Mrs Elizabeth Greenup. Elizabeth is buried in the churchyard just outside the windows. These windows are the work of Mr. F. Drake of the Cathedral Close in Exeter. He used extremely rich stained glass in his portrayal of four important and precious events in the teaching ministry of Our Lord. The main part of each window is divided into two *lights* by vertical stone *mullions.*

In the first window, the left light is of Jesus with Martha and Mary, and the inscription text "One thing is needful" is from Luke 10 v 42. The second light in the same window, is of Jesus with the woman of Samaria, at the well, and the words inscribed: "Jesus being wearied sat thus by the well". John 4 v 6

In the second window, the left hand light is of Jesus calming the troubled sea: "Even the winds and the sea obey Him", (the story set out in Mark 4 vv 37-41), and the other shows the woman with a haemorrhage, creeping up to touch the garment of Jesus whom she believed could heal her: "Thy faith has saved thee". Luke 7 v 50, but note that the story illustrated is told in Luke 8 vv 43-48.

Wonderful happenings they were indeed. Do spare some time to read the stories over again.

*Filling in the extra spaces*

The odd-shaped openings in the stonework tracery above the main lights have always been attractive to the glazier, who could use them, within limits, in his own imaginative way. Each of the windows in the north and south transepts has a *roundel* high up, filled with a small scene, and surrounded by 'conventional' cherubim, each with just a head and six wings. In the north transept windows the scenes are of 'Jesus the Good Shepherd', and 'Jesus gathering the children and blessing them'. Other small spaces are filled with coloured designs.

These 'Greenup' memorial windows were already installed when the building was re-opened on March 10th 1875. So were the three middle lights and the 'rose' of the great east window (to be described later).

*The South Transept Glass*

Here are two windows matching those in the north transept, and surely crafted by the same glazier. The subjects chosen for the main lights in the south-east one are:

(left) The visit of the Magi bearing kingly gifts for the infant Jesus:
"A light to lighten the gentiles"   Luke 2 v 32

(right) John the Baptist with his disciples, meeting Jesus.
"Behold the Lamb of God".  John 1 v 36

In the roundel above is a small picture of the Risen Christ with Peter, and the caption: "Feed my sheep"  John 21 v 17

The second (south-west) window has:

(left) A Canaanite woman (i.e. not of the House of Israel) coming to Jesus to beg him to heal her daughter. She cries out:
"Lord help me"   Matthew 15 v 25

(right) Martha and Mary at the death of Lazarus. Jesus says:
"I am the resurrection and the life".  Luke 11 v 25

In the roundel above, Jesus talks with his disciples in the 'Farewell discourses', saying:
"Peace I leave with you".  John 14 v 27

These south transept windows must have been made a little later than the ones in the north transept, for they are not mentioned in the fulsome descriptions of the new building to which the local press devoted much energy in 1875. The commemorative strips at the bottom are not visible when you stand at the foot of the windows, and if you step back far enough to see them, you need binoculars to read the details! Having done this, I can record that they were given in memory of Richard Greenup, perhaps a brother or father of Elizabeth's husband:

"This window is erected in affectionate remembrance" is at the base of the left window, and the inscription continues in the right one: "In memory of Richard Greenup who died at D'Arcey, Hey" (in West Yorkshire).

So we do know that the windows were commissioned as a set of four, around the time of the new building completion (1875). They were welcomed and admired publicly in those days; but alas, since then they have needed protection from the vandals of later generations. Strong wire screens are attached to the outside window apertures to preserve all the stained glass. The nave glass remains vulnerable to unhappy and sadly disrespectful attackers.

*In the Lady Chapel: the Raphael window*

Also not described in the Opening press descriptions, are the major works in stained glass which now embellish the *'south chancel aisle'* which became the Lady Chapel before very long.

As you step into this room from the south transept, you are immediately aware of the fine *east window*. It dates from 1885 and is a copy of a painting by the artist Raphael, entitled "The Transfiguration of Christ".

The stained glass artist, (W.F.Dixon), boldly undertook the task of fitting the picture into the stonework tracery which was already in place. It was cleverly and imaginatively done. Some of the colours are slightly different from those in the original painting, but all the components are there. They include not only the appearance of Christ in dazzling white array, and Moses and Elijah, but also, in the lower part of the picture, the story of the failure of some of the disciples to heal the epileptic boy......a scene which confronted Our Lord and Peter, John and James as they descended the hill where their high experience had taken place. Down to earth indeed!

Raphael knew his Bible and wanted to portray the whole of the story as we have it in Mark's Gospel, Chapter 9 vv 2-29. As we read it again we can perhaps get a glimpse of the glory that was revealed, and which Raphael so earnestly tried to convey.

The installation and dedication of this work took place in 1884/5

"To the Glory of God and to the loved and honoured memory of
The Rev. Orlando Manley, B.A. of Trinity College Cambridge.
for fifteen years Vicar of this Parish
this window is dedicated by his parishioners and other friends
February 1884."

There is a similar inscription on a brass plaque on the south wall nearby. It seems the glass was finished in 1885.

*In the Lady Chapel: the Altar and Reredos*

Initially, there being no screen between the chancel aisle and the chancel itself, chairs were put in the chancel aisle for some members of the congregation to use during the main Sunday Celebration of Holy Communion. This eased the difficulties over shortage of seating.

The stone carved reredos of 1825 was moved from behind the High Altar in the Sanctuary, into the south chancel aisle during the re-organisation of 1875. It was placed against the east wall, below the window to form the backdrop to a new Altar or Holy Table. This second Altar has been extensively used as an additional place for distribution of the Elements to large congregations, and for weekday Celebrations of Holy Communion.

The new Altar, or Holy Table, is made of fine oak, and carries a carved inscription on the south side:
"To the glory of God and in memory of Arthur Charles Ashby Aves"

On the front is a beautiful carving of the triumphant Lamb of God bearing his Flag of Victory. I am glad it is not covered with a frontal, for with Cross and candles on the Table there is no need for additional ornament.

This side chapel has been used regularly for Morning and Evening Prayer, the Commemorations of the Saints and for a mid-week Celebration of Holy Communion. Other suitable small meetings can take place here and it is used for private devotions, for Confession, for Services of Healing and for conversations with the priest and his helpers.

*Honouring the Holy Family*

In line with cherished tradition and popular inclination, the side chapel has become known as the Lady Chapel, where we remember especially the Holy Mother of Our Lord. It has been furnished with a handmade needle-worked kneeler for each of the chairs, and at the altar rail. These tell of many labours of love spread over weeks and months, perhaps years. The motifs employed tell us about local wildlife; some are sacred symbols, and the altar kneelers show the lilies which have long been honoured as Our Lady's special flower. Here also is kept the Mothers' Union banner (more white lilies).

Mention should be made here of a very old statue of the Holy Mother and Child, which was found stored away in the upper vestry. It is of carved old oak, and shows fragments of many layers of paint. Mary is crowned, and the Child carries the orb of the world in his hands. The history of this piece is unwritten as yet, but I hope the statue will remain in the Lady Chapel as an aid to our worship of the Word made flesh, and to show reverence for the Holy Family. It stands on the south-east windowsill.

*The Story of the Saviour of the World*

Behind the Altar is the second of our great *opus sectile* pictures; this one is a composite scene of the stable of the Nativity, together with the Visit of the Magi bearing kingly gifts.
It was designed by one of our own parishioners, named Miller, (or perhaps Muller?), and was installed in 1914. No-one seems to know what was there before this: perhaps the reredos remained plain after its move from behind the old High Altar, although it may still have framed the Ten Commandments, and Our Lord's Prayer, on painted panels.

If we start with these traditional Nativity scenes and look around this chapel we can trace the story of our salvation through the life, death and rising again of this Child. Mary's Son 'grew in grace' from childhood, to become the Son of Man who went about doing good; who was glorified in his Transfiguration on the mountain, and who accepted betrayal and humiliation, crucifixion and death at the hands of those whose Messianic hopes he came to fulfil. Symbols of his Passion are carved and painted along the top of the stone reredos: the Crown of Thorns and the Nails, the Seamless Robe and the gaming dice with which they cast lots for his garment, a Ladder and the Sponge filled with vinegar, the Hammer and Pincers.

In this chapel we have a Crucifix which helps us to recall the complete sacrifice made for us by Our Lord Christ. The saving work of Our Lord goes on beyond His earthly death, so we need to turn back to the Altar to see the *empty Cross* and the *victorious Lamb* proclaiming the truth:

> "He has been raised from the dead".

Matthew 27 v 7

And He calls us to begin a new life with Him in His risen power.

The Crucifix stands on top of the *aumbry,* a small cupboard on the wall south of the Altar, where consecrated Elements are housed, ready for use at any time of need. Nearby is suspended a candle in a white surround. When it is alight, it signifies that consecrated Elements, the essence of Christ himself, are there for us. This living flame helps us to recall Our Risen Lord's words:

> "Remember, I am with you always, to the end of the age".

Matthew 28 v 20

*Still in the Lady Chapel: the South Windows*

In 1875 at the opening ceremony, we hear that the 'South Chancel aisle' had a "four light east window and two south windows of three lights, all of which were filled with (plain) tinted Cathedral glass". They would, before long, have coloured glass. We have described the east (Raphael) window and now turn to the other stained glass put in over the next 10-15 years.

We have seen that the Lady Chapel speaks eloquently of the Resurrection of Our Lord. Not only do we have the Lamb of Victory on the altar front, but the *south window nearest to the Altar* is a celebration of the Resurrection. The centre light shows the Risen Christ in Majesty. Ministering angels attend Him on one side, while we are taken back to the first Easter morning on the other. The women come with their spices to the tomb, while at the bottom centre the Roman soldiers shrink back with amazement. There are stars scattered around and the Dove of the Holy Spirit shines in the roundel above; cherubim with golden wings carry the joyful message abroad. Almost unnecessary is the caption:

"I am the Resurrection and the Life"

John 11 v 25

"In memory of John Hearn of this Parish 1888" is written at the bottom of the glass. A brass plaque is fixed to the windowsill:

"To the glory of God and in affectionate remembrance of John Hearn who died 17$^{th}$ June 1888 aged 70 years. The window above this tablet was erected by his widow and sons".

*The southwest window* tells of the welcome and the love of Jesus for all people in any kind of need or trouble. He stands with open arms ready to receive the woman kneeling before him; gathered round are a humble soldier, a cripple, a mother with a child, sick people pleading for help, including a child with a bandaged head. And the caption?

"Come unto me all ye that labour and are heavy laden"

Matthew 11 v 28

Above, the roundel shows two angels bearing a glorified Crown of Thorns. Serving others is a costly offering. Roses in the tracery also speak of beauty beset with thorns. An inscription reads:

"To the glory of God and in loving memory of Elizabeth the wife of Sidney Lawford who fell asleep at Dawlish Feb.5 1912".

*The West Window in the Tower*

In the west wall of the tower, (the oldest part of the present building), there was a small window above the west door, but no recorded description of it survives. We know only that in 1875 the window was enlarged, and the tower arch opening into the nave was repaired. The window structure is now of Perpendicular Gothic style and is filled with coloured glass. The only persons who might be aware of it during regular times of worship are the Priest Celebrants at the High Altar! But since the changes to the west end made the upper narthex room possible, we can now go upstairs to see it at close quarters.

The picture is of Jesus and the children:

"and they brought little children unto Him......
and He took them up in his arms... and blessed them".

Mark 13 vv 13, 16

This is a memorial, as well as a story window. In the upper spaces are two angels with sashes bearing the words "Blessed are the dead who die in the Lord".   Revelation 14 v 13.  The inscription reads thus:

"To the glory of God and in memory of
Jane Vaughan Forbes-Pemmo (1819-1869) and
Mary Wilhelmina Lanyon Pemmo (1848-1872)"

*The Great East Window: "People look East!"*

It has long been the custom in western Christendom to site the Altar at the *east* end of the building, so that the congregation faces east (some say towards Jerusalem the Holy City), during public worship. (But I learn that in the time of the early Roman churches, it was the priest celebrating the Eucharist from behind the Table at the *west* end who looked eastwards). Pagan religious practice was always to pray towards the rising sun which restores and maintains life; it is only a small step for Christians to transform such a tradition into a symbolic reference to Our Lord Christ as the *Morning Star or the Rising Sun:*

*"O Morning Star, Thou splendour of eternal light, thou Sun of righteousness:*
*Come, shine forth upon those who sit in darkness and in the shadow of death".*

(from the Latin Advent Antiphons,).

So here we are, looking east towards the High Altar, and above it, in prime position, is a great window which teaches, reminds, and can help us, in our meditation and worship.

When the new Chancel was opened in 1875, of the seven main lights of the window, only the three middle ones had coloured glass, but "…but we understand that the donors also intend to fill the remaining lights…". The donors in question were members of the Hoare family of Luscombe Castle, Dawlish; we owe much to the long-standing interest, co-operation and generosity of the heads of this family.

The dedication panel on the left pillar of the window arch reads thus when translated from the Latin:

To the greater glory of God
and in memory of the greatly esteemed mother SOPHIA HOARE
Isabella Maria Hoare and Carlotta Anna Strickland Hoare
dedicated this window in the year of our Lord 1876.

The design was already established, for the whole work is said to be a copy of one in a French cathedral. The fact that nobody can now identify the original is less than important; what does matter is that we allow it to speak to us. Much of the Creed is there, and I guess many of us do follow its story during the earlier parts of the Celebration of the Eucharist: using our eyes as well as our ears.

*So look up and look east*

In the highest place is set a *circle,* symbol of the wholeness, the perfection of God. Within its orbit are eight worshipping angels, and the pattern has become a *rose* reminding us of Mary. At its heart is the sacred symbol *IHS:* Jesus, Saviour of Mankind, the Son come on earth to suffer for us in love. He is like the *Pelican* (in the trefoil to the right), which was thought to draw blood from his breast to feed his dependent chicks. Jesus feeds us too, but He makes the full sacrifice as the *Lamb of God*, yet He rises again victorious, so (in the left hand trefoil) we have the *Lamb with His Flag of Victory.* The *trefoils* also remind us of the three-fold nature of God: Father, Son and Holy Spirit. And four angels represent the whole of the heavenly host "evermore praising Thee and saying: Holy, holy, holy is the LORD of hosts".

Our generous donors did indeed make possible the completion of the seven light window telling the *Story of Jesus on earth.*

Look down first to the lowest part of the central light. Here is a lovely Nativity scene, and its position is chosen with care:
"For Jesus our treasure,
With love past all measure
In lowly poor manger was laid"

(from the carol "All poor men and humble......Come haste ye and be not afraid" by Katherine Emily Roberts).

And reading the main lights from left to right, we have:
1. The Baptism of Jesus by John.
    Look for the Holy Spirit in the form of a dove.
2. In the Garden of Gethsemane: Jesus prays while the disciples sleep.
3. Jesus carries His Cross. St. Veronica comes near to wipe His brow, while a Roman soldier looks on.
4. The Crucifixion scene dominates the whole window.
    We can only begin to enter into the grief and wonder of those who were near Him then.

5. *Christ is risen.* On the third day, silently and surely. The soldiers still sleep, but we who are awake see an empty tomb, and the Risen Christ with the Flag of victory.
6. *He appears first to Mary Magdalene:* that dear Mary whose many sins are forgiven.
7. *He ascended into heaven* ...into glory...into a cloudburst of kingly gold and purple.

This story, so powerfully brought to us again in this window, sums up the truth of God's loving relationship with mankind, and invites us to enter into that mysterious communion. Like the disciples, we are bidden to wait for the gift of the Holy Spirit, and then to

"Go in peace to love and serve the Lord".

*We* continue the unending story when with all Our Lord Christ's followers we respond with joy and shout:

"In the Name of Christ. Amen".

# CHAPTER SEVENTEEN

## *MAKING MUSIC FOR THE LORD*

Congregational singing is treasured as a way for everyone to participate and contribute actively during public worship. How we vary in our musical ability, and in appreciation of the discipline expected by composers! But whether we are 'tone deaf' or very sensitive to the niceties of pitch and rhythm, all of us should know that our offering is acceptable to the Lord. Many of us have savoured, with much amusement, the wording of Psalm 95 in the Authorised Version of the Bible:

"O come, let us sing unto the Lord:
let us make a joyful noise unto the rock of our salvation.
Let us come before his presence with thanksgiving,
and make a joyful noise unto him with psalms."

Musicians of integrity want to share the riches of their art with other people, and to offer them as a worthy part of common worship. From earliest days Christians have sung together, often as an unaccompanied art. As in many monastic communities, the unobtrusive blowing of a pitch pipe, or the voice of a gifted chorister, would set the note for the singing or chanting of each Office. A good deal of early Church music, including Gregorian chant, was written for this kind of singing in monastery, abbey and cathedral.

This was not the most natural kind of music in rural village life and worship. In village holiday (Holy Day) gatherings for feasting, dancing and folk-singing, instrumental accompaniment was provided from local talent and a variety of homely traditional instruments. It may often have been an amusing mixture of skills and zealous innovation, but it was fun! It brought joy and vigour and rhythm to these happy occasions. Fittingly, some of these local instrumentalists brought their music into the acts of worship in the church; when we recall that a number of hymns were set to folk tunes, this was a good link. Joy and rhythm and vigour go well with praising the Lord.

## The Musicians' Gallery in St. Gregory's church

The west gallery was the home of these musicians who led the singing of hymns and psalms. A pipe organ was also installed up there, perhaps as early as in the $16^{th}$ century. It was certainly there in 1618, when parish records state that a new "skynne of leather (was) bought to repair the organ". (Were the bellows damaged by hungry church mice?)

Then there was a time of musical dearth, when Puritans showed thorough disapproval of accompanied singing in church. Happily, in St. Gregory's church, the organ was not thrown out with the fiddles and bass-viols, and the leading of singing with a variety of instruments including the organ (with its hand blown bellows), and an amateur choir, eventually became the usual practice again (if indeed it was ever interrupted). We have little in the way of records of our own former musical tradition, but we know that in the 1825 building, this old organ, or a successor, was in use, and remained so until after the new chancel was completed in 1875.

## Re-organising the leading of Music in Worship after 1875

In the new east end of the building, provision was made for choir seating in the chancel, and for an adjacent organ chamber in the north aisle, east of the new north transept. The setting and timing was surely ripe for the commission of a brand new and substantial organ of the very best order. In keeping with this important decision, we were to appoint a qualified organist, and recruit a choir of men and boys who would rehearse regularly, and lead the congregational singing of responses, hymns, psalms and canticles, from the choir stalls in the chancel. A fine, broad musical tradition was being established which continues today under the able musicianship and guidance of Mr. George Elliott, our present organist and choirmaster.

*Our Pipe Organ: a worthy instrument and a valuable possession*

"The organ was built by T.C.Lewis and Co. in 1888. The firm was recommended by a curate in the parish who was a relative of Lewis. At that time, the organist was Mr R.E. West, a graduate of the Royal Academy of Music. Mr J.F.King, headmaster of Dawlish Boys School, was choir trainer and, shortly afterwards, organist. The frame and much of the woodwork, such as the swell-box, was constructed by a local carpenter, Mr Fred Marchant." (This note is by Mr W.J. ('Jim') Holman, of whom we shall read more, a little later).

Lewis "built a large number of fine organs......His fluework was particularly notable, and his diapason choruses and gedackts owed much to Schultze. The quality of his pipework was admirable and he used large quantities of tin in making his alloys. Structurally his instruments were durable and worthy".

(from the celebrated book *The Organ* by W.J.Sumner).

This all sounds highly technical information, but I include it to make the point that we have in St. Gregory's church, a very fine and valuable instrument. When the Lewis business was taken into the family firm of Willis after 1918, that new master builder cared well for the organ with its original (tracker) action. In 1951 he repositioned some ranks of pipes and added a 3-rank mixture in the 'Great' organ section.

While Mr.Holman was our organist (1945-1960s), he had the pleasure of playing an instrument which had a reliable (if heavy) action, and superb pipework. His enthusiasm and love of music and his desire to share it with everyone, led him to invite well known organists to give recitals here. Among those who have come, are Fernando Germani, George Thalden Ball of Exeter Cathedral, and Ralph Downes: all great names in the world of pipe organists. There were summer recitals, and radio broadcasts of organ playing by Alan Harverson, and John Birch of Chichester Cathedral, and the choir gave seven radio performances. We were on the musical map!

*Caring for our fine organ*

Over the course of time, an instrument like ours needs major overhauls in addition to regular tuning and maintenance. In 1973, the 'action' was rebuilt by the firm of Eustace and Alldridge of Exeter. The mechanical tracker system was replaced with an electric one, which operated the same splendid pipes, now cleaned and restored. Originally, because of the requirements of the tracker action, the console (keyboards and controls) had to be placed close to the organ built in the north aisle organ chamber. The organist sat in the chancel and played with his back to the choir. (You can still see the relevant woodwork). The change to electric action meant that the console could be moved to a better position in relation to the choir. Instead of having his back to them, the organist now sat 'sideways on' on the south side of the choir stalls, from where he could more easily conduct and communicate with the singers.

The next 25 years of use saw a slow increase in the number of technical problems, until it became clear that substantial changes were necessary in order to preserve the very high standard of reliability needed for the future. In 1998, the results of specialist consultations between Mr. Michael Farley (organ builder), Mr. George Elliott, F.L.C.M., L.T.C.L. (organist) and The Rev.Dr.John Bradshaw, were laid before the Committees of the Church for discussion. With careful confidence decisions were taken: namely, to raise the very considerable funds, and to have the work done thoroughly well. The Church carried out its commitment and raised all the required money by means of the gifts of the living, legacies and memorial tributes in thanksgiving for the dead, and by a host of money-raising activities which provided plenty of social pleasure and satisfaction through hard work and fun together, to support a worthwhile cause. Yes, these naturally included a number of concerts and recitals.

The renovation work was mainly concerned with the 'action', that is, with all the complicated devices which transmit the depression of a note on one of the keyboards to the activation of the correct pipe. The aim is to allow air at the right pressure to blow into that pipe as swiftly and smoothly as is possible, and also to shut it off smartly! Most faults arise through the failure of a pipe to 'speak', or when the air supply does not cut off as it should, when we will hear a whistle or 'cipher' (the organist's nightmare), which then interferes with the continuing music. The installation of a sophisticated new electrical action made life a great deal easier for the player. Built into the system was the ability to 'pre-set' changes of stops or combinations of them, which could then be activated by touching easily reached buttons around the keyboards.

The setting up of this system, the re-voicing and tuning of some of the pipes, and complete cleaning, took place over many months of hard work by organ builder Michael Farley and his team of specialist technicians. The resulting electrical operation panel is impressively complicated, and is adorned by coloured light emitting diodes. We offer you our thanks Michael!

On completion of the work, we had in our care a first class and robust instrument to enjoy, and a worthy gift to future users.
The Vicar at that time, The Reverend William Lark, was (and is) as gifted a musician as his avian counterpart, and in happy co-operation with George Elliott and the Choir (now a company of men and women able to sing in four-part harmony), we were offered a feast of traditional and innovative music as part of the worship during the main Parish Communion, and a Choral Evensong. Carefully chosen hymns, sensitively accompanied and supported by the organ tones, bring the whole congregation together in worship. Good music in worship is indeed a great joy to most of us, even if we do not regard ourselves as 'musical'.

*Music is offered as part of Worship*

Sadly, we notice that not everyone uses the quiet, meditative music played as we take our places, as a help in preparing to worship; likewise the often majestic brilliance of a complex postlude goes unheeded as conversation breaks out. This, I am told, is quite unlike the practice in Germany, where nobody moves or speaks until the musical offering is completed. But here, in recent times, there is spontaneous applause for George at the end of some of his rich and ambitious postludes: music from the great composers like J.S.Bach and many others both ancient and modern. These are indeed a shout of praise and thanksgiving as we go on our way.

*Remembering Jim Holman*

St. Gregory's Church remembers a former organist with great affection. He was popularly known as 'Mr. Dawlish'. Jim Holman was Organist and Choirmaster for many years in the middle of the 20th century. He was a strict disciplinarian as far as the young choirboys were concerned, but they all knew there was a twinkle in his eye as he schooled them, and set a demandingly high standard for music in worship. Jim perpetuated the fine musical tradition which was inaugurated when the new east end of the building was opened in 1875. His notes (quoted above), were "recalled from memory", for in his later years Jim became blind, a handicap which was not allowed greatly to curtail his many and energetic activities. Formerly the owner and editor of The Dawlish Gazette, his wide knowledge of Dawlish, and his interest in its resident families endeared him to a great many of us. His detailed memory was phenomenal: latterly, long after he had lost his sight, if you sat with him at Evening Prayer, he would ask you for the first words of the set Psalm, and then sing the whole of it without faltering. His appreciation of the importance of local history led him to write a number of papers and published articles about Dawlish families, businesses and interesting events. These are now in the care of Dawlish Local History Society.

Jim Holman's skills and devotion are commemorated in the gift, by his daughters, of the rich covering for an altar in the crossing; we treasure his musical legacy which includes his wisdom in helping us all to value a fine instrument and to fund generously the necessary maintenance and up-dating work.

(The 'Specification' of the present day organ may be found among the appendices to this book).

*Other Musical Instruments*

Within the families in any parish, there will be members who are skilled in the playing of instruments other than the organ, and also children and young people who are at various stages of learning to play. For them to be invited to take part, as a musical group, in making music in a service, is a fine way of encouraging them to know they are wanted and appreciated. Many churches hold Family Services in which worship is less formal (but no less sincere), than in the full Liturgy of Holy Communion. In such a more relaxed setting, music groups can effectively accompany hymns and songs of many types, and find space for solo items. Preparing for this by rehearsing under the guidance of a leader, makes a happy item in the week for those involved. I hope we will welcome the chance to have *some* joint services, perhaps at the great Festivals? People coming to *either* a Family Service *or* Parish Communion, still belong together: we are one church, and surely should show this by *sometimes* coming to worship together at the same time, and using all kinds of music-making.

*What is a Hymn?*

"......a hymn is intended for singing, and for singing together. Its subject must therefore be worth singing about, and it should express the common faith of Christendom. Nothing is so worthy of our singing as the glory and majesty of God, His creative power and redeeming grace......The singing of a hymn is an act of corporate worship, and, as our fellowship is not only with each other but with the saints above, our reach will often exceed our grasp......"

From the preface to "Congregational Praise", (1950).

What a happy choice of name for the hymnbook of the Congregational Church! In 1972 this Church formally joined with the Presbyterian Church and the Churches of Christ, to form the United Reformed Church. In due time their new (and current) hymnbook was published (1991) with the even happier title of "Rejoice and Sing".

Leaders of all parts of the Church, through specially convened Hymns and Music Committees, take immense care to have what they believe is good material in their hymnbooks. To be included (or retained) in a collection, a hymn has to be theologically and musically sound, poetically satisfying and a means of enabling people of all ages to join in worship with sincerity and thoughtfulness. Some hymns pass these tests time and time again, and can be used for many centuries; others are quickly 'dated' and if sung today would give rise to well deserved mirth or bafflement. Words can indeed change their meaning!

So the updating of hymnbooks is essential if we are to avoid the perpetuation of inadequate ideas that can mislead new seekers after truth. Much more positively, we need to bring into our worship the many beautiful compositions in music and poetry which are taking shape day by day. With discernment, let us *add* to our time honoured treasures, some of the creative writing of present day artists. Their work too, will stand or fall in due course, but their message is for today and we should hear it. Given the desire to understand what moves other people, we may all discover fresh inspiration from both older and younger friends.

New music and poetry can enrich the offerings of young and old. But there is a need for caution. Woven into the fabric of all new means of expression in worship must be the underlying awareness that it is an offering to the Lord. In that spirit, even if we do not immediately like what we see and hear, there can be mutual tolerance embracing everybody in the Church family, traditionalists and innovators alike. We learn from each other. For example, while I deeply enjoy singing the ancient hymn:

> "Come Holy Ghost, our souls inspire,
>   and lighten with celestial fire,
> Thou the anointing spirit art
>   who dost thy sevenfold gifts impart......"

Latin 9th century, translated by John Cosin in the 17th c.

a modern equivalent has become equally precious:

> "Be still for the presence of the Lord
>   the Holy One is here......
>
> Be still for the glory of the Lord
>   is shining all around;
> He burns with holy fire,
>   With splendour he is crowned......
>
> Be still for the power of the Lord
>   is moving in this place:
> He comes to cleanse and heal,
>   To minister his grace......
>
> In faith receive from Him......"

David J Evans: (in Kingsway's Thankyou Music). 1986

Perhaps it is true today, more than ever before, that each generation requires, or at least demands, its own hymnbook. Such an edition will be a collection of words set to music which anyone who comes to church can enjoy singing with other people. Music that is easy to learn, and which lets us all rejoice and sing the great truths of the Gospel; music which draws us to praise and honour the Lord our God, and to bring our prayers before Him.

*Embellishing our Musical Offering*

Readers will have looked around the church building with me and been encouraged to think about the contributions made by architects, sculptors, carpenters and glaziers and many others who determine the *appearance* of the place. It is not quite as easy to gather up the importance of the *sounds* we meet when we are in it. They can be just as important as the visual impact.

Our worship includes times of silence; we join in spoken responses and prayers, listen to the spoken Ministry of the Word, greet each other with a word of peace, and happily, we all sing!

> "Thou didst ears and hands and voices
> For thy praise design;
> Craftsman's art and music's measure
> For thy pleasure
> All combine".

Francis Pott, 1832-1909

Some of us have special gifts to offer, and among them are the musicians who lead our singing, after careful rehearsals. Choir members take their calling to include sharing more advanced and complex music with all who will listen, both within services, and in concert settings. They give pleasure and often raise money for the work of the Church. The same is true of organists and other instrumentalists. They are well placed to introduce anthems and new songs to us all during worship. Should we ask more of them? It is good to hear new songs, but are we not neglecting some of our musical heritage? The art of chanting Psalms and Canticles as part of Morning and Evening Prayer is being edged out as Holy Communion becomes the main service in many places. Look through any hymnbook and see how many fine hymns are available, but which we never use. There is food for thought here: perhaps choirs can be our good stewards.

*We will all go on making music for the Lord.*

# CHAPTER EIGHTEEN

## ON THE KEEPING OF RECORDS

*Caring about the Past*

The need for officially recognised records of the lives of citizens led to the compilation and careful preservation of factual documents about people, institutions and land ownership, from the time of the Anglo-Saxon Chronicle and the Domesday Book onwards, to the establishment of the series of National Censuses and other legal data in modern times. The County Record Offices, Diocesan records and Cathedral Archives are rich mines of information about people, parishes and church buildings. The searching out of personal family origins and links is of growing interest, and an institution such as St. Gregory's Church is quite frequently approached for information.

The Church has its own system whereby Registers have been kept of Baptisms, Marriages and Burials solemnised in each Parish. These are of historical, personal and social importance, and are much used today in family and legal matters. In St. Gregory's Parish our earliest entries are for Burials (1627) and Baptisms (1652). These are in addition to the established practice of the keeping of accounts, the minutes of Parochial Church Council meetings and Churchwardens' business. In the church we keep a plan of the burial plots in the churchyard, and an alphabetical list of names and dates of those buried there.

Although many local church documents were lost or destroyed, especially after the Reformation, (and sometimes indeed, records were not properly kept), it remains true that most record keeping was taken very seriously. Much contemporary writing remains to give us lively pictures of the past in village and Church life, and names were preserved. These documents enable us to feel our kinship with so many who have worshipped in this place. And we should be glad that today's registers and accounts of *our own* decisions and feelings will be accessible in future years.

*Publicly visible records on the walls of St. Gregory's church*

Mention should be made of some of the wall tablets now preserved *inside* the building. We have in the nave a number of memorials to people who died in the 19th century and who came from other parts of the country. This indicates the popularity of Dawlish as a resort, and then a desirable place of residence, after the coming of the turnpike roads and the railway in the 1800s.

There are two marble tablets made by celebrated sculptor John Flaxman (1775-1826), given in memory of Elizabeth Pennyman, (the builder of 'The Rise'), who died in 1801, and Frances Mary Hunter (d.1805). The oldest tablet we have is now mounted on the south wall of the Lady Chapel. It gives thanks for the Reverend John Trosse, Vicar of Dawlish, who died in 1678, and his son Francis who died in 1674. In the north transept we learn of John Schank (1740-1823) who had a notable career in the Royal Navy, and of Sir William Grant (1755-1832) who was Master of the Rolls for 16 years from 1801. These memorials have all been relocated during the rebuilding of the nave walls and arcades in 1825, the construction of the Chancel and transepts in 1875, the final removal of the galleries in 1897, and the changes to the west end in 1981 when the Narthex was made.

*The War memorials:  "We will remember them"*

It is fitting that we pay tribute to those who, in two World Wars in the 20th century, and in further conflicts since then, have given their lives to preserve our freedom. Their names are inscribed on the granite War Memorial in the garden adjacent to the church. Here, many of the people of Dawlish assemble on Remembrance Sunday, to lay wreaths, to remember with gratitude and to pray for peace. Inside the church we have a Remembrance plaque on the north wall of the north transept, beside which are laid up the flag of the Dawlish branch of The British Legion, together with that of our local branch of The Royal Air Force Association.

*References for research purposes*

Our Victorian forbears had what sometimes seems to be a morbid interest in funerary monuments and such things; their descriptions of St. Gregory's church had long lists of wall tablets which many of us find tedious now, but for those carrying out research these lists can be located as follows:

(1) In the West Country Studies Library, Castle Street, Exeter:

Davidson, The Revd. James. After visiting many Devon churches he wrote a book in about 1846 and it contains an account of his visit to St. Gregory's Church, Dawlish on July 6th 1846. There is a list (occupying five A4 sheets of typescript!) of all the then wall tablets in the 1825 building.

Carter, F.J. "Notes on Old Dawlish, 1588-1850"
        First published 1938, also later as:
      (Dawlish Museum Society Publications No.1 1976)

*Old Guides to Dawlish Parish Church:* several are available for scrutiny. They are based on Davidson's account. The most recent *Guide to the Parish Church of St. Gregory, Dawlish (1981)* and its updating slip (1984) were compiled by Dr. Chris Penn and R.W. Hill, using the work of Lt. Col. Theo Lloyd who sadly died before his carefully researched writing could be published. There are many copies of this Guide on sale in the church foyer.

(2) The Devon County Record Office has recently been re-housed in a new, air-conditioned building on the edge of Exeter. Here are stored original documents as well as microfiche copies of Parish registers, accounts, correspondence and minutes of official meetings, and a great deal more besides! Exeter Cathedral archives are now preserved here. A Research Service which will, for a fee, trace and copy records for you, is also available. Go to,

or apply to: The Devon Record Office, Great Moor House, Bittern Road, Sowton, Exeter. EX2 7NL).

*Our ancient churchyard and burial ground*

It is probably the case that our burial ground is older than the succession of buildings for worship. Maybe it was already used as a sacred burial place before the coming of Christianity. Throughout the Saxon, Norman and Mediaeval periods, and during and after the changeful years of the Reformation as well as of the Commonwealth and Restoration of the Monarchy, this was the only burial ground in the township and the wider Parish. It was also the locus for many activities on the part of the living, as we saw earlier.

Mr. F. J. Carter writes thus in 1938:
"The old churchyard was of much less extent than at present. It was originally enclosed by thorn hedges except on the east side where it abutted on the tithe barn and the houses near the east gate. These hedges were a constant cause of trouble and expense: '1607. Pd. for that the churchwardens were cited because swyne hoggs were in the churchyard. Vjs ijd  (6s and 2p)'.

"It was not until 1822 that the west churchyard wall was built, and in 1824 the north wall (alongside the mill leat).

"There was a very celebrated double row of elm trees in the churchyard, remarked upon by all the old writers about the church. That they were of some antiquity may be inferred from the following extract from the parish accounts:
'1588-89. Paid to John More for makynge of the bynch (bench) aboute the elme in the churchyard. Vjd (6 pence)'.
"Some of the elms were removed at the re-building of 1824, and more in 1873.

"There were originally three gates to the churchyard, of which the east one was a lychgate with a stone or tiled roof and provided with a stile. This old gate dated back many years, but was removed in 1824 on the extension of the churchyard. It was replaced by an iron gate between two octagonal pillars, and part of the new boundary...consisted of iron railings. The north gate was a wicket gate, and the south gate what was then known as a trap stile, which stood originally much nearer the church than at present". (*Author's note:* it is preserved to this day as the 'kissing gate', beside the tall iron gates which allowed better access for wide skirts, invalid chairs, or family groups; and maybe egress for funeral parties and the hearse on the way to the new cemetery in Oakhill).

*Marking the Graves*

It was during the 17$^{th}$ century that the provision of long-lasting headstones became customary; before then, the ordinary parishioner's resting place might have a simple wooden cross or board which had disappeared in a generation or two. As the ground in the relatively small churchyard became used up, the usual practice was to inter mortal remains *on top of* older burials. So the ground level gradually rose over the centuries, especially on the favoured south side of the church. As you enter our churchyard from the town (east) end, you will see this higher level on your left hand side. North of the building (in the shadow cast by the walls), the ground is three or four feet lower.

Today we have in the churchyard an array of gravestones, many of which are gently becoming very difficult to decipher. Yes, they have social and historical value, but of equal importance to me is the knowledge that those there laid to rest are members of our own fellowship of Christians in Dawlish. Men, women and children like us today, of varying fortunes and opportunities and abilities.

In the grassy plots we have stones commemorating prominent citizens and their families, while others tell tragic stories of the prevalence of infant and maternal mortality, and of early deaths in battles on land and at sea. I'm told that there are, by the west wall, the graves of French prisoners taken during the

Napoleonic Wars, while nearby, the headstone of Commander William Pye R.N. marks the final resting place of a Trafalgar veteran. Some members of the old Devon sea-faring family, the Frobishers, are here. Many stones recall various ordinary, but fairly well-to-do families, whose names (such as Tripe, Cole and Beard) appear in older churchwardens accounts, and who obviously gave long and faithful service to the Church.

In the south-west corner is the Mausoleum, (designed by Sir George Gilbert Scott), of the Hoare family of Luscombe Castle. The family's generous support of the church has already been noted. This 'private', walled off burial plot is tended by the family. An ecclesiastical faculty (permission) grants them the right to lie there undisturbed. Within the churchyard walls of course, for they are part of our Dawlish Church family.

Two of the oldest gravestones are now mounted on the outside south wall of the church, near the east gate. Gilbert Clapp (1663-1733) was a "Master Mate of seven ships of war", and his wife Avis died in 1731 at the age of 65, a good age for those days. She was much loved and her stone is inscribed thus:

> "And she that here hath left this life
> was a tender mother and a vertuous wife"

If you are interested in finding a particular grave, you will be glad to know that in the late 1980s the Council for Christian Care, in Exeter, employed a group of young people to research and list the graves in this churchyard. In addition to the plan kept in the church, a copy is held by Dr. Christopher Penn of Teignmouth. To trace a grave in the 'new' Dawlish cemetery farther up Oak Hill, you need to telephone the Teignbridge Parks and Cemeteries Department, whose current telephone number is 01626 361101.

*"And some there be which have no memorial......"*

The most carefully compiled registers and family trees are likely to be incomplete, for all kinds of reasons. As travel, and marriage beyond the immediate social circle of acquaintances became more frequent, so was it more possible for someone to 'disappear' and be lost from the records of family or State. For whatever reason: unforeseen happenings, or intentional 'escape' from burdensome reality, or sadly, uncaring neglect resulting in a lonely death, there are many people whose names *we* have lost and forgotten, who lie in unmarked graves somewhere. There must be some of them in nearly every churchyard, because it was, for a long time, the 'right' of a person who died within the parish boundary, to be buried in the churchyard there.

As Christians, we do not believe that, for those who have no memorial,......*"they are perished as though they had never been"*, (Ecclesiasticus 44 v 9), but rather that *"...the souls of the righteous are in the hand of God......they are at peace".* (The Wisdom of Solomon 3 vv 1and 3).

During the Prayers of the People in the Liturgy of Holy Communion, we remember before God "...those who have died in the faith of Christ", often adding "and those whose faith is known only to God", and we pray "...grant us, with them, a share in your eternal kingdom". *We* cannot name more than a small number, but we believe that *all* are called by name by the all-knowing Father, and that they remain in his loving care. They are all in *His* complete records.

*Extending the churchyard*

As the population of Dawlish increased, it was not only the provision of seating in the church that became inadequate, but also the availability of places where the dead could lie peacefully in the churchyard.

Because it was the only burial place in the town, people of all denominations were interred there. Marked with an obelisk is the grave of the Reverend Ebeneezer Pardon who laid the foundation stone of the Methodist church in Brunswick Place. Mr.Pardon's sister-and brother-in-law Mary and William McDiarmid, benefactors of the Methodist cause, lie close by. That was all very right and good, and done with the approval of the resident priest. (This 'permission' was needed after the Vestry, getting very anxious about the shortage of burial plots, had in 1797, passed a minute saying that "It's the request of the Parishioners that no stranger be admitted to be buryed in the Church from this Day". This was duly challenged, and 'strangers' memorials continued to be placed in the church and graveyard).

The graveyard was slightly enlarged in 1825. This did not solve the problems engendered by the increasing population, the growing numbers of members of other denominations, and the deaths from a number of disease epidemics. In 1852, parishes had been empowered to elect Burial Boards for the maintenance of local cemeteries. By 1882, the Dawlish Board had purchased land on Oak Hill for the new cemetery to serve the whole area. It was consecrated on March 22$^{nd}$ 1884, and in that same month the graveyard around St. Gregory's church was closed to burials.

It remains a very special place. A Garden of Remembrance has been set out, where the Interment of Ashes after Cremation is permitted. The old public 'right of way' through this parish land gives many local residents and visitors a pleasant walk around the church, to cross the old mill leat and on to the streamside paths and the Newhay meadow. We are glad we all share this amenity. A usual meeting place for high-spirited and amorous young people was indeed the churchyard for centuries (we still have a 'kissing gate'), but sadly there is today, too much thoughtless behaviour in the form of litter and vandalism which costs us, the guardians of this parish possession, a lot in terms of labour and money.

*The Churchyard is full of Life!*

For those who enjoy birdsong and trees and flowers, and who savour the scents and colour which attract butterflies, bees and many other amazing insects and other wild creatures, the churchyard is a little haven of interest and delight. You will find articles on the wildlife here, (another facet of our recorded history), in an appendix at the end of this book.

## Giving thanks and remembering

All over *inside* our present building are plaques telling about additions to the fabric made possible by special donations. These brass plates are tucked away and are not obvious to the hurried visitor. Most are left unpolished and are hard to read, but in the windows to which some refer, you can read the main messages. Many of the individual gifts are tokens of the affection of families for their church, for their loved ones, and in appreciation of people whom they felt had been particularly significant in the story of the Church in this place. We have inherited some beautiful things, and it is good to be thankful for those who were able to contribute in these ways. After a search, (sometimes on hands and knees!), I now offer a more easily scrutinised record of some of these items.

Firstly, at the steps leading up from the nave into the chancel, brass handrails have been fitted, and decorative open brasswork on the low 'screen' walls. These were given in addition to the most important contribution, the handsome Lectern which stands to the right, in the 'crossing' area. A plaque on the base of the screen nearby records these gifts:

"To the glory of God and in loving memory of Charlotte Dick. This brasswork and lectern were presented to the church by parishioners and friends. 1889".

Next we can move into the Lady Chapel to the open doorway into the Chancel near to the steps up to the High Altar. At the base of the stone pillar by this doorway you may read:
"This stone was laid on May 28 1874 by Peter Rd. Hoare Esquire of Luscombe, lay Rector.  Rev. Orlando Manley, Vicar.
William Tapper and Francis Lee Church Wardens".
This is the foundation stone for the new parts of the building set out during 1873-5.

It was the intention, in 1875, to build a screen between the choir stalls (in the chancel) and the south aisle, thus converting the eastern part of the south aisle into the chapel which has become the Lady Chapel. For some reason the builders did not complete the screen which was itemised in the contract. A brief word in the press report merely states that "The only parts of the works of the original design not carried out are the *iron grills* in the side arcades of the chancel". The present *woodwork screen* was put in place in 1916, when the following was carved on it:

"To the glory of God these screens were erected in loving memory of Sir Edward Wills, Baronet K.C.B. by his daughter Violet Edith Wills. ANNO SALUTIS 1916".

Further panelling on the south wall of the Lady Chapel was added in 1926, in memory of:

"Jane Bush Alford who was a regular worshipper in this place".

(The Reverend William Powell Alford was the Vicar from 1895 to 1917. The small window south of the Altar, allowing plain daylight to illuminate the Sanctuary, was named in his honour as late as in 1953. This family expressed continuing affection for the church of St. Gregory).

In the *south transept*, in the part now used as the Memorial corner:
"This carpet was given in loving memory of
Dr. Robert Arthur Sammons, who died February 14 1978"

The display case made to house the Book of Remembrance in the same area is inscribed:
"In loving memory of Winifred Joan Page
who died 31$^{st}$ July 1977"

The memorial Candle stand against the pillar at the entrance to the south transept reminds us of a much loved Server, Ben Paul. To light a candle as a symbol of prayers offered for the well-being and peace of loved ones, has continued to be an act which brings relief and strength to many churchgoers. The inscription on the stand reads thus:

"Dedicated to the memory of Benjamin Arthur Paul
5$^{th}$ Jan 1927 – 27$^{th}$ June 2000
from his daughters Celia Louise Maddona Sandra
Intro-Ibo ad Altari Dei"

Then there are various oak 'ecclesiastical' chairs, used in the Sanctuary, the Lady Chapel and near the recent Nave Altar. Two of these came from St.Mark's church and bear its name on the arms, while a large and very heavy one is used as the Bishop's chair, on which he sits during Services of Confirmation and when a new priest is installed. Another oak chair is inscribed:
"In memoriam
The Rev. F. W. Barrows M.A.
1861-1934"

These gifts are but examples of the continuing generosity of loving and loyal parishioners. Special they may be, and welcome, but apart from such bequests and specific money-raising efforts, *the upkeep of the Church and its building is in the hands of those who solemnly undertake to provide funds to maintain its worship and work by regular, dedicated giving from their income.*

# CHAPTER NINETEEN

## *TOWARDS THE PRESENT DAY*

With the installation of the Transfiguration window in the Lady Chapel in 1885, which gave thanks for the life and ministry of Orlando Manley, and following the inauguration of the new organ and choir, we might think that the congregation would have been content to rest and recuperate! But the later Victorians were alert to changing possibilities and desirable improvements. They didn't sit still for long!

Year after year, new features and decorations were added in the chancel and crossing areas: the Lectern in 1889 (see p.114), the pulpit, of carved Bath stone in 1890, although the nine sculptured figures of Old and New Testament characters were not yet ready. They took their places in the prepared niches, in 1902. (see p.115). The last ten years of the $19^{th}$ century were marked by almost continuous work on the fabric and furnishing of the building. Most striking was the dismantling of the huge galleries.

*Let there be Light!*

For the building was still dark and overloaded by the remaining sections of the north and south galleries, which were not much used by then. So plans were laid to remove them altogether, and this immense task was completed 1895-7. What a tremendous upset this was to the normal activities in the building! Perhaps the congregation joined with people worshipping in St. Mark's church for a while.

The cost of this work was defrayed by a single generous donor who wished to remain anonymous. We give thanks for the giver, and for his or her artistic sensibility, devoted to beauty in worship.

When the galleries were gone, there was general pleasure in the improved appearance of the whole building. An article in the Parish Magazine read thus:

"The removal of the galleries was generally acknowledged to be a greater improvement than could have been anticipated. There was more light, more air and space, which gave dignity to the whole building; and the pillars, though somewhat slender according to their period, are thrown up by the removal of the ponderous galleries which (had) destroyed any grace they had".

Inevitably the next move was an extensive interior redecoration. Illumination for evening services was provided by a series of graceful branched light holders mounted on twisted brass standards. I have a rather poor picture of these, taken after 1902, but I cannot tell whether the lights were candles, gas jets or very early electric bulbs. (Probably candles at this date). We certainly did have gas piped into the building, for the old fittings and pipes for gas lights can still be seen on the walls of the Lady Chapel. They had lasted for some 25 years. Barton Villas, Terrace, and Crescent, very near to the church, were still lit by gas street lamps in 1906. Electric lighting was soon to be installed in all public places, including the church.

All this work being completed, there was, in 1899, a grand re-opening ceremony. An illuminated scroll was produced to mark the celebration, but this does not seem to have been preserved.

*Royal Celebrations marked by a loyal Parish*

The approach of the end of the century coincided with nationally important happenings which affected us all: life was not dull during these times.

1897 saw the whole nation celebrating Queen Victoria's Diamond Jubilee. Sixty years a Queen, and many were the street parties and special commemorative events and projects to mark such an outstanding reign. Among the Dawlish happenings was the renovation of the tower of St. Gregory's church. The lovely red stonework, dating from 1400, was cleaned and carefully re-pointed. The spiral staircase, giving access to the belfry and the roof, was repaired and made safe again. (The lead sheeting on the roof of the tower had already been removed, melted down and re-laid and stamped with the year date, in 1879).

We joined in mourning when Queen Victoria died in 1901, and on the death of King Edward V11 in 1910.

*Bells to celebrate a New Monarch*

To commemorate the Coronation of King George the Fifth in 1911, our peal of six bells was enlarged by the addition of two new bells. This brought the ring up to the present peal of eight. The rearrangement would have entailed cleaning, tuning and re-hanging all the bells. Apart from the enforced silences during two world wars, the art of bell-ringing has not faltered, and is attracting new young ringers to this day. We should pay tribute to Tower Captains, and the teams of faithful and skilled ringers and learners. Without their keenness and patience this art would be lost. Long may it continue! The ring of bells in St. Gregory's tower is well known all over the county, and we welcome a number of teams of visiting ringers.

Over the small arched doorway giving access to the tower, there is a carved wooden panel which reads:

"In memory of George Henry Marchant
for over 65 years a ringer in this church
who died November 8$^{th}$ 1947, aged 86.

"Ring out the old, ring in the new
Ring out the false, ring in the true"

I think George must have been brother to the Fred Marchant who made the organ case and swell box in 1888. They were a local family of carpenters, and it is interesting to see that the memorial to George is of good carved wood rather than of marble.

## The bell of "Peace and Good Neighbourhood"

Early in the 20th century, Beatrix Cresswell made a survey of the churches in the Kenn Deanery. Her published 'Notes' (1912) include comments on the peal of six bells in St. Gregory's tower, which had been recast by Pennington in 1784:

"The first three have inscriptions:

"Peace and good neighbourhood. IPCP 1784";

"Richard Whidbourne and John Paddon, Churchwardens IPCP 1784"; and,

"Thomas Prowse, Vicar, Richard Inglett Fortesque Esq. IPCP 1784".

(I think the letters IPCP must be the initials of the head of the firm of Pennington).

I do not know which of the bells carried the peace message; perhaps the ringers do? Every time the bells were rung, this message was sent out all over our beloved town and countryside!

## The Tragedy of the First World War

But alas, within three years of the installation of the new, and the restored bells, our country was at war. Dawlish families saw their younger menfolk leave to fight for King and Country. They were followed by both men and women who worked in the various supporting services. Many of them would never return. When peace was declared in 1918, Dawlish joined with the rest of the country in mourning its dead, and in making preparations to honour them. Church land was set aside for the War Memorial and garden (see page 170). At the opening of the garden and dedication of the inscribed granite cross, on February 19 1921, there was a great procession from all parts of the parish. Then, led by the Vicar, The Reverend Frank Simmons, the Service of Remembrance brought together people of all denominations and organisations in the area. It opened with Charles Wesley's hymn:

> "Let saints on earth in concert sing
> with those whose work is done;
> For all the servants of our King
> in heaven and earth are one."

Inside the church, on the windowsill nearest to the altar in the Lady Chapel, there is a memorial plaque in honour of a father and two sons, who must have been among the very earliest casualties in the war. It is inscribed thus:

> "To the Glory of God and in memory of
> Captain G.A.Browning and his two sons Kendal and Hamilton
> The Altar rails and prayer desk
> are given by his wife and sons. All Saints' Day 1914

Two years later, the screen dividing the chancel from the Lady Chapel was completed at last. This is the Wills Memorial, made in 1916. On the south wall, matching panelling was fitted in 1926 as part of the Alford family tribute (see p.178, and below).

*Reviving devotion to our original Patron Saint*

Since about 1860, the church had become known as 'St. Michael's', though nobody is quite sure why the change from the first dedication to St.Gregory the Great, came about. (The author's thoughts on this are set down on p.136).

In 1924, the Vicar, The Reverend Frank Simmons, having considered the history of the Parish and consulted the lay representatives and the Diocesan authorities, offered to hold a Re-dedication Service. This move met with general approval.

The Western Morning News reported, under the heading "Mistaken Dedication", that:

"The Rev. F. Simmons preached and stated that for 60-70 years the dedication was said to be St. Michael, but proof of the original dedication to St. Gregory should now be recognised.
A service to mark this was held on Wednesday, on St. Gregory's Day." (1924)

We kept St.Michael in his niche on the sixth pillar of the north arcade. It was given in 1902 when he was regarded as our Patron Saint. The vicar of Dawlish is, by long established pattern, also the patron of St. Michael's Church in Teignmouth, and the link is meaningful.

*The Feast of St. Gregory*

This is set on March 12 in the Ecclesiastical calendar; in recent years we have tended to celebrate his life on September 3, the date of his 'translation', that is, of his being made Pope. In the chancel, we have a woven and embroidered banner displayed. This is carried in procession on special Deanery and Diocesan occasions and at the annual Patronal Festival. It bears the inscription: "Servus servorum Dei", (Servant of the servants of God), which was how he chose to be styled. We should continue to honour him for his urgent desire to spread the Christian faith to distant lands, a zeal that made possible the founding of our Church here in Dawlish. We have weathered many changes during our long existence, but in company with Saint Gregory, we know that "The Church's one foundation is Jesus Christ her Lord".

At the end of our Prayers of Intercession, we may use this form from "Common Worship":

"Rejoicing in the fellowship of St. Gregory and all your saints, we commend ourselves and the whole creation to your unfailing love"

Continuing a very old tradition, we have a statuette of St. Gregory, not on the Altar as in former times, but set on the south pillar of the chancel arch. It is Italian work and was given to the church in 1961. When first acquired, its colours were rather gaudy, but it has now mellowed to more gentle tones. I hope nobody will attempt an inappropriate repainting.

*A Second World War*

George Stanley Trewin became our Vicar in 1936 and bore with us the anxieties, hardships, terrors and griefs of the war years (1939-1945). Every town and city in our land has its own precious records made by local people detailing their experiences and feelings.

In Dawlish many names were added to a new plaque on the War memorial. Sadly, other names are still being added as members of Her Majesty's Armed Forces continue to fight for peace and stability in the world. I understand that the current Mayor of Dawlish, The Rev. Dr Thomas (Tom) E.C. Bush, is to make his 'special' work for the town this year (2006-7), the addition of an appropriate plaque gathering up the names of more recent casualties. We will remember them: men and women who went in our name to try to bring stable and just government to troubled people and places.

*The Limitations accepted by this Author.*

I did not come to live in Dawlish until 1991, (though my father, The Reverend Frank Quick M.A., a Congregationalist Minister, was born here in 1896). So I have some roots here, but I do not, and cannot, know the personal stories of local families and happenings, in the same lively and detailed way as do many of those who have been here for much of their lives. As I approach more modern times, I recognise the fact that there is a great wealth of information about which I am not competent to write. And the hope I treasure is that other Dawlish people will want to add to the store of knowledge that is already being built up by individuals, and organisations such as the Dawlish Local History Group, and Dawlish Museum. All who contribute in writing and speaking and in the collections of pictures and sound recordings, are making a valued contribution to a personalised and interesting record of this community. This will be stored for the use of future friends who come to live here, and who may want to make 'real' and accessible, the links that join us all together over many generations. Perhaps some of my readers will see their way towards enriching the 'archives of Dawlish'. After all, the writing of this story of our Church has been possible only because of the availability of carefully kept records.

What this implies is that I have decided to limit the rest of *my* story of 'The Church in This Place', to a brief chronicle of the changes which were made in respect of St.Mark's Church, and the structural alterations within the St.Gregory's building in the years since 1945. But first, a word in recognition of our benefactors.

*In appreciation of our Benefactors*

We have seen much in our building which acknowledges our many benefactors. The dedicatory plaques, almost without exception, bear the words: *"To the Glory of God......and in memory of......"* There is an essential 'rightness' about this sequence in the wording, and we give thanks for both the proper devotion, and for the material generosity on the part of the donors. Both help us to be thankful for the lives of those who give, and of those who are thus commemorated.

We remember the long continued support which has been give by the Hoare Family of Luscombe Castle, extending over several generations. Charles Hoare bought Luscombe farm in about 1786 and added to its land, to form the present Luscombe Estate. Their careful land ownership and use, has preserved much of west Dawlish from becoming over-developed. Some land was provided for the new cemetery in 1882, and some was leased for a West Cliff area housing estate (where the author now lives and enjoys the splendid view across the estate to the top of Little Haldon Hill and the whole catchment area of Dawlish Water). The major part of Luscombe Estate remains an area of well tended fields and woodland whose seasonally changing colours and growth give delight to all Dawlish residents as we look inland.

St. Mark's Church was endowed by the Charles Hoare of another generation, in 1851. In addition, several large monetary gifts have helped the programmes for the major alterations to St.Gregory's building to proceed smoothly. The friendly relationship has been expressed in several pleasant and less formal gestures: a large Christmas tree, supplied for the church every year, from the Estate, and a brace of pheasants hung on the door of the vicarage as Christmastide approached; St. Gregory's choir invited to sing in Luscombe Castle chapel, and the Vicar to officiate there at a family Marriage Service. The Castle is opened on several occasions each year, particularly for helping local and national Charities. It is a pleasure to be invited to visit and to enjoy the garden.

In 1948, Sir Peter Hoare Bt. gave to the church a silver Altar Cross and Candlesticks. Sadly, these were stolen, then found in a country lane hedge. Someone, perhaps with fearful regret, had abandoned them. The Cross was irreparably damaged, but we still have the candlesticks in our care.

*Maintenance and Renovation work after 1950*

We all needed a time of recovery and refreshment after the war years, and this was true also for church premises and fabric. In 1949, a complete re-decoration of the interior of the building was carried out. The following year the tower bells and frames were subject to a detailed inspection, and some necessary repairs completed. Then it was the turn of the pipe organ. The firm of organ builders, Willis & Co., made changes in the position of some pipes, and added to the 'Great' organ section to increase its power and brilliance. Over the next few years we were treated to some fine recitals by famous organists (see p. 161).

Then we were saddened by the decline in health, and the early death in 1952, of King George the Sixth. Our sense of loss was followed duly by widespread expressions of loyalty to our young Queen Elizabeth the Second.

Within the Sanctuary of the church building, a two-light plain window allows extra daylight to fall upon the high Altar from the south side. At the foot of the window is a stained glass strip telling us that it was dedicated in 1953, the year of the Coronation of Queen Elizabeth the Second. It also bids us remember the life and ministry of The Reverend William Powell Alford, Vicar from 1895-1916. Mrs. Alford had given money for the installation in the church, in 1938, of a new electric light system: this gift is also recorded as being in memory of her husband.

*Trying to make the best use of our resources*

In the early 1970s, it was becoming increasingly obvious that the parish of Dawlish could not continue to support a church additional to the parish church. Major structural repairs to the St. Mark's building were pending. After long and intense discussion and consultation, the decision was reluctantly taken to close St. Mark's, our Chapel of Ease in Brunswick Place. The building was demolished in 1975 and the site sold for re-development.

A much loved and highly regarded Deaconess Bunce who died in the 1950s had been honoured by the interment of her ashes within the church building. Before demolition workers could begin their task, this good lady's remains had to be moved, and they were re-buried near the southeast door of St. Gregory's church, and a commemorative stone slab marks the place.

*Ongoing reminders of St.Mark's Church*

Although the name is perpetuated in the title of the new building on the former church site, 'St. Mark's Flats' is a completely independent business concern. In the courtyard through the access arch, you can see the fine stone work shoring up the near vertical terrace wall which was behind the church.

When St. Mark's church building was taken down, stone by carefully shaped stone, various firms and individuals acquired the material piecemeal. A few former members still treasure bits of the fabric, and some is on display in Dawlish Museum. Of the interior fittings, some items were transferred to St. Gregory's church. These include oak chairs used by the servers and visiting preachers, also a pair of fine brass candelabra which were set on the High Altar in St. Mark's, and now in St. Gregory's, to give visible Glory to God and to remind us of Christ the Light of the World. These had been given in memory of a faithful St. Mark's churchwarden, and are so inscribed. Members who had previously worshipped in St. Mark's treasure this link and the combining of sacred, meaningful material resources as the two congregations melded together.

I understand that the priestly vestments were made available on a 'loan' basis, to Manaton Church on Dartmoor, but I have not been able to trace the whereabouts of the Font or the Communion Table or the Communion Plate. The two-manual pipe organ travelled into Cornwall, to a church in the Falmouth area, and the belfry carillon found a home in the United Reformed Church steeple across the Dawlish Lawn.

A contribution to the Booklet produced to mark the 60th Anniversary (in 2005) of the Consecration of St. George's Church, Holcombe (within the parish of St. Gregory's), records that "the actual choir seats have been rescued from the demolition of St. Mark's Church in Dawlish".

The link here is with the lovely and ancient village in the next valley, and its Church which was accorded "District Church status, within the Parish of Dawlish", in the 1990s. The delightful booklet describing the story of this happy and devoted congregation, its building and its place in the life of the village, continues to be available at that church. It is a pleasure and a privilege to go to worship there sometimes.

*Using the proceeds of the sale of the valuable St. Mark's site*

"It was agreed that part of the proceeds of the sale would be made available to the parish for essential capital works in the future. The existing parish room, in Old Town Street, had many deficiencies in its role as the educational and social centre of the parish...... Many plans were accordingly examined for a new parish centre, to be built adjacent to the church (St. Gregory's). But the very high cost of building in stone, and of running a separate building, precluded this approach. It was then investigated and found feasible to create the necessary facilities, using little-used space within the actual fabric of the church.

"In this way we are able to meet the growing needs and demands of the Christian family who worship at St. Gregory's, but in addition provide a meeting and activities centre for our organisations. The development provides a much needed reception area where the exchange of those very necessary social courtesies can take place, both before and after services, without disturbing the devotions of those within the church. These facilities also improve the comfort of all those who use the church on other occasions......weddings or funerals, (and) those special services of thanksgiving or remembrance when the whole community turns to the Parish church, or when the church is in use for concerts or other performances of the arts."

This quotation is taken from the up-dating slip added to the St. Gregory's church brochure in 1984, by Dr. Christopher Penn, so that visitors and 'regulars' could study the building and its furnishings accurately after the changes.

*The Narthex Development: an old practice up-dated.*

The quite large spaces brought into new use by the bold internal structural changes, became known as 'The Narthex'.

This a term used in the early Church to signify a porch or vestibule extending across the width of the nave at the opposite end from the Altar. In that space, in those long ago days, new seekers, and those under instruction and perhaps not yet ready to partake of the Elements in Holy Communion, could watch and join in the early parts of the Liturgy *only*. They were required to leave the building before the Consecration of the Elements, but would certainly have received a Blessing.

Whatever good reasons made that rule desirable *then,* we do not follow such a restrictive practice now. Everyone who wishes to do so may occupy a seat in the nave itself, and hear and watch and be open to the impact of the full Liturgy. The Celebration of Holy Communion is not at all like the exclusive ritual of a secret society (many of which existed in the days of the early Church). For nowadays, any "Baptised persons who are communicant members of other Churches which subscribe to the doctrine of the Holy Trinity, and are in good standing in their own Church" are welcome to partake of the Bread and Wine offered at the Table of Our Lord, here. It is the privilege and pleasure of the local congregation to be joined at the Table by fellow Christians from elsewhere. Any child or adult who is moved to do so, is invited, unconditionally, to come to the Table with the full communicants, to receive an individual Blessing.

Today our new narthex is not used as a means of shutting people out, but of welcoming them in! The purpose of the rooms in the upper and lower narthex is the provision of space for use in getting to know newcomers, and sharing in what they offer us by who they are, and what are their own experiences. When we use these rooms to offer instruction in the Christian faith, we enrich our own understanding and strengthen our own commitment. We are being drawn together as fellow pilgrims within the fellowship of St. Gregory's Church in the 20$^{th}$ and 21$^{st}$ centuries. The use of the narthex in these ways continues, opens up and widens the purpose of the early Church provision. So with this understanding of the word *narthex,* the choice of the name was a happy one. So what was involved in the practical implementation of this plan?

*The Structural changes*

     The first bay of the west end of the nave is now closed off by a full height glass screen, above and continuous with a lower wall with access doors to the main worship area. This one-bay-deep space, together with the way into the building through the tower, gives at ground level, good room for reception and greetings, small group Friendship meetings, a Mother and Toddler session on a weekday, a coffee bar, toilets, church office, notice boards and stairway to the next floor. Up there, a soundproofed (nearly!) meeting room commands a splendid view, through the glass screen, of the whole of the nave and chancel. Here, children can have a story and teaching activities during part of the Parish Communion service, before rejoining parents and friends and coming to the altar for a Blessing. Here on a weekday, the larger committees can meet conveniently, the Mothers' Union members gather, as do the St. Gregory's Art group and the various Youth Groups.

     There is room here too, for lectures, gatherings for study and preparation for outreach, for ventures such as the Alpha Courses. The new floor extends into the tower space (where there are comfortable armchairs), and also into a fitted kitchen where clever Catering Committee members and helpers can prepare hot meals for up to 60 people seated in the main room. Coffee and refreshments may be arranged here for those who have travelled for weddings and funerals, and in the intervals during concerts. Every Sunday this room is used for coffee after the Parish Communion Service: a good chance to be with others to share news and views.

     If you look up when in the tower space of this upper room, you will see a fine timberwork ceiling. Above this is the bell-ringers chamber, and above this again, the bell-chamber. Until 1984 the bells were rung from the ground level of the tower. I am told that there was a wooden screen in the north porch, which was moved in 1961 to become the 'tower screen' which partitioned off the ringers from the assembling congregation who, at that time, came in through the south porch, and not, as now, through the west door in the tower. To see and meet the bell-ringers now, you must needs ascend the spiral staircase during rehearsal or ringing times: you will be made welcome for your interested support.

On the south wall of the tower, at the entrance to the ground floor of the narthex is a tablet marking the dedication of all the new work:

> This Narthex was dedicated by
> The Right Reverend Eric Mercer
> Lord Bishop of Exeter
> May 29th 1984
>
> Robin Taylor, Vicar
> William Bryant. Derick Elson. Churchwardens
> Michael Ford. Architect.

*The Royal Arms*

On the new screen, facing into the nave, is our interesting Royal Arms. The practice of setting up the Royal Arms dates from the Reformation, recognising the sovereign as a monarch both spiritual and temporal. It was re-emphasised under Elizabeth I and at the Restoration of the monarchy in 1660 (James I), and again with the Hanoverian succession in 1714. Students of heraldry will note that at that date, the arms of the Elector of Hanover were super-imposed in an escutcheon ensigned with the Electoral Bonnet, on the shield of the Royal Arms. In 1816, however, Hanover became a kingdom, and the bonnet was replaced with a crown. As no woman could succeed to the throne of Hanover, the link with the British crown ceased in 1837 with the accession of Queen Victoria. This coat of arms is therefore somewhat of a rarity since it dates from between 1816 and 1837. When the old galleries were removed from the church, the Arms were installed above the Bench in the Vestry Hall (Central Hall) where the Petty Sessions were held; they were eventually returned to the church after World War Two, when the Vestry Hall was sold, and the Sessions were moved to the new Council Chamber in the manor house. (These facts were compiled by Lt. Col. Theo Lloyd T.D., and confirmed by Mr. Jack Batten).

*Moving the Font*

We saw that the narthex development involved a lot of re-location, and it was not only at the west end of the church. The proposed cutting off of the first bay by the full height screen would result in the Font being left outside the main worship area. Although it meant that we lost the visible symbolic link made by seeing the Font as we *entered* the building, (which reminds us that it is by receiving the Sacrament of Baptism that we *enter* and become members of the world-wide Church), it felt right to seek, and to accept, permission to move the Font into the north transept. It was most carefully set there in the correct orientation. The Vicar, The Reverend Robin Taylor, supervised the move, insisting that meticulous precision was necessary. (see p.133).

In this location, the Font can be seen by much of the congregation, throughout Services of Worship. When Baptism is administered during the Parish Communion Service, everyone present takes part in confession and cleansing, profession of our Faith, and in the promises of commitment to helping the child or adult to grow in grace. There is also room for members of the family and more of the congregation to gather around the Font, the better to witness and appreciate in detail, the actions of the presiding priest. On a lighter note, the plug in the Font has had to be sealed into its drain hole because the runaway into the old well was not re-established! From that time onwards, the consecrated water has had to be carried out in a vessel, and so returned to the good earth of the churchyard, where, in truth, the story of *The Church in This Place* had its beginning.

# CHAPTER TWENTY

## *AT THE END OF THE SECOND MILLENNIUM*

"Peace on the earth, goodwill to men
From heaven's all-gracious King......

Yet with the woes of sin and strife
The world has suffered long
Beneath the angel-strain have rolled
Two thousand years of wrong;
And man, at war with man, hears not
The love song which they bring:
O hush the noise ye men of strife,
And hear the angels sing".

Edmund Hamilton Sears, 1810-1876.

The latter part of the 20th century saw the pace and complexity of daily life increase to a point such that it has become hard to maintain a measure of peace and quiet. The eternal quest for a 'philosophy of life'— (What does it all mean? Why is there pain and unhappiness? What makes a good society?)- is seemingly abandoned by many people who allow themselves to be driven by relentless commercial pressures, and the demands of those who see wealth and 'instant gratification' as the key to their happiness. Yet power-seeking and greed are often at odds with consideration for the needs of others: these things and uninformed intolerance lead to local and international warfare.

The age-old wisdom of setting aside a weekly day for rest and renewal, and for thinking carefully about the great questions, is being ignored. Some of us feel we are the poorer because of losing the former pattern of Sunday observance. The days when coming to church was compulsory, are long gone, and voluntary attendance seems to be, for many families, an irrelevancy. Many children are growing up without regular instruction in a Christian way of life, and adults drift aimlessly without moral signposts.

Paradoxically, there is a general expectation that the Church will be there when needed. In times of national crisis, and major natural or accidental disasters, people expect Church leaders to voice a Christian opinion and comment and encourage support for helping agencies. They look to the Church for words of consolation, or simply to provide locally a place where they can be quiet and thoughtful. Personal crisis may draw some to the local church to find a listening ear and sympathetic company. May it always be here to minister to those with needs of this kind. It tries to do so through public worship, and the friendly greetings and concern of those who are near them in church; by the pastoral care offered by ordained men and women, and in organisations which are enjoyed and made possible by the efforts of lay people. There are many forms of ministry which are extended freely and naturally by 'ordinary' members of the Church Family.

So, what is it that sustains and nourishes the continuing life of 'The Church in This Place'?

*Why we come and what we believe*

Those who come to church regularly, do so because we feel a need for a comprehensive way of relating our own lives to the mystery of the world in which we are set, and to seek ways of making possible a life of peace and happiness for everybody. We come together to worship God, the Creator of "all that is, seen and unseen"; to pray together, to hear readings from the Holy Scriptures which we know can helpfully guide us; and to re-affirm what we believe:
> (Words within quotation marks are from the form of the Nicene Creed used in 'Common Worship').

*We believe* ......that the Bible tells of the Covenant made between a loving God, and all men and women. It shows the fulfilment of Old Testament searching and Prophecy and Law, in the person of Jesus Christ who is "......of one substance with the Father......and was made man". Jesus was both a human person *and* the divine presence of God. His earthly life of showing to everyone the nature of a loving Father God, was eclipsed when, to show the full extent of his love for us, he went on our behalf, to a cruel death at the hands of those who chose not to grow beyond hardened tradition and self-interest. But the shadow of an eclipse does not last for long: that was not the end. Jesus came back from the tomb, and met, ate and talked with his astonished disciples and followers for a short while, setting them on the road to a new kind of life. His promise to them and to us is that He is alive, and is our Friend and Guide for ever.

By his rising again, he offers us the reviving hope of God's confidence that, with his help, we are capable of beginning to make the journey from incompleteness towards perfection.

The early disciples were shown that they could be open to God himself, and in touch with him, in a fluid, two-way relationship which we usually call the 'working of the Holy Spirit'. That gift has been on offer to us ever since. The love of Jesus for his fellow men and women, even unto death, tells of the length to which God himself will go, to show us that he yearns for us to respond with mutual love and respect. As we accept that Our Lord Christ has redeemed us from being slaves to a self-centred, incomplete nature, and has set us free to grow towards our full stature with his continuing help, we can enter a new life full of meaning and hope, and of goodwill towards each other. Our response must be to acknowledge, and to accept God's forgiveness for our self-centred shortcomings and wrong-doings. Then, as we stand with awe and humility, in the presence of our God, the King of Love, we can worship him, and begin our God-given new life as we obey the all-embracing commandments:

"You shall love the Lord your God", and,

"Love your neighbour as yourself".

*The Church lives on to offer this life to others too*

To grasp the fact that we are *all* wanted, loved and needed, is to know that each of us is a part of God's wonderful, limitless act of creation. To exist in this mode is to live a life that is *not* snuffed out at the point of physical death, but which is a permanent and recognised part of the awesome purposes of God the Creator. Such a life is open to all people today.

Members of the Church are called by God to reach out to bring this Good News to the many who rarely, or never, set foot inside a church building. We must go out and meet people *where they are* today; they may, and we hope they will, want to join us in church later.

*So how does a Church like St. Gregory's prepare its members?*

It is the worship of God that binds us together as a Church. All of us need to develop and deepen our faith as we grow both physically and spiritually, and the form that our worship takes may helpfully reflect our needs at different stages. As Christians we are always reaching out to the new and mysterious, and are growing and learning! The full Liturgy draws us on to search further, but most of us need help in exploring its riches. The result of searching for ways of encouraging newcomers to step confidently into the Christian family is a series of less formal acts of worship and teaching. Hopefully those who take part will be led on to want to experience the quiet joy, dignity and inspired wisdom of the full Liturgy in due course.

Our continuing to learn implies that we need to be ready to change our minds about long-held assumptions, in the light of more accurate translations of the Scriptures, and unfolding knowledge, and to be aware of our own personal needs and motives which have such a powerful effect on how we relate to other people. Preferences that have become prejudices must be examined with a view to judicious pruning to favour healthy growth from the main stem which does not change or falter.

We should all try to be aware of what is happening in local and world situations. We need to sift media presentations in order to discern a balanced picture and to be touched by the triumphs and the tragedies of people like ourselves. Overall, and especially in our immediate situation, some of us may have to struggle very hard indeed to understand the mode of life and thought of other people, but it is essential that we make the attempt: who knows what we could enjoy and learn in the process? It shows too, that we care enough about a person or family when we meet them, to want to share what *we* have found to be life-giving.

A Church whose members worship and pray and study together, and enjoy each others' company, will enable those members to *live* their faith attractively. An inner peace which is unshaken by adversity and sadness; the outward signs of enjoyment of this strangely beautiful world; the genuineness of the respect we show for people whom we meet in any of the ordinary happenings of daily life: these things will not go unnoticed. Many whom we encounter may be in need of encouragement and comfort; some will be delighted to share with us their own 'special event' news and happiness; those who are desperately searching for meaning in their own lives, may get a tremendous lift simply because we noticed them in the street and smiled or said "Good morning".

The intermingling of Town and Church which was so close in former centuries, continues today in this way, and also by the involvement of Church members and Clergy of all denominations, in secular town committees and public activities both sober and of Carnival type. We are all hoping to promote "Peace and Good Neighbourhood", to share concerns and responsibilities *and* to enjoy fun and laughter and common interests together.

*Giving thanks for the Clergy and their Ministry*

Members of the Church are aware of their need for leadership and guidance, and personal support of a special kind. To give such help, some members of the Church have been called to train to become the Ordained Ministers of the Word and

Sacraments. They have been drawn to special ways of service, in presiding over acts of worship, and in the *cure* (or care) of souls. Their vocation is to be *ministers,* that is, *servants* of Our Lord, who said of himself that he had come to serve: that he was a servant. Those who enter the priesthood are humbly proud to bear that title. Remember that St.Gregory's chosen ascription was "Servant of the servants of God". The period and depth of training which priests undergo is long and demanding. They will agree that their open-ness to fresh learning, like that of all Church members, should continue throughout their years of Ministry. So also to go on cultivating ways of being open and accessible to all in their care, and with whom they work to spread the Gospel. May all who are elected to this special office be humbly worthy of their calling.

The clergy are our instructors in the Faith, our leaders in worship, and they bring to us and our families the blessings of Grace, Mercy and Peace, especially at the peak experiences in our lives. They also encourage lay members to take part in the leading of worship by reading the Scriptures and leading the Prayers of the People. 'Duly authorised' lay men and women are privileged to serve by administering the Wine of Holy Communion to those who are in church, and by taking the consecrated Elements to the sick and housebound of the Parish in their homes. It seems good that we serve together in these and other ways, when priest and people support and learn from each other.

The priest, together with our lay delegates, forms a link with the wider organisation of Deanery and Diocese and beyond. The names of the Bishops of the Diocese of Exeter are inscribed on a marble tablet on the wall of the lower narthex. There too, are the names of all the Vicars of Dawlish since 1272. The lists are reproduced in an appendix to this book. We give thanks for the unbroken chain of ministry in this Parish of St. Gregory, Dawlish.

*Appreciating the Retired Clergy and their continuing Ministry*

Dawlish being such a pleasant place in which to live, it is hardly surprising that retiring clergy, as well as lay people, come to live here! Many of them seek the Bishop's 'Permission to Officiate', that is, to conduct worship (by invitation of the relevant incumbent), in local and district churches; this continuation of their ministry is greatly valued. They bring many years and a great variety of experience to share with us in the leading of worship, and in friendship within the family of St. Gregory's Church. In the 1990s they contributed to a series of scholarly 'Lent Lectures' which were attended by many members and a substantial number of interested townspeople. One could not forget the firsthand descriptions of the Holy Land and its history which was brought to us by The Reverend Prebendary John Parkinson who had served as Honorary Chaplain to the British Embassy in Israel for 5 years, and as Assistant to the Bishop of Jerusalem. Others have served in overseas chaplaincies in Bahrein, Dubai, Cyprus, and other places. The Reverend Dr. John Bradshaw was for 10 years Principal of Malua Theological Training College in Western Samoa, and all have served in pastoral charge of Churches in this country. Some use their available time and abilities in writing, and as 'speakers', and in town organisations such as the Twinning Association. Dawlish has its twin in the town of Carhaix in Brittany, and exchange visits take place regularly. One of our retired priests, The Reverend Canon Colin Evans, a fluent French speaker, travelled to Carhaix not long ago, having in his 'luggage' two Dawlish black swans, and a locally grown Lucombe oak tree sapling, these being the very happily chosen gifts from the town to our friends there!

People living in small villages whose churches are grouped together in the care of one priest who cannot be everywhere at once, welcome the visits of 'retired' ministers who give them increased opportunities to take Holy Communion in their local setting, in buildings which are often ancient records of that community. The nature of the countryside around Dawlish is such that one can only admire the courage and determination of our older priests, who are prepared to drive considerable distances along beautiful but hazardous narrow lanes in order to accept the invitation to assist in the rural ministry.

*Just before the Millennium*

It seems good to put on record something of the way in which Public Worship was conducted during the final years of the 20$^{th}$ century.

On Sunday there was a quiet 8.00a.m. service of Holy Communion according the Book of Common Prayer provision.

The Parish Communion Service at 10.00 a.m. was a choral Celebration for *everybody*. During the Ministry of the Word, the First Lesson was read by a lay person; after a hymn or psalm, the Bible was carried down among the congregation, in a procession with candles (often carried by children). There the Gospel was read aloud by a priest. We all stood and turned to face the reader. For many of us, this was a high point in our worship.

Then the first part of the preaching of the Word, by the priest, was an often lively and memorable talk to the children who came up to sit on the floor in the 'crossing' at that point. The *teaching of children* was seen as part of our worship. Children of Church families, and the friends they brought with them, gathered in the south transept, and were very much part of the scene. They experienced what it was like to be in the awe-inspiring place of worship with people of all ages; they watched the choir process in, and sang a hymn of praise in the church, listened to the Bible readings, and then had their own special talk, given by one of the priests. (This was much appreciated by adults too, the message often well remembered). Then they left for lessons and activities elsewhere, in their different age groups, before returning to come to the Altar with everyone else, for a Blessing. They belonged, and felt that they belonged, in amongst us all. Give thanks for their devoted teachers and all the imaginative hard work involved in this ministry of care and instruction of children.

The Sermon, which was delivered from the pulpit, was teaching and leading us in our thinking about the set Bible passages, and would be carefully related to any significant local or international events. Our building is of such a size that we have found it essential to have a public address system so that all can hear what is read and said and take part as fully as possible. The provision of a printed pew sheet each week also gives everyone the chance to follow the Bible readings visually, and to take their copies home for further reflection.

From 1980 to 2000 we followed the provisions of the Alternative Service Book. During the Ministry of the Sacrament of Holy Communion, we began, in these years, to offer one another a sign of peace by handshake and greeting. The Bread and Wine were carried up through the nave to the Table, by lay members, before our gifts of money were also 'set before God' and blessed. Within the Eucharistic Prayer, we thankfully began to enter into the full meaning of the Bread and Wine, those tangible things which were consecrated, set apart for this Holy use. When those symbols were lifted up to God, and shown to the people, these essential actions were marked by the sounding of the Sanctuary bell. Distribution of the Elements took place at three altars in those years: the High Altar, a north aisle one and the one in the Lady Chapel. We were free to choose where we partook. There were always enough clergy who would robe and serve; some particularly liked serving at the north aisle altar where the children came for a blessing.

After the Parish Communion Service, the upper narthex room was much appreciated as a place where coffee, tea and soft drinks were on hand (with home made biscuits too). Here, strangers were made welcome, news and views exchanged. We could often see the pictures and models which the children had made during their Sunday School department time up there. It was a happy time of just being together, which pleased and warmed us all, but especially the lonely, and the elderly people who lived on their own for most of the week.

A need was made known for a less formal meeting for prayer and praise in song, the telling of the Gospel story, and perhaps the sharing of the personal witness of committed

Christians. Such an act of worship took place at 5.30 p.m. It attracted young people, families, and people of any age who were 'seekers', or who did not feel comfortable in other ways of worship. Room here for novel music: songs and friendly amateur instrumental accompaniments.

Sunday Services concluded with a Choral Evening Prayer, with sermon. This has always been a meditative Act of Worship by a relatively small congregation, and much treasured for the chance to savour the literary gems and devotional offerings of The Book of Common Prayer.

*Weekday activities*

During the week, there would be Holy Communion on Wednesday and Saturday mornings, and Celebration of the major Saints' days and other festivals on the appointed days throughout the year. Morning and Evening Prayer were said daily in the Lady Chapel; the vicar at that time (The Reverend William Lark), being musically gifted, would sometimes *sing* the Office for sheer pleasure. It was known that to come at these times was a good opportunity to talk privately with the Vicar.

The building was open for many regular activities. Interested strangers might call in just to see what the building was like, to do family research, or even to shelter from the rain. Sadly, as the years passed, thefts and vandalism increased to the point where we had to bow to instruction from our insurers, and lock the doors when there was no responsible steward present. We would have much preferred to have the building always open as in former times, for anyone to come to pray or meditate.

*House groups* gave members an opportunity to meet regularly in each others' homes in small numbers, to consider in detail the set Bible readings for the forthcoming Sunday, or to follow a pattern from available guides such as those of the Bible Reading Fellowship. Or, more simply but no less importantly, to be a company of friends who come to eat and drink, converse and pray and sometimes sing with one another. One such group was often attended by the Vicar, who welcomed the input from us lay members, and would remember our questions and contributions and sometimes bring them into his sermon next Sunday.

## The Church's Ministry to Young People

The Church supported, financially and practically, a *Youth Worker*, (Ruth Cawood), whose enthusiasm led her and several helpers to meet and talk with young people wandering about the town in the evenings. In winter, talking often began where there was hot soup and coffee on hand. A brave ministry in response to a perceived need, for by the end of the 20$^{th}$ century, membership of the uniformed organisations like Scouts and Guides, had declined. These groups had been giving good training for the young of all ages, encouraging friendship, loyalty, teamwork, and the fun of working hard to acquire practical skills and to develop special interests. They upheld the ideals of thoughtfulness for others, self esteem and discipline, as necessary in a good society. Almost all were linked with a local church where Church Parades brought many children to experience worship with people of all ages. Sadly, it seems that these movements declined because of difficulties in providing and retaining dedicated leaders, as well as because of all the powerful attractions competing for the time, money and interests of children and young people.

As the 21$^{st}$ century drew near, the members of St. Gregory's Church were increasingly feeling the call to expand the outreach to children and young people, to build up Church Youth clubs for a range of age groups. Our Vicar was about to retire after 13 happy years with us. We knew that there were changes in the air, not only in familiarising ourselves with 'Common Worship', and changes in the peripheral features of some of our worship, but also so that we could support additional Youth leaders (who would have to be qualified and accredited in the light of the necessary laws protecting minors from abuse). We hoped that the next priest to serve with us, would see new youth work as an important part of his or her ministry in Dawlish, in addition to caring for us all.

*The Church is a Worshipping Family*

We have thought a lot about 'The Church in This Place'; about the land, the buildings various, the stones and tiles, the bells and the furniture. Yet, much as we may love them, if some catastrophe should reduce the building to dust, the Church would continue, for *The Church is the People.* And under-pinning the whole life of the people of St. Gregory's Church, is the worship that we offer to God the Father, Son and Holy Spirit. To come, Sunday by Sunday with a sense of joyful anticipation, and to go out refreshed, renewed and re-inspired, and with joys and burdens shared: this is Family Worship, and surely pleasing to our God.


*(Turn to the next page to read the Epilogue......)*

## *EPILOGUE*

*Two Thousand Years since the Birth of Our Lord*

*The Dawlish Churches of all denominations marked the beginning of the new millennium with a Service of Thanksgiving and forward-looking commitment. It was held in the Parish Church, which could barely contain the press of people wanting to be part of this public declaration of loyalty to the Christian heritage, and the shared hope for the future wellbeing of our common life, especially here in Dawlish.*

*At the close of a happy time of worship, we celebrated with an outburst of fireworks from the top of the church tower. It was echoed from all round the hill slopes surrounding the Old Town; every home and family wanted to shout the excitement. The church bells rang out, their merry sound not quite drowned by the noise of exploding rockets and bangers. It was a night to remember!*

*A new century, a new millennium, had begun. Who knows what is in store? Our tale is still being told and we travel on with a prayer in our hearts:*

"Father let me dedicate
  All my days to Thee......

Let my glad heart, while it sings,
  Thee in all proclaim
And whate'er the future brings,
  Glorify Thy Name".

Laurence Tuttiett, 1825-1897.

This seems a good time to gather up all the rememberings we have shared in this book, and to bring the work to a close. It will be the task, and pleasure, of someone else to be the narrator for the years of the new millennium. There will be in my present offering, I am sure, things I have left unsaid, some inaccuracies lurking in what I have culled from records and copies of papers, and the reminiscences of my friends in Dawlish. For all my imperfections and unintentional errors or misunderstandings, I apologise, and ask for your kindly indulgence.

The following prayer was printed in several former editions of the brochure entitled 'History and Guide to the Church of St. Gregory the Great, Dawlish'. It seems good to offer it again as this book is sent on its way. May God bless us all.

*A Prayer of St. Gregory*

*"O Lord, I offer and present unto Thee myself and all that is mine, my deeds and words, my rest and my silence.*

*Only O Lord do Thou take me and lead me: move my hand and my mind and my tongue to those things which are well pleasing in Thy sight.*

*Turn me from all things from which Thou wouldst have me abstain.*

*Grant this O Lord for Jesus Christ's sake through whom I pray to Thee. Amen."*

# APPENDICES

## *GLOSSARY*

AISLE…a 'wing' (Latin), a sideways extension of the nave to make a broader seating area. The term is also used for the walkways giving access to the pews

ASHLAR…masonry or squared stones in regular courses: as used in the outer walls of the new chancel and transepts built for St. Gregory's church in 1875

AUMBRY...a cupboard where the consecrated Elements may be kept

BAY… the nave is divided across into sections by pillars of the arcade; each section is called a bay

CAPITAL…the wider topmost portion of a pillar, often decorated with carving

CHANCEL…the eastern part of the building, formerly divided off by a screen. It includes the Choir, and the Sanctuary where stands the Altar. See page 104

CHEVRON…a zig-zag pattern in stone, much used by the Norman masons

CORBEL…a bracket, often carved, which projects from a wall to support the beams of the roof, the ribs of a vault or a statue

CROSSING…the space at the intersection of nave/chancel and transepts

CRUCIFORM…cross-shaped

DYKE… a man-made earth work to mark out property rights or to act as a defence wall. (see Castle Dyke p. 2)

INDULGENCE…(in pre-Reformation times)…a remission of anticipated punishment (such as time to be spent in Purgatory), granted by Papal Authority in recognition of 'good works' or major gifts to the church

JAMB… the upright side member of a door frame

LINTEL…the horizontal member above a door

LIGHT… a distinct section of a window, outlined by vertical stone MULLIONS. TRANSOMS are horizontal dividers, of stone or iron, often used to strengthen a large area of stained glass

NARTHEX…an entrance/annex at the west end of the nave. (see p. 191)

NAVE… the main body of a church. (from the Latin word for a boat)

PISCINA…(Latin: a fishpond)…a washing and draining bowl carved into the wall near the Altar (see p.140)

RED-LETTER DAYS…The great Festivals and major Saints' days were marked on the Roman Church calendar in red pigment (rather than ordinary black), and were celebrated with High Mass and a public holiday (Holy Day)

REREDOS…a panel behind the Altar, usually decorated with devotional pictures or symbols

ROOD… a carved Crucifix, set on the top of the screen dividing the nave from the chancel in every church in pre-Reformation times

ROUNDEL…a circular feature in a window or carved stonework. The term is also used in needlework and tapestry design and in paintings

SCREEN...an often elaborate barrier separating off parts of a building reserved for special purposes, e.g. chancel from nave, chancel or nave from side chapel, or organ chamber from transept

SEDILIA...seats cut in the chancel wall near to the altar: for the use of priests and servers. (see p 140)

STRING COURSE...a projecting band of stones or mouldings along a wall. Often a decorative feature on an outside wall or tower

TRACERY...patterns formed by the interweaving of stone mullions at the top of a window or screen

TRANSEPT...that part of a cruciform church which projects at right-angles to the axis of the main building, usually to north and south, and forming the arms of a cross. It is sometimes called a cross-aisle

TYMPANUM...a semicircular or semioval slab filling up the space between the lintel and the arch of a doorway. Used by Saxons and Normans who built with rounded arches, but later set into the magnificent main doorways of Mediaeval cathedrals. This was a prime location for highly significant carvings (see p 18)

VOTIVE CANDLES...in pre-Reformation days, candles were offered to fulfil a vow of dedication to a particular Saint; they were lit on one of the many Altars to favourite Saints, or in front of statues. They burned continually in the ROOD LOFT above the chancel screen, except during Lent, when the Rood was veiled.

In recent times, many have welcomed the opportunity to light PRAYER CANDLES...to mark special petitions for the needy, in memory of loved ones and to give thanks for many blessings

# APPENDIX TWO

## LIFE IN THE CHURCHYARD

Our churchyard is a small haven for wildlife. Within its old stone walls grow flowers in profusion, protected from the munching of farm animals, the plough and hopefully also from weed and insect killers. Recently we have accepted the services of Council staff to help with regular grass cutting — this is a difficult job because of uneven grave surrounds. Prior to this arrangement, we had a grand midsummer tidying up which did not take place until after many of the flowers had bloomed and set seed, making secure the next year's abundance. Encouraging a diversity of wildlife *and* desirable neatness involves a delicate balancing act! Recently a team effort by one of the churchwardens with pupils from a local Special school cleared back overgrown shrubs and trees from the west wall and revealed a cluster of rather rare Earth Star fungi. Better light will benefit our native Primroses, while trimming of rampant nettles has allowed a bed of Sweet Violets to flourish and scent the air.

In 1998, in early June, I spent a happy and sun-drenched afternoon among the gravestones, listing the plants to be found there. The trees were full of the songs of a Robin, Blackbirds and many of those elusive 'little brown birds' busily food-gathering for hungry chicks. Close by, the call of a 'yaffingale' (Green Woodpecker) echoed across the grass, and a startled Pheasant fled from almost under my feet. I was in good company, for I was surrounded by the great family of the Children of God who had lived in this parish: our fellow heirs with Christ. Here they lie, in this sacred place, which teems with on-going life. I was reminded effectively of Our Lord's very words: "I am the resurrection, and I am life".

This book is a record of many things. It seems good to add my catalogue of plants, and the list of birds which was complied by Colin and Margaret Evans. I list the plants by English names, for that is how I first learned them from my mother.

## *The Trees*

English Yew (spreading)
Irish Yews (upright branches)
Hawthorn (white and pink)
Wild Cherry
Blackthorn (Sloe)
Guelder Rose
Elderberry
Alder
Horse Chestnut

Cypresses
Ash
Beech
Oak
Laurel(s)
Cherry (or Portugal?) Laurel
White Poplar
Lilac
Hazel

## *The Ferns*

Hart's Tongue
Polypody
Wall Spleenwort

## *The Wild Flowers*

Stinging nettle
Pellitory of the wall
Knotweed
Common Sorrel
Broad-leaved Dock
Greater Stitchwort
Common Chickweed
Creeping Buttercup
Meadow Buttercup
Lesser Celandine
Traveller's Joy (Wild Clematis)
Common Poppy
Cuckoo Flower (Milkmaids)
Garlic Mustard (Jack-by-the-hedge)
Hedge Mustard
Shepherd's Purse
Hairy Bittercress
Wavy Bittercress
Thale Cress
Whitlow Grass
Swinecress
English Stonecrop
Biting Stonecrop (yellow)
Blackberry
Barren Strawberry
Wild Strawberry
Dog Rose
Herb Bennet
Tormentil
White Clover
Hairy Tare
Bush Vetch
Birdsfoot Trefoil
Black Meddick
Spotted Meddick
Hop Trefoil
Red Clover
Yellow Oxalis
Herb Robert
Meadow Cranesbill
Shining Cranesbill
Cut-leaved Cranesbill
Dovesfoot Cranesbill
Dog's mercury
Sun Spurge
Portland Spurge
Dog Violet
Sweet Violet
Great Willowherb
Broad-leaved Willowherb
Ivy  (the climbing kind)
Hogweed
Cow Parsley (Queen Anne's Lace)
Ground Elder
Primrose
Scarlet Pimpernel (Poor man's weather glass)
Greater Bindweed
Common Bindweed
Goosegrass (Cleavers, Sweethearts)
Field Forgetmenot
Green Alkanet (bright *blue* flowers)
Ground Ivy (purple flowers)
Red Deadnettle
Ivy-leaved Toadflax
Woody Nightshade (Bittersweet, with purple flower, red berry
Black nightshade (white flower and black berry)
Germander Speedwell

d

| | |
|---|---|
| Field Speedwell | Field Thistle |
| Thyme-leaved Speedwell | Dandelion |
| Greater Plantain | Sow Thistles |
| Ribwort Plantain | Hawkweeds |
| Red Valerian | Hawkbits |
| Cornsalad | Nipplewort |
| Honeysuckle | Greater Burdock |
| Daisy | Common Cat's Ear |
| Ox-eye (Moon-daisy) | Wild Garlic (Ramsons) |
| Scentless Mayweed | Snowdrop |
| Yarrow | Cuckoo Pint (Lords and Ladies, Jack-in-the Pulpit…and many very rude names!) |
| Ragwort | |
| Groundsel | |
| Spear Thistle | Stinking Iris (Gladdon) |

## *The Grasses and Fungi*

These are not included in this amateur study of our churchyard plants. One day perhaps, somebody with specialised interests may come to live in Dawlish and be able to study them all the year round.

## *BIRDS in the CHURCHYARD*

### *(a contribution to the Parish Magazine)*

"Did you see the redwings and fieldfares swarm to eat the yew berries in November? They came in great numbers, cleared the berries, and left — and we even heard one redwing singing — rather like a thrush. Then, soon, we hope to hear the first chiff-chaff (its name describes its song), greenfinches are already making their 'chumping' noises, as well as all four sorts of tits: coal, blue great and long-tailed; and of course, blackbirds and thrushes. Wrens are there most of the time, creeping in the low bushes, like hedge mice, as well as chaffinches, goldfinches if you are lucky, and the ubiquitous magpies and starlings. Cormorants, rooks, crows or herons, fly over but do not stay.

"Later, there will be swallows, swifts and house martins to see – but none seem to nest here; neither do jackdaws, although we have a tower to attract them. And we do not seem to have a resident predator: no kestrel, often a characteristic bird of churchyards, nor a visiting sparrow hawk. We do have wood pigeons and the smaller, beautifully buff-coloured, collared doves (called palumbo dekaocto, because their call sounds like the Greek for 18), and, when rain is about, you may hear the laughter-like call of the green woodpecker (sometimes called the 'yaffle'), and may even see one coming down for ants. We've heard, but not seen, a nuthatch, but have not heard the drumming of the spotted woodpecker – though they should certainly be about in the Luscombe grounds, as should moorhens.

"Pied wagtails, or grey ones, (which perversely, have a chiefly yellow appearance, with grey-blue heads and wings), are there from time to time, as are hedge sparrows (a much nicer name than the official 'dunnocks'), robin sized, brown-ish, delicate little birds, with a delicate song too. And of course robins themselves. We have one or two scarce house sparrows, and sea gulls, common in town, mostly give us a miss.

"No doubt, if you have really sharp eyes, you might see some of the other warblers pass through on migration, and you might see a blackcap (the female's head is brown) at any time of the year, for they have taken to over-wintering with us for these past twenty years or more, and have a lovely spring-time song. And ducks sometimes waddle through, in the spring, and the odd pheasant.

"But for all that we are so close to Luscombe grounds, and have quite a good bit of cover, those are all we have seen: do tell us of others you have seen".

Margaret and Colin Evans

## EVENING LIFE around the TOWER

Very early in September 2000, a quarter-peal was rung to wish Godspeed to our Vicar on his 'retirement'. Seated comfortably (and respectfully) on a grave with an upright headstone to lean against, I watched and listened as the sun set, and dusk fell. It was a beautiful, warm and calm evening, and the swifts had delayed their departure for warmer lands, for an unusually long time. There were swarms of insects on the wing, and the swifts made good use of the chance of a feast to build up a good reserve for the long flight ahead of them. In their dozens, they wheeled around the church tower in the last of the sunshine and the updrafts near the warm red stonework.

When the sun had gone, so too had the swifts, but the show went on with another cast taking over the stage. Enter the bats – a score or so, of our commonest species, the pipistrelle. They took over what remained of the insects still on the wing, and continued the amazingly acrobatic flying display. Quite undeterred by the huge volume of sound pouring out through the louvres of the bell chamber, they dipped and soared without respite until darkness fell and I could see them no longer. (There have been no reports of 'bats in the belfry', I'm glad to say, for they make a terrible mess!)

When the peal came to its triumphant final flourish, and the bells fell silent, the tower itself continued to *hum* for a full minute and more. It was an awesome sound, and eloquent of the tremendous stresses and strains put upon ringing towers like ours. The architects and builders of more than 600 years ago certainly had great wisdom and technical skills. We salute them! It was a wonderful evening there in the lively churchyard setting, thanks to them and the life outside and inside the tower.

# APPENDIX THREE

## VICARS of DAWLISH

1272  W — (register damaged)
1273  Robert
1279  John de Sancto
1312  David de Molton
1339  Mylo
1340  William de Brokelond
1341  William de Heghes
1344  Joscelyn de Suetsham
1346  Thomas de Beauforest
1349  (the year of the Black Death)
      Hugh de Comb
      John Andreu (1$^{st}$ May)
      John Payewel (8$^{th}$ May)
1351  Robert de Luttertone
      Robert Bilbard
1381  Thomas de Burleigh
1383  Thomas de Wydecomb
1383  John Caynok
1411  Thomas Fayforde
1424  John Frensh
1425  Walter Chiterwell
1438  John Sarger
1457  Philip Skinner
1490  Roger Sydall
1492  John Forde
1523  John Street
1558  William Marwood
1561  Hugh Trevor
1567  John Symonds
1610  John Marker
1627  Elizeus Coke
1644  Henry Westlake
1662  John Trosse
1679  Richard Long
1690  Humphry Harvey
1730  Thomas Prowse
1789  William Ralfe
1807  John David Perkins

1846  Edward Fursdon
1864  John Rashdall
1869  Orlando Manley
1884  John Allen Bullen
1887  Henry Vyvyan
1895  William Powell Alford
1917  Frank Simmons
1936  George Stanley Trewin
1947  William Hammond Croft
1955  Albert William John Delve
1969  Leo Shirley Price
1974  Robin Taylor
1988  William Lark
2001  Jerry Bird

# THE BISHOPS of CREDITON and EXETER

909 Eadulf
934 Aethelgar
953 Aethelwold
973 Sideman
977 Aelfric
988 Aelfwold
1012 Eadnoth
1027 Lyfing
1046 Leofric
(1050  See transferred to Exeter)
1072 Osbern
1107 William Warelwast
1138 Robert Chichester
1155 Robert Warelwast
1162 Bartholomew
1186 John the Chantor
1194 Henry Marshall
1214 Simon of Apulia
1224 William Briwere
1245 Richard Blondy
1258 Walter Bronscomb
1280 Peter Wyville or Quivil
1292 Thomas Button
1308 Walter Stapleton
1327 James Berkely
     John Grandison
1370 Thos Brentigan
1395 Edmund Stafford
1419 John Catterick
1420 Edmund Lacy
1458 George Neville
1465 John Booth
1478 Peter Courtenay
1487 Richard Fox
1493 Oliver King
1496 Richard Redman
1502 John Arundel
1505 Hugh Oldham
1519 John Harman (or Voysey)
1551 Miles Coverdale
1555 James Turberville

1560 William Alley
1571 William Bradbridge
1579 John Wolton
1595 Gervase Babington
1598 William Cotton
1621 Valentine Cary
1627 Joseph Hall
1642 Ralph Brownrigg
1660 John Gauden
1662 Seth Ward
1667 Anthony Sparrow
1676 Thomas Lamplugh
1689 Jonathan Trelawny
1708 Offspring Blackall
1717 Launcelot Blackburn
1724 Stephen Weston
1742 Nicholas Clagget
1747 George Lavington
1762 Frederick Keppel
1778 John Ross
1793 William Buller
1787 Henry Reginald Courtenay
1803 John Fisher
1807 George Pelham
1820 William Carey
1830 Christopher Bethell
1831 Henry Phillpotts
1869 Frederick Temple
1885 Edward Bickersteth
1901 Herbert Ryle
1903 Archibald Robertson
1916 Lord William R. G. Cecil
1936 Charles E Curzon
1949 Robert Mortimer
1973 Eric Mercer
1985 G Hewlett Johnson
2000 Michael Langrish

(2004 Robert Evens was consecrated Suffragan Bishop of Crediton)

# APPENDIX FOUR

## *THE ORGAN IN THE CHURCH OF ST. GREGORY THE GREAT, DAWLISH*

STOPS, as shown on engraved heads on the console

*PEDAL ORGAN*

| | | | | |
|---|---|---|---|---|
| 1 | KRUMMHORN | 4ft | CH | |
| 2 | TRUMPET | 8 | CH | |
| 3 | CONTRA OBOE | 16 | SW | |
| 4 | TROMBONE | 16 | EXT | |
| 5 | CHORAL BASS | 4 | CH | |
| 6 | FIFTEENTH | 4 | EXT | |
| 7 | OCTAVE QUINT | 5 1/3 | | |
| 8 | BASS FLUTE | 8 | | |
| 9 | PRINCIPAL | 8 | | |
| 10 | BOURDON | 16 | | |
| 11 | VIOLONE | 16 | | |
| 12 | OPEN WOOD | 16 | | |

13 SWELL TO PEDAL 4
14 SWELL TO PEDAL
15 CHOIR TO PEDAL
16 GREAT TO PEDAL

*SWELL ORGAN*

17 OCTAVE
18 SUB OCTAVE
19 TREMULANT
20 CLARION 4
21 OBOE 8 EXT
22 CORNOPEAN 8
23 CONTRA OBOE 16
24 MIXTURE 15.19.22 III
25 FIFTEENTH 2
26 FUGANA 4
27 VOIX CELESTE 8
28 VIOLA DA GAMBA 8
29 ROHR FLUTE 8
30 GEIGEN DIAPASON 8

*CHOIR ORGAN*

31 OCTAVE
32 KRUMMHORN 8
33 TRUMPET 8
34 LARIGOT 1 1/3 EXT
35 TIERCE 1 3/5
36 PICCOLO 2
37 NAZARD 2 2/3
38 OPEN FLUTE 4
39 DULCIANA 8
40 CLARABELLA 8

41 SWELL TO CHOIR 4
42 SWELL TO CHOIR

*GREAT ORGAN*

43 TRUMPET 8
44 MIXTURE 17. 19. 22 III
45 FIFTEENTH 2
46 TWELFTH 2 2/3
47 SUABE FLUTE 4
48 PRINCIPAL 4
49 HARMONIC FLUTE 8
50 OPEN DIAPASON II 8
51 OPEN DIAPASON I 8
52 CONTRA GAMBA 16

53 CHOIR TO GREAT 4
54 CHOIR TO GREAT
55 SWELL TO GREAT 4
56 SWELL TO GREAT
57 SWELL TO GREAT 16
58 GREAT AND PEDAL
    PISTONS

i

# APPENDIX FIVE

## ANGELS and ARCHANGELS
(the author's contribution to the Parish magazine in 1999)

Emily was four years old. She came into the church building with a child-minder one afternoon when I was a summer steward. Life for Emily was one huge treasure-hunt: the world sparkled for her and she drank in new experiences with an infectious enthusiasm. She wanted to go everywhere, and gazed up at the so-high pillars, the coloured glass and the shiny brasswork. She peered down from the upper narthex to get another view of this vast building. It was obviously something quite out of the ordinary for her, (though I suspect that nothing is ordinary when you are her age!) But it was the font that really held her attention. She found the ANGELS.

Now you need to see the world from Emily's eye-level in order to find them. They are right down under the bowl of the font. When she found the first one she went very quiet, and hesitated, looking up at me as if to ask "May I touch it?" Reassured, she ran her fingers over the face and hair, and stroked the outspread wings. Solemnly she moved all round the font to find eight of them, and each in turn claimed her full attention. The watchers could only wonder, perhaps with longing, what she was thinking: her feelings of delight and awe were written all over her face and figure. Then quite suddenly she was off and away out into the sunshine like a butterfly, and the 'magic moment' was over.

I confess I was relieved not to have been asked "What is an angel?" What would you have said?

Since then I have given some thought to the matter. I roamed all over the church and counted the number of angels portrayed in stone, wood and glass. To my astonishment the number grew rapidly to 98! (see list which follows). Just why are angels so important and persistent? To me the answer goes something like this:

Since the dawn of civilisation man has distinguished between himself as part of the created universe, and the mysterious God who brought it all into being. A God so powerful, so holy, that men were afraid to approach him, yet they longed to do so. How could the gulf be bridged? So, (it seems to me), a belief grew up that there were other 'orders' of beings who were holy enough to be close to God, but who also had enough human-ness for mortal man to feel in touch with them and so with God. Such ANGELS were the intermediaries, the messengers between God and man, and man and God. This is what the name 'angel' means. We know that in early Old Testament times, God's Name was felt to be too holy to be spoken. Perhaps the actual 'presence of God' was meant when word 'angel' was used. (Try re-reading Genesis 16 vv 7-13 with this alternative in mind.)

j

In the Bible we read of the work of the angels:

Firstly: To worship God continually.
Secondly: To carry God's commands and instructions to all men, and to convey to God their response.
Thirdly: To guard, comfort and cherish those who search for God and try to do His will.

How do Christians feel about such 'Old Testament' ideas? Surely, we might well say that Our Lord Christ has opened for us a safe highway joining God with man, man with God? Should we now dismiss belief in angels as a heresy? Well, I don't think so. There are other ways of trying to understand these creatures. Jesus himself did not openly discourage the popular belief in angels. Rather, he carried the idea of an immortal, spiritual communicator forward into the reality of the Holy Spirit who is
God-with-us eternally.

In order to appreciate the place of these angels, perhaps we should remember the immense value of *symbols* to lead us further in our understanding. Symbols are triggers or switches that have an impact on us through our physical senses, but which lead into those realms of truth which are beyond our usual experience: to the places where we are indeed 'lost for words'. Some symbols seem to have universal appeal and can help us to respond to fundamental truths that might otherwise remain shrouded in mystery. The Liturgy of Holy Communion is plentifully adorned with such symbols. And yes, the angels are there in full flight! Like other symbols they enable us to fly beyond the 'five senses' boundaries of our earthly existence; they are like booster rockets to our questing imagination, and they bear us up as we try to respond to "The gracious calling of the Lord". Like fledgling birds uncertainly poised on the edge of the nest, so *we* discover our wings and find we can fly……even into the Holy of Holies.

"……Therefore with angels and archangels,
and with all the company of heaven,
we laud and magnify thy glorious name,
evermore praising thee and saying,
Holy, holy, holy Lord, God of power and might……"

So thank you Emily for your vitality. Thank you for laboriously writing your name in our Visitors' Book. I hope you will come back and become one of the family here. I think the angels that you love will stay on in our church, calling us all to blend with them in doing the work of the angels:

to worship, to be God's evangels, to cherish each other.

k

## THE ANGELS IN THE FABRIC OF ST. GREGORY'S PARISH CHURCH

### IN THE NAVE
Carved stone angels above each of the main pillars (15th century)………10
(the westernmost pair have been cut in half by the narthex screen)
The Archangel Michael, a carved statuette on the 6th north pillar…….1

### IN THE NORTH TRANSEPT
*2 north windows* glass: above the main lights are 2 roundels, each surrounded by 5 small lights of angels with head and 6 wings only. (19th century)………………..10
On the FONT: below the bowl itself are 8 carved angels on the angles between the 8 side panels. (probably 15th century)…………... 8

### IN THE CHOIR
South side, on the screen which separates the choir from the Lady Chapel, 8 wood-carved angels watch over the choir and organ console. (20th century)……….8

### IN THE SANCTUARY
In the 'rose' of the east window……8
in the main tall light 2nd from left….1
in the quatrefoils at the foot of the window (19th century)………….4

### IN THE UPPER NARTHEX
In the west window, (visible now only from the sanctuary and the upper narthex): 2 in the main lights, and 3 in the top ones………5

### IN THE SOUTH TRANSEPT
In the south windows: around the upper roundels are 10 more 'heads and 6 wings' angels matching those in the N Transept..10
On the screen through which you pass into the Lady Chapel are more wood-carved angels……………….4

### IN THE LADY CHAPEL
In the *east window*, surrounding the stained glass copy of Raphael's painting of the Transfiguration of Christ, are 2 angels in the upper trefoils and 4 at the window foot….6
In the *south-east* window are some brilliant angels with head and wings only (top lights)…………………….2
and in the main tall right hand light are the angels of the Resurrection…2
*On the windowsill* are 2 small angel figurines, someone's very personal offering, I think…………………….2
In the *south-west window* the central top light shows angels holding the Crown of Thorns……………...........2
*Three seats on the north side of the altar* carry angels beautifully carved in wood: their history is a bit of a mystery…………………….3
*The north screen* between the Lady Chapel and the choir has 8 angels facing into the chapel…………….8
*The west screen* between the Lady Chapel and the south transept has another 4 facing into the south transept……………………………4

*GRAND TOTAL*………98

# APPENDIX SIX

We are invited to share this letter which is part of a series written to the Editor of the Magazine of The Prayer Book Society. The author has asked to remain anonymous, but is surely known by name to God himself: "I have called thee by name, thou art mine" (Isaiah 43 v.1). We give thanks to God for him, and for this glimpse into the spiritual life underpinning his work as a Parish Priest—a ministry marked not only by the desire to enable all to draw near to God in worship, but also by the willingness of a dedicated craftsman, to share in the uniquely personal journeyings of some of us, helping us towards clearer vision, and enabling us, with humility, to travel a little further along the road towards perfection.

His letter is about the priceless heritage of the Liturgy: the distilled wisdom and faith of leaders in the Church over many centuries, and the effective offering of these things to God and his people 'in perpetuity'.

## *LITURGICAL WORSHIP*

"There have been one or two articles recently about liturgy—perhaps a word or two from an elderly priest might be added, for it was the Book of Common Prayer that helped bring me into the Church of England when I reawoke to Christianity, and its ordered use has carried me on into the newer forms of service, for the timeliness of well-ordered liturgy does not really change, except in changing circumstances, in order to remain the same.

"It can seem curiously impersonal: the priest, for example, prepares himself (or *her*self —and so throughout, because we have not yet devised a usefully inclusive way of doing this) with care, putting his whole person into it. He draws on the week's pastoral contacts to inform the style and content of the preaching and prayers, and yet, at the same time, endeavours to be as unobtrusive a presence as possible, using his robes, and the customary, familiar gestures to show that it is not him, as a particular person, who is leading the worship, but rather that he is the responsible, authorised celebrant, his own specific personality at most the vehicle for this. It takes a few years to be able oneself to worship while being the celebrant: but until it has become second nature, one has to be content with doing one's part as carefully and well as may be, which is itself a real satisfaction of the spirit.

"As to the congregation, of which he comes increasingly to know himself an integral part, and which somehow tells him and teaches him what it is to be a priest, the regular, reliable, expected order of known words, known ceremony, all with sound seasonal variation, and carefully articulated readings from Scripture—in a word, all that ordered liturgy entails, all this comes to be a way of allowing the whole person to be drawn nearer to the presence of God, to whom it is all addressed in worship. For the busy surface of the mind does not have to be perpetually watchful, lest it miss something: one relaxes, somehow slots in, and is carried along; and the upper part, maybe the cerebral part, is somehow combed through and realigned, and the deeper part of one's being is opened. One drops down deeper, and in a perhaps fleeting way— not to be exaggerated, nor specifically sought after, but real all the same—one's spirit is touched and accepted by the Spirit himself. One cannot exactly do this to order, and many Sundays may go by with one having been aware of gladly doing no more than one's bounden duty—but something of that order is a true part of the nature of it all, for priest and people alike.

"So too the sermon. Set as it is in the context of giving oneself over to God, one's guard is down, one is open to hearing things that one might miss, or even resent, if said in the high street. The preacher is himself included in this—and it is not so much that he is preaching the Word of God (though, may he be preserved, that is what he is doing) but rather that a word from God often forms itself, not so much in the mind, as in the heart of preacher and people alike; and strangely, it is not always the brilliant sermon that allows this to happen.

"All this does not immediately reveal itself to the casual enquirer: liturgical worship does not yield up its treasures so easily—but treasures they are, rich, deep and true, and they suffice for a lifetime. Maybe today's danger is that the world around us is used to instant satisfaction, and thinks this should be the norm in worship, and some clergy, with great integrity, think we must try to offer worship in this way. But it seems to me that if people are convinced of the need to seek God and worship him—and he does continue to call people—they will not thank us if we give them half rations, liturgically or otherwise, and forget the over-riding duty of stewards to be found faithful."

**INDEX:** Page numbers

Aisles, 46, 47, 81, 95
Altar, 17, 82, 99-100, 104, 109, 138, 204.
    See also: Communion Table, Holy Table.
Altar rail, 83, 85, 137
Angels, 43, Appendix Five
Arches, 39, 41, 43, 77, 80
Augustine. St., 7, 8-9
Aumbry, 153
Axe carving, 17

Baptism, 49, 123-129
    See also: Font
Beer stone, 42, 81, 129
Bells, 33-36, 182-183
    Change ringing: 36, 110
Bible, The Holy Bible, 114-115, 116-122.
    Ministry of the Word, 114-115
Black Death, 31
Book of Common Prayer, 56-57, 63
    Appendix Six
    See also: Prayer Books
Book of Hours, 52
Bosses, ceiling, 82
Buttresses, 47, 80

Candles, 30, 39, 50, 58, 137, 178
Capitals, 18
Carving, 17-18, 40, 132, 135
Cathedrals, 31, 40
Chalice, 84
Chancel, 81, 101, 104, 1o6
Chancel Arch, 106
Children in Worship, 203
Choir and choir stalls, 105
Churchwardens, 29, 85, 131
Churchyard, 172-176
Clock, 70
Colour: in the Norman church, 28
    in Mediaeval times, 40, 145

Colour (cont'd) in stained glass, 145ff
    Liturgical colours, 142-3
Commemorative plaques, 170, 171
Communion Plate, 40, 57, 84
Communion Table, 85, 86
    See also: Altar, Holy Table
Confirmation, 49, 123
Congregationalists, 72, 186
Consecrated Water, 125-6
Corbels, 18-20
Credence table, 140
Creed, 6, 24, 156
Cross: the Empty Cross, 137, 153
    Processional Cross, 110
    Preaching Cross 53
Crucifix: by the pulpit, 116
    in the Lady Chapel, 153

Dawlish Water, 2, 4, 69, 71
Domesday Book, 14
Doors and carving, 18, 80

East window, 156-158
Ecclesiastical Courts, 20

Flag and flagpole, 36
Font, 44, 49, 127, 129-136, 195
    See also: Baptism
Frescoes, 50

Galleries, 71, 74-75, 77, 83, 86
    Dismantled, 180-181
Gargoyles and Grotesques, 18, 37-38
Gates, 172
Gothic architecture, 39, 41, 155
Granite, 53, 106, 184
Gravestones, 172
Graveyard, 172-176
Gregory the Great, 8, 10, 21-22, 136
    Statue, 186
    Patronal Festival, 185
    A Prayer of St. Gregory, 209

High Church Movement, 95, 101-105
Hoare Family, 100, 156 174, 177, 187-8
Holman, Jim, 164
Holy Communion, 112, 137
Holy Family, 151-2
Holy Matrimony, 17
Holy Water, 27, 29
Host, 51
Hymns, 72, 73, 165ff

Industrial Revolution, 65, 87-92
Ironwork, 178
Itinerant Preachers, 53

Lady chapel, 103, 151-4
Lectern, 112, 114
Lighting:
    Torch and candles, 17, 39
    Gas, 107, 181
    Electric, 189
Liturgical colours, 142-3
Liturgy, 48, 111, Appendix Six
Lock on Font, 27
Lych gate, 82

Marriage, 17
Mass, 16, 17, 24, 28, 29, 30, 57-8
Mass dial, 47, 80
Maypole and Morris bells, 29
Mediaeval times, 27, 29-30
Methodists, 72, 175
Michael, Saint, 19, 136, 184-5
Monumental wall tablets, 170ff
    See also: Graveyard
Music and Musicians, 71-74, 159-168

Narthex, 191-194
Nave, 50, 101, 107
Non-conformists, 60-63, 72
Norman building, 16-20, 24, 28

Opus sectile work, 94, 138-9, 141, 152

Organ, 71, 82, 160-165
Organ recitals, 161

Parish, Saxon, 11
Parish Clerk, 29
Parish Priest, 20, 24, 25
Parish Priests:
    List of Vicars of Dawlish:
        See Appendix Three
Parish Registers, 169
Paten, 84, 142
Patron Saint, 10, 22, 136, 184-186
Patronal Festival, 185-6
Pews, 70, 74, 84, 86, 103, 107
Pillars, 39, 41-43, 77, 80
Piscina, 140
Plan of the church: see Picture insert
    between pp 112 and 113
Pope Gregory,.. 8-9, 10, 136
    See also: Gregory the Great
Poor Laws, Poor Rate, 67-8, 89, 90
Poverty and Poorhouse, 89-91
Prayer books, 55-57, 63, 99, App. Six
Preaching Cross, 53
Processional Cross, 56
Prophets, 139
Pulpit, 70, 83, 95, 112-115
Purgatory, 32, 52, 54, 144
Puritans, 59, 74, 80

Railway, 1, 88
Raphael window, 150
Records and Registers, 169, 186-7
References for research, 171
Reformation, 54-60, 84, 104, 107
Reredos, 60, 81, 82, 151
Rood, 50, 57, 59
Rood Screen and loft, 50, 59, 80
Roof, 47, 63, 77, 78, 82
Royal Arms, 194

St. Mark's Church, 94-95, 189-191
St. Michael, 136, 184-5

Sacraments, 96, 99
    Baptism: 96, 123-127
    Holy Communion, 96, 99, 109,
        112, 137-8
Sacristan, 142
Sanctuary, 81, 82, 105, 137
Sanctuary bell, 204
Schools, 78
Screens, 50, 51, 82
Sedilia, 140
Sermons, 95, 97, 84
South 'tower', 46, 80
Spiral staircase, 35, 46, 182
Stained glass, 59, 79, 145-150,
    153-158
Stocks, 48
Sundial, 34, 47, 80
Symbols, 38, 99, 135,
        Passion Symbols:152

Ten Commandments, 25, 60, 85, 152
Tiles, 107, 141
Tithe barn, 11, 46, 79
Tithes and tithing, 15, 21
Tithes abolished (1836), 79
Torch and candle lighting, 17, 81

Town Boards, 75-6, 87
Tower, 32, 33-38
    Renovation: 182
Tracery, 31, 147, 148, 150
Transepts, 80, 82, 84, 103-104
        N and S transept glass:148-149
Turnpike roads, 65, 90
Tympanum, 18

Vaulting, 39
Vestments, 56, 57, 58
Vestry, (for robing), 66, 79, 82, 103
Vestry, (the executive body), 66-8, 77
Vestry Hall, 87
Vicarage, 69
Vicars of Dawlish, Appendix Three

Wall tablets, 170, 171
War Memorials, 170, 183-4, 186
Wildlife in the churchyard,
    See appendix Two
Windows, 144ff
Workhouse, 90

Yew trees, 125, Appendix Two